Outward, Visible Propriety

Studies in Rhetoric/Communication
Thomas W. Benson, Series Editor

OUTWARD, VISIBLE PROPRIETY

Stoic Philosophy and
Eighteenth-Century British Rhetorics

LOIS PETERS AGNEW

The University of South Carolina Press

© 2008 University of South Carolina

Published by the University of South Carolina Press
Columbia, South Carolina 29208

www.sc.edu/uscpress

Manufactured in the United States of America

17 16 15 14 13 12 11 10 09 08   10 9 8 7 6 5 4 3 2 1

LIBRARY OF CONGRESS CATALOGING-IN-PUBLICATION DATA

Agnew, Lois Peters.
  Outward, visible propriety : stoic philosophy and eighteenth-century
British rhetorics / Lois Peters Agnew.
    p. cm.— (Studies in rhetoric/communication)
Includes bibliographical references and index.
ISBN 978-1-57003-767-2 (cloth : alk. paper)
  1. Stoics—Influence. 2. Common sense. 3. Rhetoric—Great Britain—
History—18th century. I. Title.
B528.A29 2008
192—dc22   2008030339

This book was printed on Glatfelter Natures, a recycled paper
with 30 percent postconsumer waste content.

CONTENTS

SERIES EDITOR'S PREFACE

In *Outward, Visible Propriety: Stoic Philosophy and Eighteenth-Century British Rhetorics*, Professor Lois Peters Agnew offers an important and challenging rereading of the primary British rhetorical theorists of the eighteenth and early nineteenth centuries. She argues that the theories of language and rhetoric in the works of Anthony Ashley Cooper, Third Earl of Shaftesbury; Thomas Reid; Adam Smith; Henry Home, Lord Kames; George Campbell; Hugh Blair; and Richard Whately were shaped, often in ways that remain implicit and unstated, by the principles of Stoic philosophy, found especially in the ethical thought of Epictetus, Marcus Aurelius, and Seneca and given explicitly rhetorical treatment by Cicero and Quintilian. Agnew demonstrates that the British writers' theories of common sense, taste, sympathy, and propriety take on a new coherence when understood as adaptations of Stoic ideas brought to bear on rapid and unsettling cultural and economic changes in the eighteenth and nineteenth centuries, when concepts of civic virtue, ethics, and community were threatened by a new emphasis on bourgeois individualism, competitive economic rationality, and increasingly sharp distinctions between the public and the private.

The British theorists, Agnew argues, sought to establish a synthesis that acknowledged contemporary scientific, religious, and cultural thought, which they adapted to their understandings of Stoic philosophy to sustain an integrated depiction of both the individual and community as part of the natural order. She writes that "many eighteenth-century thinkers were not prepared to grant the sharp division between public and private that has come to be a defining feature of modern life." "The theories of Campbell, Blair, and Whately," she maintains, "in large part represent attempts to struggle against the turn toward individualism that eighteenth-century society seemed to be taking." Agnew demonstrates that Stoicism offered to these theorists an intellectual and ethical framework connecting the virtues of discipline and restraint with the "more fundamental objective of harmony among individuals, society, and nature."

Professor Agnew makes possible a reading of eighteenth-century rhetorical theory that is theoretically integrated and historically situated. But, she points out, the coherence achieved by the Stoic frame lasted only briefly. She concludes by tracing how the Stoic frame was soon displaced by nineteenth-century assumptions of the central role of human subjectivity.

THOMAS W. BENSON

PREFACE

This book argues that the work of prominent British rhetoricians from the eighteenth and early nineteenth centuries was significantly informed by key principles from Stoic philosophy, particularly the ethical systems articulated in the writings of Epictetus, Marcus Aurelius, and Seneca and developed in the rhetorical theories of Cicero and Quintilian. This influence is evident both in eighteenth-century theorists' direct citation of Stoic sources and in their reliance upon a Stoic framework that indirectly shapes their assumptions concerning the role of the natural order in providing human life with meaning. The Roman Stoic view that virtue develops only through civic responsibility and an acknowledged connection with others was particularly compelling to eighteenth-century theorists struggling to find social stability in the midst of a modern trend toward privacy. Their incorporation of Stoic perspectives encouraged their development of rhetorical theories that emphasize aesthetic judgment, sympathetic interactions, and appropriate conduct, which are all seen as components that simultaneously contribute to private and civic virtue.

In order to understand how Stoic thought functions in eighteenth-century theories of language and rhetoric, I focus on the writings of Anthony Ashley Cooper, Third Earl of Shaftesbury, Thomas Reid, Adam Smith, Henry Home, Lord Kames, George Campbell, Hugh Blair, and Richard Whately, all of whom adapt Stoic ideas to the particular challenges of their era. The introduction and the first four chapters explore the Stoic presence in eighteenth-century theories dealing with common sense, taste, sympathy, and propriety and demonstrate how an understanding of that influence significantly illuminates the assumptions that guide those theories. Chapter 5 explores the turn away from the Stoic ideal of sensus communis during the nineteenth century, a move that ultimately detaches language from public life in ways that subsequent scholars have perceived as a rejection of rhetoric. This trajectory demonstrates how Stoic thought provides a basis for better understanding eighteenth-century rhetorical theories, recognizing the presence of earlier rhetorical strains even in nineteenth-century theories that appear to have little connection with the past, and at the same time appreciating how the grounding of rhetoric in character and culture sets the stage for a significant transformation as British rhetoric moves into the nineteenth century.

This endeavor poses a number of challenges. The philosophical influences on rhetorical texts are difficult to ascertain, in part because of disciplinary divisions that have come into being relatively recently. The long-standing disinterest in rhetoric on the part of many philosophers has stood in the way of their inquiry into the infusion of a broad range of ancient philosophical concepts through developments in rhetorical theory. At the same time, the tendency on the part of rhetorical scholars to align notions of "classical thought" with principles found in classical rhetorical treatises has artificially narrowed the network of ancient influences that shaped eighteenth-century rhetorical theories. This process generates accounts of the history of rhetoric that implicitly assume that eighteenth-century theories that fall outside the line of direct descent from particular classical rhetorical principles reflect modern and scientific assumptions, a view that has at times neglected the complicated interweaving between ancient and modern thought found in those theories—and ignores ways in which this dense pattern of ideas reflects theorists' efforts both to benefit from and to resist scientific advances.

To acquire a more complete understanding of this complexity holds merit that justifies the effort involved. While it is undoubtedly impossible for contemporary scholars to read historic texts completely "in their own terms," examining the many influences that inform the thought of eighteenth-century theorists can at least promote a more fully contextualized understanding of their work. Such an enterprise can seem daunting, because the immersion in classical sources that now seems so foreign was something that people in previous eras took for granted. Knud Haakonssen notes that Reid's frequent failure fully to cite and elaborate upon his philosophical premises reflects Reid's assumption that many of his sources were too well known to his audience to merit direct reference. Haakonssen adds, "The main difficulty in understanding the ideas that past thinkers have thought original enough to justify publication is precisely the retrieval of the background ideas that were too common to be worth publishing but that have now been lost sight of."[1] This project seeks to retrieve some of the background ideas "that have now been lost sight of" in order to pursue a more complete understanding of eighteenth-century British rhetorical theories. Of course, accounts of history are always grounded in present concerns and brought to life using the lenses of present ideas. Although this means that grasping the thought of other eras "in their own terms" is an unlikely prospect, adding layers of complexity to historical interpretation can facilitate a confrontation with the particularity of the past in ways that offer useful insight into the complex challenges the present continues to offer.

ACKNOWLEDGMENTS

I would like to express my appreciation to a number of people who have supported my work on this project in important and varied ways: my colleagues at Syracuse University, particularly Cathryn R. Newton, dean of arts and sciences, Carol S. Lipson, and Eileen E. Schell; Richard Leo Enos; the anonymous readers at the University of South Carolina University Press; Linda Fogle, Jim Denton, Bill Adams, Jonathan Haupt, and other members of the University of South Carolina Press staff; and Alexa Selph, Stephen McKenna, and Beth Manolescu. I also want to acknowledge my late parents, Lloyd and Maxine Peters, whose belief in me has sustained me throughout my life. Special thanks go to Pete, Elizabeth, Peter, and Mike for the patience, love, and support that have seen me through this process.

Portions of this book derive from the following articles that I have previously published:

"Walter Pater and the Rhetorical Tradition: Finding Common Sense in the Particular." *Advances in the History of Rhetoric: The First Six Years.* Edited by Richard Leo Enos and David E. Beard. West Lafayette, Ind.: Parlor Press, 2007. © 2007 by Parlor Press. Used by permission.
"'Unstifling the Rhetorical Impulse': Style and Invention in Thomas De Quincey's Rhetoric." In *Rhetoric, the Polis, and the Global Village.* Lawrence Erlbaum, 1999. Used by permission of Taylor and Francis.
"The 'Perplexity' of George Campbell's Rhetoric: The Epistemic Function of Common Sense." *Rhetorica* 18, no. 1 (2000). Used by permission from the University of California Press.
"The Stoic Temper in Belletristic Rhetoric." *Rhetoric Society Quarterly* 33, no. 2 (2003). Used by permission of Taylor and Francis, www.informaworld.com.

INTRODUCTION

The eighteenth century constitutes a turning point in the history of rhetoric, a moment many scholars characterize as one in which classical rhetorical principles were integrated with or in certain respects superseded by modern epistemological concerns. In describing the components of this integration, most accounts of rhetoric's history have identified two strains of influence on eighteenth-century British language theorists: classical theories of civic discourse, primarily developed by Aristotle, Cicero, and Quintilian, and the scientific and philosophical doctrines of modern theorists such as Francis Bacon, John Locke, and David Hume. These strains are clearly relevant to rhetoric's development, but this should not obscure other influences that have a significant part in rhetoric's history during this period.

One of these influences is Stoic philosophy. This book argues that the history of British rhetoric cannot be understood without attending to Stoic strains in influential language theories of the eighteenth and early nineteenth centuries. Stoic thought can be seen as an important frame of reference for a group of prominent British intellectuals whose thorough classical study facilitated their integration of this philosophical system with their own ideas about the social function of language—leading to theories that promote key concepts in rhetoric's history. Stoic ethical principles infuse the thought of eighteenth-century language theorists in many ways: through their extensive familiarity with Stoic texts, their appreciation for the application of Stoic ideas in the rhetorical theories of Cicero and Quintilian, and their participation in intellectual circles that directly and indirectly use Stoic thought as a frame of reference for responding to eighteenth-century concerns.

These networks of Stoic influence consistently exist in a complex relationship with modern ideas that eighteenth-century theorists found both compelling and problematic. The Stoic influences can be seen as both direct and indirect—categories that Gloria Vivenza also uses in her study of classical influences on Adam Smith. In examining these influences, I share Vivenza's sense that indirect influences can be seen as having particular power, as they reflect a thorough immersion in systems of thought that ultimately lead to a distinct way of viewing the world.[1] Although eighteenth-century writers frequently cite Stoic philosophers directly, there are many other instances where the Stoic system is embedded in the outlines of their thought, as they make ancient ideas their own in responding to modern problems. The process of integrating ancient and modern ideas occurs seamlessly, both due to the writers' familiarity with ancient thought and to their participation in a restricted intellectual community that shares a common reservoir of sources and perspectives. Knud Haakonssen notes that Thomas Reid's frequent failure fully to cite and elaborate upon his philosophical premises reflects Reid's assumption that many of his sources were too well known to his audience to merit direct reference, concluding that "the main difficulty in understanding the ideas that past thinkers have thought original enough to justify publication is precisely the retrieval of the background ideas that were too common to be worth publishing but that have now been lost sight of."[2] Recapturing those sources "that have now been lost sight of" is this book's central objective.

The significant presence of Stoic thought can be seen early in the century in the writings of Anthony Ashley Cooper, Third Earl of Shaftesbury, and Francis Hutcheson, both of whom examine issues of language, ethics, and aesthetics through a Stoic lens and in ways that both support and challenge contemporary developments in science, religion, and philosophy. Interestingly, Stoic principles prove to be sufficiently malleable to accommodate different and at times opposing ideological positions. Citing religious historian George T. Buckley, James Herrick describes Stoicism's appeal "to rationalistic approaches to religion," as it establishes an emphasis on religion and the rule of nature that eighteenth-century skeptics such as Shaftesbury found appealing. At the same time, Herrick reports Buckley's observation that Stoicism was also "advanced by its apologists as an aid to Christianity, and the churchmen, unable to condemn it because of its lofty sentiments, saw little to which they could object. Thus in a way Stoicism actually enjoyed the protection of the church."[3] Hutcheson explored this compatibility between Christianity and Stoicism, creating a fusion of the two that had a lasting impact on the development of British moral theory and ultimately on rhetoric.[4] One exemplar of Christianized Stoicism was Reid, whose interest in Stoic thought shaped his philosophical response to eighteenth-century skepticism; his development of Scottish commonsense philosophy has much in common with Stoic sensus communis, even as it builds on contemporary philosophical and scientific insights. Several prominent figures, including Adam Smith, Henry Home, Lord Kames, Hugh Blair, George Campbell, and Richard Whately, bring Stoic ideas squarely into the history of rhetoric, as they draw both upon their own encounters with Stoic thought and upon the work of Shaftesbury, Hutcheson, and Reid in placing their rhetorical theories within a Stoic framework. In tracing the significant presence of Stoic principles in the work of these theorists, I do not intend to represent this influence as one that simply unifies the eighteenth century with ancient thought but instead to demonstrate how conditions specific to the eighteenth century encouraged rhetorical theorists during that period to turn consistently to Stoic thought as a resource that guides their response to social instability.

In spite of the fact that they approach Stoicism from different ideological positions, key Stoic principles can be seen as central to the rhetorical vision of the theorists included in this book. All of them were drawn to the Stoic notion of an ordered universe in which virtue will ultimately prevail. They also found comfort in the assurance, particularly characteristic of Roman Stoicism, that human society provides a structure through which individuals may achieve a more complete understanding of their place in the natural order. They were committed to exploring ways in which rhetoric could foster this constructive relationship between individuals and their community. Such a relationship seemed particularly vital in a period marked by dramatic political change. The 1707 Act of Union between Scotland and England resolved the issue of accession to the throne, provided both nations with reason to hope for new prosperity and stability, and strengthened the social ties that bound the two nations. In the decades following the union, new economic prosperity would entail the shift from an agrarian economy to an industrial one, changes in the class system, and new ways of defining personal and collective identity as the model for citizenship shifted from political participation to economic success. Various factors expanded earlier efforts to explore the potential of the autonomous individual to acquire meaningful knowledge of the world, including scientific empiricism, the rise of print culture, and new interest in religious inquiry. At the same time, many people sought to preserve a role for collective action in order to check the fragmentation that seemed inevitable to a society experiencing such rapid change. The intellectual energy surrounding this period reflects the anxiety as well as the optimism of a society in transition.

These rapid social changes had a significant effect on conceptions of the individual's relationship to society. Michael Warner argues that notions of the public sphere inevitably reflect the dynamic moments in which they are situated: "Almost every major cultural change—from Christianity to printing to psychoanalysis—has left a new sedimentary layer in the meaning of the public and the private."[5] The "new" rhetoricians of the eighteenth century were daily experiencing what Jürgen Habermas describes as a shift from more clearly defined boundaries between "public" and "private" to a modern public sphere composed of private individuals brought together in an effort to acquire authority in communicating about public issues. According to Habermas, individuals who would previously have been situated in the private realm therefore began to see themselves as participants in a public sphere shaped by new commercial relations and authorized to develop informed opinions concerning state policies: "The bourgeois public sphere may be conceived above all as the sphere of private people come together as a public; they soon claimed the public sphere regulated from above against the public authorities themselves, to engage them in a debate over the general rules governing relations in the basically privatized but publicly relevant sphere of commodity exchange and social labor."[6] Habermas depicts the individual's use of reason as central to the formation of the public sphere, as those engaged together in critical reflection established new rules for deliberating with each other about the courses of action that might be of the greatest public benefit. He argues that this emphasis on reasoned deliberation also provided a mechanism for resisting domination and for expanding the realm of public participation. While the fact that only literate property owners were entitled to participate in public debate certainly limited the scope of this "public," Habermas suggests that the existence of the new public sphere nevertheless involved a deliberative process that had certain democratic elements, as people communicated "in their common quality as human beings and nothing more than human beings."[7] Although eighteenth-century salons and coffeehouses implicitly reinforced middle-class values, Habermas maintains that these venues nevertheless removed people from an immediate concern with social standing, as the critical discussions that took place there "established the public as in principle inclusive. . . . The issues discussed became 'general' not merely in their significance, but also in their accessibility: everyone had to be *able* to participate."[8]

This apparently free and open participation proved to be a source of both excitement and concern to those invested in public discourse. Eighteenth-century Scottish novelist Tobias Smollett satirically captures the anxieties underlying this expanded discursive realm in *Roderick Random,* where the narrator's observation of the impressive conversation at "a certain coffee-house" convinces him that he has fulfilled his goal of surrounding himself with "a set of good acquaintance."[9] Random's realization much later that his companions were all poseurs and did not in fact possess "the illustrious birth, and noble education"[10] that he had attributed to them reveals both the democratic potential of the coffeehouse—and the underlying concern that such expanded access undoubtedly provoked in those who hoped that coffeehouses would provide a venue that would enable them to encounter "good acquaintance."

Many of Habermas's critics have acknowledged this tension and have pointed to gaps between the public participation his theory describes and the increasingly rigid class boundaries that developed during this period. The works of eighteenth-century theorists reside at the crux of this transitional moment, as they simultaneously reflect an expansive vision of rhetoric and a desire to harness rhetoric's power for the purpose of preserving social order. The emergence of new sites for negotiating ideas did at least provide theorists with hope that the collective consensus that had been the goal of classical rhetoric could be preserved even in a society that was rapidly changing. Yet for rhetoricians, this hope was offset by anxious reflection about how rhetoric might best adapt to the challenges and opportunities of a new era. Warner states that during the eighteenth century, "both public and private were redefined, and both gained enormously in significance following the conception of state power as limited and rights as vested in private persons."[11] The question of how to ensure that private persons used the power accompanying their rights responsibly was one that eighteenth-century theorists sought to address. Devising a rhetorical consciousness of the rules governing the language of "civil society" and preparing citizens for such participation posed unprecedented challenges for eighteenth-century theorists. Their writings demonstrate both their appreciation for the apparent progress represented by scientific ideas, the widespread distribution of print, and the expansion of literacy and their awareness that these changes might threaten the public consensus they still believed to be possible.

Various sources of anxiety are evident in the writings of rhetoricians during the latter decades of the eighteenth century. Their basic adherence to classical views concerning language's role in forming a strong community raised urgent questions about the impact of industrialization on the social stability that had historically both guided and been preserved by language use. Many eighteenth-century thinkers believed that the increased literacy available through print provided new opportunities for creating the collective harmony they saw as their ideal. In some respects, the isolated act of reading provides the opportunity to imagine a community that could not exist in any other way, a view Warner supports in his study of the rise of print culture in eighteenth-century America: "It becomes possible to imagine oneself, in the act of reading, becoming part of an arena of the national people that cannot be realized except through such mediating imaginings."[12] Eighteenth-century adaptations of rhetorical principles that could accommodate written as well as oral speech reflect attempts to take advantage of the possibility that print might facilitate collective unity.

At the same time, their society's literary orientation was the cause for some unease among people of the late eighteenth and early nineteenth centuries, as they feared that the detachment and impersonality associated with written communication could diminish the vitality they had experienced as part of a predominantly oral culture. In his 1762 *A Course of Lectures on Elocution*, Thomas Sheridan attributes the tendency to lose sight of the affective side of human life to the growing emphasis on written discourse, insisting that oral language, a direct gift from God to humanity, is better suited for correctly forming the human mind than written language, which represents an artificial system.[13] Although Blair holds significant responsibility for the shift from oratory to belletristic rhetorical instruction, he forcefully maintains the classical view of language as a collective rather than a solitary enterprise: "What we call human reason, is not the effort or ability of one, so much as it is the result of the reason of many, arising from lights mutually communicated, in consequence of discourse and writing."[14] While this claim reflects Blair's willingness to consider writing a legitimate form of reasoned communication, he at this moment sets aside the ways in which an increased reliance upon writing might jeopardize the shared communication of common goals that had at least seemed to be possible in a society oriented toward oral communication. However, Blair is conscious of the distinct characteristics of speech and writing and acknowledges ways in which each form alters the nature of the communicative act. While he applauds the capacity of writing to further "the instruction of mankind" and describes its superiority as "a more extensive, and a more permanent method of communication,"[15] he maintains that "spoken Language has a great superiority over written Language, in point of energy or force. The voice of the living Speaker, makes an impression on the mind, much stronger than can be made by the perusal of any Writing."[16] Blair thus acknowledges the distinctly dynamic quality inherent in the spoken word, even as he embraces the potential of writing for the development of civilization.

Rhetoricians of the eighteenth and early nineteenth centuries perceived the fragmentation associated with technology and the practical needs of industry as not only generally detrimental to society's health but also specifically threatening to the principles of reasoned deliberation that had at least apparently sustained the rhetorical tradition for centuries. Fears concerning the loss of community inherent in a world governed by the anonymity of print, coupled with long-standing assumptions concerning rhetoric's civic function, inevitably raised new questions about rhetoric's role. Just as the expansion of print and opportunities for literacy helped to promote the evolution of a public sphere distinct from the political structures that had previously defined classical notions of the "public," new lines of thought emerged concerning the individual's potential role in shaping "public discourse." In some respects, changing conceptions of "public" and "private" seemed to grant new authority to individuals through raising awareness of public issues and offering diverse forums for making those interests known. Lockean insights about the value of individual perception in the formation of knowledge also elevated individual experience above the classical search for consensus. At the same time, the modern diffusion of political power through new public spaces and technologies expanded opportunities for competing perspectives to be heard.

Eighteenth-century rhetoricians, all too aware that economic competition challenged notions of rational consensus that had been the classical ideal, were interested in determining how such competition could be constructively managed. Classical consensus had assumed the possibility of open debate among people committed to reaching judgment that would enact their notion of the common good—a value now threatened by individualism and the very competition that in some respects seemed to ensure rhetoric's continued vitality. George Campbell contrasts the responsible rhetorical strategies he proposes with the dominance of "party-spirit," which he perceived as a polarizing outlook that replaced constructive argumentation with biased discourse that fails to promote genuine understanding of other points of view.[17] In his 1828 publication of *Elements of Rhetoric,* Richard Whately expresses a similar desire to prepare the orator to counteract the biases associated with party-spirit and attributes the strength of this phenomenon to the growing influence of the press: "One of the strangest phenomena of the present day is the kind of deference shown by men of each party for the authority of the Newspapers of their respective parties; both in respect of fact and of opinions. . . . A stranger from a distant country would probably suppose that the writer to whom he saw thousands habitually surrendering their judgment, must be a person well-known to them, and highly respected by them. He would be much surprised to find that most of them did not even know who he was."[18]

Issues of public and private knowledge were also central to scientific discourse of the seventeenth and eighteenth centuries, and the desire of eighteenth-century rhetoricians to preserve rhetoric's public function in part affected their positions with respect to modern science and philosophy. While they consistently sought to incorporate contemporary scientific insights about the workings of the human mind into their theories, these rhetorical theorists consistently resisted the implication that individuals hold primary responsibility for acquiring meaningful knowledge about the world in isolation from other persons. Campbell and Whately agree with Bacon's preference for inductive reasoning but at the same time maintain a determined focus on the imagination that challenges the pure scientific emphasis on fact advocated in Thomas Sprat's *History of the Royal Society.* The curriculum of Scottish universities focused heavily on mathematics and science from the early decades of the eighteenth century, with Newtonianism taking a particularly strong hold; Reid was a proponent of Newtonian theories and, like many religious figures of his day, saw science as a valuable resource for proving religious principles, due to what he and other Christian advocates interpreted as its capacity to demonstrate God's ongoing presence in the natural world.[19] Yet Newton's influence, along with Locke's role in the development of epistemological rhetorical theories, must be seen in relief against Reid's insistence that the principles of modern science and philosophy, though worthwhile, had become too abstract to bene-fit humanity at large. Reid's desire to develop a philosophy that acknowledges "principles which irresistibly govern the belief and the conduct of all mankind in the common concerns of life"[20] reflects the dilemma of those who sought to benefit from scientific knowledge while preserving the type of consensus that had been central to the classical world.

Scientific rationalism had also created challenges for those who sought to uphold the humanizing influence of reason while arguing for an essential human quality that could not be restricted to the workings of science. Although their appreciation for the centrality of reason is fully in keeping with Stoic and Enlightenment assumptions, many eighteenth-century rhetorical theorists also resisted the trend to associate rational acts with self-interest, as advanced in the theories of Thomas Hobbes and Bernard Mandeville, whose ideas are sys-tematically attacked by Francis Hutcheson and described by Adam Smith as "wholly pernicious."[21] Their encounters with such ideas presented eighteenth-century rhetoricians with the challenge of maintaining the idea "that moral authority in a community is located in the public consensus of its members rather than in their individual private convictions,"[22] even as they drew upon modern scientific, psychological, and philosophical insights in seeking a better understanding of how those private convictions might be reached and directed toward the formation of responsible civic judgments.

Further complications emerged from the role of rationalism in raising ques-tions about religious revelation, which supports Herrick's observation that Sto-icism was a resource skeptics drew upon in support of religious insight gained through the use of reason rather than authority.[23] However, Christian theorists also interpreted the notion of a collective intuitive judgment of the world as implicitly supporting Christian arguments concerning the value of testimony and of the reservoir of community beliefs that form the basis for interpreting truth—a position Whately adopts in using "common sense" to locate the bur-den of proof in favor of Christian perspectives agreed upon by the community. Christian thinkers also found value in the Stoic virtues of duty, self-control, and the notion of an innate ethical sense. The range of possible approaches to Stoic thought helps to account for its appeal across varied cultural moments and helps, in the present case, to account for its presence in the writings of Shaftesbury, a noted skeptic, and Christian clergymen such as Reid, Campbell, Blair, and Whately. Thus, even as Shaftesbury helps to perpetuate questions about reason and Christian belief that were anathema to thinkers such as Reid and Campbell, their shared interest in promoting an ethical community involved Shaftesbury and the clergymen who followed his lead in pursuing the sensus communis described by Stoic philosophers.

Tracing the strains of Stoicism in later thought is a complicated undertaking. Although Stoicism originated as a highly structured philosophical system, its coherence diminishes over several centuries of development, particularly as it begins to be appropriated in contexts distinct from its ancient origins. Founded by Zeno of Citium, who was born in 334 B.C.E. and established the first Stoic school in Athens in 300 B.C.E., Stoicism evolved in three distinct phases across the following five centuries. This evolution included a shift in its central axis from Greece to Rome that began in the Middle Stoa in the second and first centuries B.C.E. and was completed in the Late Stoa in the first and second centuries C.E. Significant variations in its precepts emerged as Stoicism evolved across several centuries, in different locations, and under different leaders. However, Stoic thought was a major influence in the ancient world[24] and has consistently maintained a strong presence in the development of Western ideas at several moments in history. This presence can be seen as particularly significant during the eighteenth and early nineteenth centuries in Britain, when key principles of Stoic thought, particularly as developed through the ethical teachings of Roman Stoics, provide the framework for British theories about language and community.

The central tenets of Stoicism consistently revolve around the need for people to orient themselves toward finding a meaningful place within the divine order, which leads to a complex exploration of the relationship among physics, which generally includes the study of the external world, logic, the systematic study of the processes by which humans acquire knowledge, and ethics, which comprises theories about how people should apply their knowledge to benefit themselves and others. From its inception, Stoic philosophy emphasized the cultivation of an appropriate response to external circumstances. This in part involves a focus on an internal sensibility that allows the individual to maintain an appropriate perspective on the distractions of the external world. At the same time, the foundation of the Stoic ethical system is the assumption that people's lives are intricately connected, which means that each individual can only fulfill his or her divine potential through discovering the connection between the harmony that resides in nature and the harmonious function of the social life for which humans were created. Marcia L. Colish notes that "the Stoics see no gap whatever between the ethical fulfillment of the individual, the ethical fulfillment of the entire human race, and the rational law of nature."[25] These assumptions resonate with eighteenth-century anxieties, which often centered upon questions related to whether people are naturally disposed to good or evil, the role of public knowledge in a world increasingly guided by individual experience, the role society plays in the development of human nature, and the individual's ability to overcome the sense of isolation and instability that seemed to be a danger of modern life. Stoic ethics therefore provided a model for eighteenth-century theorists interested in finding a way to acknowledge the importance of the individual's perception of the world while maintaining the commitment to shared understanding that had served as a fundamental precept of rhetorical theories from the classical period forward.

Stoic ways of connecting nature, beauty, and virtue provide a foundation for a long tradition that assumes similar links among nature, sensory experience, expression, and moral development. Although the Stoics clearly had little use for rhetoric as a formal discipline, their ethical system relies upon language and education in ways that resonate with other strains in the rhetorical tradition. The potential significance of this connection for rhetoric is developed in the writings of Cicero, who was strongly influenced by his study with the Stoic Posidonius at Rhodes, and Quintilian, whose notion of *vir bonus,* "the good man speaking well," also has Stoic roots.[26] The austerity typically associated with Stoic style represents the historical antithesis to Cicero's eloquence, but Cicero's rhetorical philosophy nevertheless draws upon Stoic ethical principles in defining rhetoric's potential to cultivate public and private virtue.[27] The appropriation of Stoic thought by both Cicero and Quintilian provides rhetorical theorists with early and influential models for assigning Stoic ethics a role in rhetoric's civic work.

While the profound influence of Cicero and Quintilian on subsequent rhetorical theorists brings Stoic thought into the history of rhetoric at various cultural moments, the Stoic ethical system becomes particularly significant in rhetoric's history through the work of eighteenth-century theorists. In part, the presence of Stoic thought among these rhetoricians reflects the general influence of Stoic philosophy on British literature and culture, particularly during the eighteenth century. Yet, in spite of the recognition of the place of Stoic philosophy in eighteenth-century culture, little has been written about its presence in the evolution of British rhetoric. The appropriation of Stoic ethics by British rhetoricians, including the notion of sensus communis, represents an important strategy for resolving tensions between the emerging priority of individual self-interest, most notably advanced by Hobbes, and the classical rhetorical emphasis on the pursuit of the public welfare. For theorists concerned with these questions, Stoic philosophy provided a framework for negotiating the tensions between sense and reason and for reinscribing inextricable connections between public and private decision making. The Stoics had consistently maintained that the basis for the community's strength lies in sensus communis, the common values that people share, rather than any political system, and that individuals dedicated to a virtuous life will ultimately discover deep bonds with others that transcend the immediate limits of their social circumstances. This philosophical outlook therefore prescribed a type of internal reflection that to some extent protected the individual from social upheaval but at the same time maintained the civic commitment that had been a central precept in British rhetoric's evolution. Stoic arguments about the role of individual perception in discovering the virtuous course of action and sharing that vision with the community effectively addressed eighteenth-century anxiety about individual isolation in the midst of social upheaval and promoted an optimistic vision of social cohesion in the midst of radical change. Thus Stoic insights about the role of individual deliberation in social transformation provided eighteenth-century rhetoricians with a useful framework for addressing contemporary concerns—and for attempting to establish order in the midst of what must at times have seemed to be a chaotic environment. Their appropriation of Stoic philosophy in exploring these intersections provided eighteenth-century theorists with a means for responding to specific cultural challenges while still invoking the stability associated with an ancient and respected philosophical tradition.

This response acknowledged the new public significance of "private" life, as they emphasized private perception and reflection as first steps in strengthening public discourse. In their view, engaging in thoughtful reflection should help to overcome the artificial boundaries, exemplified in party-spirit, that divided people from each other and to strengthen the natural connections people discovered through the immediacy of personal interactions. In light of such concerns, eighteenth-century theorists sought to devise a new version of rhetoric that defined the rhetorical function of personal reflection and interpersonal interactions, a world that had previously been considered private but had now become public. In adopting this course, they attempted to adapt rhetorical theory to changing social conditions even as they reinforced notions of civic discourse that had been central to rhetoric's development from the sixteenth century forward. Their strategy involved developing a vocabulary that created a bridge between the world of private perception and reflection and public life—a vocabulary heavily shaped by their engagement with Stoic ethics.

The writing of eighteenth-century theorists reflects awareness of the tension between the pursuit of individual objectives and public duty, and they found in Stoicism a historic model for constructively resolving this opposition by demonstrating that nature has ordained that individuals can only flourish when their interests are connected with those of the community. Richard B. Sher comments that, in the 1783 history of Rome that Blair described as "out of all sight the best Roman History that we have,"[28] Adam Ferguson, professor of natural and moral philosophy at the University of Edinburgh, depicts the philosophical struggle between Stoicism and Epicureanism in the late Roman republic as "essentially a struggle between self-interest and public virtue, carried on with all the intensity of a religious crusade."[29] Stoic thought can be seen as one philosophical alternative British rhetoricians locate in their efforts to develop theories that would provide the necessary balance between personal autonomy and civic virtue as they carried out their own crusade against the dangers of self-interest. Exploring the presence of Stoic philosophy in the writings of eighteenth-century British theorists therefore brings into focus the persistent exploration of style, ethics, and civic virtue that form the vocabulary they use in seeking to define the relationship between the individual and society in response to the social and intellectual challenges that they find consuming.

Their thorough familiarity with ancient thought enables British rhetoricians to draw upon Stoic ideas both directly and indirectly in developing distinctly eighteenth-century ideas about how rhetoric could not only accomplish specific practical goals but also prepare people to fulfill their ethical potential. This public and private mission is enacted through the development of four important rhetorical terms during the late eighteenth and early nineteenth centuries: common sense, taste, sympathy, and propriety. Although these eighteenth-century terms do not in themselves have direct correspondence to Stoic philosophy, they are deployed in eighteenth-century rhetorical theories to support the broader Stoic objectives of individual vision, achieved through self-discipline, and civic harmony, thereby serving as focal points for observing how Stoic concepts are adapted to address modern concerns. The writings of major theorists of the late eighteenth and early nineteenth centuries who make these terms central to their theories of language and rhetoric, including Shaftesbury, Reid, Smith, Kames, Campbell, Blair, and Whately, maintain important ties to Stoic thought, even as their particular cultural circumstances transform the ways in which these terms are used.

It has been something of a commonplace in history of rhetoric scholarship to depict eighteenth-century preoccupations with psychology, aesthetic appreciation, sympathy, and taste as signs of an "inward turn" that abandons classical rhetoric's civic mission in favor of a modern elevation of individual experience. This transformation has been attributed to various causes: scientific views of knowledge as empirical and based in individual experience; an evolving class system that glorified self-improvement, supported by a professionalized educational curriculum; and Romantic notions of creative genius developed in isolation from others. Many studies of eighteenth-century rhetoric have focused primarily on ways in which such contemporary philosophical and scientific principles guide the development of belletristic rhetoric. Several scholars have focused on links between belletristic rhetoric and contemporary French thought. Wilbur Samuel Howell's landmark *Eighteenth-Century British Logic and Rhetoric* depicts eighteenth-century British theories as sharply departing from classical assumptions. Howell identifies both scientific empiricism and contemporary French theories as dominant influences on "the new rhetorics" of the eighteenth century, specifically tracing the roots of belletristic rhetoric to

François de Salignac de la Mothe Fenelon's expansion of the province of rhetoric to include poetry[30] and to the popularization of Charles Rollin's term *belles lettres* among English speakers.[31] Thomas M. Conley's survey of the history of rhetoric also stresses the significance of French thought and fashion in shaping British intellectual discourse.[32] Conley describes Claude Buffier's use of the term *common sense* as a foundation of Thomas Reid's commonsense philosophy, which in turn establishes the groundwork for the "philosophical" rhetoric of George Campbell,[33] and he identifies Blair's primary influences as Nicolas Boileau's translation of Longinus and the writings of Buffier and Henry Home, Lord Kames.[34] Barbara Warnick's extensive examination of the French forerunners of British belletristic rhetoric points to the significance of aesthetic reception in belletristic rhetorical theory, as she argues that aesthetic appeal provides the basis for a new conception of invention, which she identifies as a "sixth canon," in the works of Smith, Blair, and Campbell.[35] This understanding leads her to argue that belletristic rhetorics can best be appreciated not by viewing them through a "neoclassical lens" but "on their own terms, as products of the intellectual climate of the Enlightenment and as reflections of a desire to improve taste and discernment in Scottish culture."[36]

H. Lewis Ulman echoes this view in his assessment of how eighteenth-century theories of language are grounded in particular goals relevant to a society attempting to standardize English usage: "Eighteenth-century rhetorical theory traditionally addresses the persuasive effect of particular forms of language, supporting the dominance of standard varieties over 'barbarous' dialects and discourses."[37] Lloyd F. Bitzer notes parallels between the thought of Campbell and Hume, even as Campbell participates in Reid's commonsense response to Hume's extreme religious skepticism.[38] Douglas Ehninger stresses how changing intellectual and social conditions led eighteenth-century rhetorical theories to depart significantly from classical rhetorical principles.[39] Thomas Miller also focuses on contemporary influences that shaped eighteenth-century rhetorical theories, as he examines in depth rhetoric's participation in "the educational transmission of the dominant culture"[40] that shaped what Scottish intellectuals perceived to be morally and aesthetically valuable.

In placing eighteenth-century theories of the individual mind and experience firmly within the realm of contemporary thought, such interpretations legitimately posit for eighteenth-century theorists an absorption with questions generated within their immediate cultural moment. However, understanding their responses to those questions also requires situating their theories within the broader intellectual context that surrounded the people who created them. Eighteenth-century intellectuals were vitally concerned with the changes that were taking place around them, but their academic foundation in ancient sources was both a cause and an effect of their unwillingness to yield entirely to the worldview advanced by the modern era. For many of these theorists, modern science and philosophy represented, on one hand, an intriguing avenue to certain truths about the world, including a resource for defending religious faith, and, on the other, a potential threat to social tradition and religious belief. To focus on the scientific and psychological orientation of eighteenth-century theorists neglects to account for their appreciation of a range of classical texts not simply as the means to acquire education and culture but also as resources for understanding human experience in a way that actively addressed the pervasive tensions and conflicts found in modern thought. Encountering the work of these theorists does involve acknowledging that their works cannot be seen as part of a timeless neoclassical succession, but it also requires taking into account the complete intellectual context from which their thought emerges. Broadening the scope of influences beyond rhetoric's immediate origins can add valuable depth to the study of eighteenth-century British rhetorics and illustrate ways in which changing views of the individual's relationship to society emerge only gradually over time—and through complicated networks of historical and contemporary theories and disciplines.

One of the complicating features of any effort to sift through the strains of influence constituting such networks has been the long-standing tendency to simplify and streamline the various strains that comprise ancient theories of language. A number of contemporary scholars have initiated work that challenges earlier accounts that present ancient rhetoric as monolithic; such accounts often conflate Aristotle's rhetorical theory with all Athenian rhetoric and in turn use Athenian rhetoric as the model for all ancient rhetoric.[41] The argument that the Stoic strain fusing ethics and rhetoric merits recognition in the history of rhetoric contributes to efforts to expand the rhetorical canon, a response to Susan Jarratt's call for histories that "entail the appropriation and redefinition of texts currently 'held' by other disciplines,"[42] an endeavor that underscores the dynamic and intricate relationships between rhetoric and culture. Acknowledging the complexity of these relationships across time supports Richard Leo Enos's claim that "works are best understood when viewed not as isolated and autonomous events, but as intertextual, that even discrete texts are part of a diachronic chain of being."[43] This chain of textual relationships presents an important resource for expanding scholarly assessments of the ancient principles that guide eighteenth-century rhetorical theories, which include texts that fall outside the classical rhetorical canon.

At the same time, the effort to trace the philosophical influences on eighteenth-century rhetorical theories should not be interpreted as willingly participating in previous approaches to scholarship that have tended to subsume rhetoric's history under the umbrella of philosophy. In their critique of the work of P. Albert Duhamel, Richard Graff and Michael Leff argue, "Duhamel threatened to obscure tradition by burying it beneath philosophical foundations. Rhetoric as a teaching practice commands little attention when we concentrate on the epistemological and metaphysical grounding of 'rhetorical systems.'"[44] Although arriving at a more complicated understanding of the philosophical roots of eighteenth-century rhetoric undoubtedly might appear to fall under the category of an "influence study," the purpose of this inquiry is neither to substantiate rhetoric's authority through its connection to a long philosophical tradition nor to establish a line of theoretical descent for rhetoric that has only an esoteric significance. Instead, I seek to demonstrate how eighteenth-century theorists draw upon Stoic ethics in response to their perception of the cultural changes that surround them. It is my hope that a more complete awareness of the philosophical influences that shape eighteenth-century rhetorical theories will not end as a contribution to an intellectual history removed from the immediate social concerns that have always been central to rhetoric's disciplinary identity. My interest in tracking the appropriation of Stoic thought in eighteenth-century theories reflects the conviction that this intersection helps to bring into focus the significant material implications that emerge from changing conceptions of rhetoric's role in society.

The philosophical orientation of eighteenth-century theorists both reflects their educational training and shapes the pedagogy they advocated. Part of the particularity of eighteenth-century British education involves an emphasis on classical training that served not only as a marker of intellectual acumen but also as a resource for understanding the world. Because classical sources were so central to their worldview, many eighteenth-century thinkers were not prepared to grant the sharp division between public and private that has come to be a defining feature of modern life. Acknowledging the Stoic underpinnings that inform eighteenth-century thought about the link between the individual's experience and civic life helps to distinguish eighteenth-century rhetorical theories from later appropriations of those theories that are found in the development of nineteenth-century composition. Many rhetorical scholars have accepted James A. Berlin's argument that the popularity of Campbell, Blair, and Whately in the United States can be attributed to "their not being altogether incompatible with the American belief in individualism."[45] However, this interpretation fails to recognize that the theories of Campbell, Blair, and Whately in large part represent attempts to struggle against the turn toward individualism that eighteenth-century society seemed to be taking. These theorists defied early signs of a cultural shift toward individual autonomy, pursuing classical notions of civic virtue that had not yet been entirely eroded by what Sharon Crowley has described as the nineteenth century's "bourgeois project of self-improvement."[46] Although notions of taste and aesthetic appreciation were later appropriated by those who sought to advance this "bourgeois project," these terms originate in the work of eighteenth-century theorists whose efforts to resist the instability of their cultural moment in part involved reinscribing the classical belief in the possibility of civic consensus—efforts supported by Stoic expressions of the natural link between individual and society. Thus eighteenth-century theorists can be seen as transitional figures in what Gregory Clark and S. Michael Halloran describe with reference to the United States as the transformation of oratorical culture, which locates standards of morality in the hands of individuals rather than collectives, a "general shift of the public realm from a setting for socialization to a setting for individuation."[47] The role of eighteenth-century British rhetorics in the construction and deployment of contesting cultural images makes fertile ground for inquiry into the principles that preserved ancient views of rhetoric's public function in one era and facilitated the modern emphasis on individual expression in another. Moreover, this line of inquiry offers broader insight into the ways in which changing cultural environments persistently redefine perceptions of the complex relationship between the individual and the social.

The Stoic roots in eighteenth-century rhetorical theories not only complicate the division between individual and social but also challenge the precise alignment of the categories of "ancient" and "modern" in the study of eighteenth-century ideas. Eighteenth-century theorists at times demonstrate a striking confidence in "progress" and argue stridently for "civilized" standards in comparison with what they conceive of as the inferior mental disposition of "savages." At the same time, many eighteenth-century theories of taste juxtapose the pure standards of natural beauty against the false refinement of society, and eighteenth-century language theorists refer to the imaginative power and simplicity of primitive society in ways that seem to support Jean Jacques Rousseau's image of the "noble savage." They also demonstrate their allegiance to nationalistic aims and a view that their role as educators obligates them to provide their students with the cultural refinement that contributes to economic success, even as they uphold classical ideals of a virtue that transcends purely material aims. Understanding the link between Scottish common sense and Stoic sensus communis offers a vehicle for understanding how the scientific and modern aims of these Enlightenment thinkers might coexist in an uneasy partnership with the optimistic vision they had received through their classical training. For eighteenth-century theorists, Stoic thought provides a means for restoring harmony to their chaotic world through applying time-tested principles to new social challenges.

Recognizing the infusion of Stoic ideas in eighteenth-century notions of language therefore both complicates and elucidates the eighteenth-century transition between classical and modern innovations in rhetoric. Adam Potkay has aptly described this transition as the "tension between a nostalgia for ancient eloquence and an emerging ideology of polite style" that dominates eighteenth-century British discourse, as he traces the emergence of new ideas about communication in response to the changing political environment in eighteenth-century Britain.[48] In "Blair's Ideal Orator: Civic Rhetoric and Christian Politeness in Lectures 25–34," Arthur E. Walzer argues that Blair can be seen as a figure whose work reflects the transition from an educational system grounded in the ideals of civic republicanism to one preparing students for polite society. Walzer notes that politeness in the social order of post-Union Scotland maintains a moral function, as it represents not simply a set of social rules but instead reflects a strategy for developing social relationships, which include developing "restraint by controlling the violent emotions, such as anger, cultivating the social emotions, such as sympathy, and subduing zeal and suppressing enthusiasm."[49] Stoic values can be seen as an important presence in providing polite discourse with its ethical force; these values function significantly in mediating the transition between ancient notions of virtue and the demands of modern society, providing vital ties to the ancient world even as eighteenth-century theorists identify ways in which the classical framework of oral public debate seemed to have lost its viability in modern public life.

The philosophical foundation of Stoicism brought ethical depth to polite society. As J. G. A. Pocock has pointed out, the culture of politeness was not in itself sufficiently powerful to ward off the chaos that eighteenth-century theorists perceived to reside just beneath the surface of their society: "The Europe-wide cult of Ossian, rivaled only by the personality cult of Jean-Jacques Rousseau, revealed . . . the historical fragility on which the philosophy of polite and commercial society was built. Was not the enlightened and sociable modern threatened with specialization and distraction, effeminacy and corruption? Was not the heroic and virtuous ancient a regression to feudalism and a slave economy, barbarism and savagery? Where in the historic process might unity of personality be found?"[50] Such unity was not entirely available through Stoic thought, but Stoicism did at least offer a way of connecting the attributes of discipline and restraint with the more fundamental objective of harmony among individuals, society, and nature. The search for harmony and control has both political and religious significance; Sher identifies the appropriation of Stoicism by the moderate literati of Edinburgh as playing a central role in the "cultivation of polite yet impassioned eloquence in the service of virtue and happiness."[51] Eighteenth-century adaptations of Stoicism therefore revised and revitalized "ancient eloquence," as they created a philosophical basis for discourse that was both grounded in ancient principles and oriented toward the discipline, restraint, and propriety that eighteenth-century theorists perceived as useful in bringing order to modern life—and guiding humanity toward a more meaningful existence.

Thus, in the midst of social trends that seemed to emphasize individual success and material advancement, eighteenth-century theorists sought a connection to classical notions of civic virtue that would increasingly be called into question in subsequent generations. Certainly the changes in their world had made these theorists aware of the challenges they faced in advocating the acquisition of civic virtue; however, they found in Stoic philosophy a vocabulary that allowed them to establish a case for this possibility in the midst of an era in which moral truths seemed to be threatened from all sides. Eighteenth-century rhetorical theorists drew upon a Stoic framework in seeking to transform the fractured and restricted "public sphere" into an expansive and vibrant entity capable of transcending the immediate social problems that surrounded them.

The eighteenth-century attempt to blend rhetoric with Stoic philosophy in order to reinscribe strong social relationships was to have a short life. The inexorable advance of modern ideas resisted the efforts of eighteenth-century theorists to find a balance between modern and scientific insights and older notions of social unity. Stoic notions concerning the role of nature in providing a mystical order for human life were gradually superseded by the nineteenth century's perception of truth as firmly situated in human subjectivity. The theories of Campbell, Blair, and Whately continued to be influential well into the nineteenth century, but the adaptation of their theories for the development of nineteenth-century composition curricula altered the complex philosophical premises of their work. The growing influence of the press altered people's understanding of what constituted "public discourse" and contributed in significant ways to suspicions that rhetoric had been placed in the service of self-interest and factionalism. Warner describes the establishment of a disinterested public as an eventual consequence of this change, arguing that "as private persons came to be seen as driven by self-interest, the public came to be defined as disinterested. Those aspects of people's lives that particularize their interests came to be seen as inappropriate to public discussion."[52] The cultivation of an ethical disinterestedness guided by Stoic self-control and modified by a commitment to sensus communis was gradually replaced by a more complete detachment that had come to be seen as the only viable remedy for party-spirit. The vitality of the new industrial economy and the durable social changes that accompanied it led many nineteenth-century thinkers to abandon the hope that rhetoric could promote the free exchange of ideas that they believed to have been associated with the public of an earlier era.

Of course, the freedom and access associated with earlier versions of the public had always been limited, as only the privileged few had been invited to participate in forming the consensus that eighteenth-century theorists idealized. The nineteenth-century turn away from the oppressive potential of consensus constitutes a rhetorical position that deserves careful attention. Tracing the eighteenth-century appropriation of Stoic thought and the nineteenth-century rejection of the possibility of sensus communis holds the benefit both of providing insight into eighteenth-century rhetorical theories and of helping to fill gaps in British rhetoric's history as the nineteenth century progresses.

The transformation of nineteenth-century British rhetoric reflects a response to social conditions that were changing rapidly and dramatically. While contemporary generalizations about Victorian society tend to be problematic, historian Robin Gilmour notes that such generalizations were common among the people who lived through that period: "No previous generation of people had been so conscious of the uniqueness of the times they were living through as the early Victorians, so drawn to compare themselves with their ancestors, or so aware of their time as an 'age' requiring definition."[53] He goes on to assert that Britain in 1850 was "a different place—socially, culturally, intellectually—from the Britain of 1800."[54] There are substantial reasons for accepting the Victorians' own view that their era was characterized by unprecedented change, but the very fact that they perceived this to be the case helps to explain possible reasons for their doubts about the viability of the cohesive community that people of previous eras had pursued so diligently.

Although the era has frequently been characterized as a time of religious revival, Gilmour says that the established Church was also beset by raging internal conflicts and by new challenges initiated by the rise of science—conflicts that had begun centuries before but that achieved new force during the Victorian era. As a result, the period "witnessed a decisive separation of the moral sense from the religious institutions which had once expressed it."[55] Gilmour explains that as fundamental uncertainty about religion accompanied broad economic, social, and political changes, "the Victorians confronted their unique historical exposure without the security of a confident world-view (Christianity being in crisis) until science began to provide one in the 1860s and 1870s."[56] Many Victorians seem to have been all too aware that they had numerous causes for anxiety.

Although the scientific worldview continued to offer exciting vistas of knowledge, the eighteenth-century ambivalence toward science continued to gain strength in the nineteenth century. Many intellectuals firmly believed in science's capacity to improve the quality of human life, but the rise of science also raised questions about individual agency in a complicated world. As James Eli Adams points out in his study of Victorian conceptions of masculinity, more sophisticated forms of technology and communication during the Victorian era created a conflict between, on one hand, the perceived need to assert personal autonomy (specifically related to gender roles, in the case of Adams's study), and, on the other hand, the impulse to withdraw altogether from the threat associated with public scrutiny.[57]

Eighteenth-century language theorists had experienced similar tensions, and they drew upon Stoic thought in order to resolve what appeared to be shifts in the nature of the public sphere and accompanying changes in the relationship between the private and the social. The accelerated pace of social change in the nineteenth century exacerbated the challenges that eighteenth-century writers sought to address and ultimately undermined the optimistic spirit that had propelled the evolution of British rhetorical theory from the sixteenth century forward. Although Victorian critics did not totally abandon the ultimate goal of sensus communis, their cultural surroundings pushed them toward a vision of language that acknowledged and at times even embraced the chasm between private perception and public expression.

This position stands in sharp contrast to eighteenth-century theorists' persistent attempts to negotiate and heal the potential rift between individuals and their society. Rhetorical theories during the eighteenth century had sought sensus communis through identifying common ground that could serve as the means for maintaining social stability. Mounting social unrest during the first half of the nineteenth century created the urgent sense that positive transformation, not the mere maintenance of the status quo, was urgently needed. Many nineteenth-century intellectuals perceived the formal structure of rhetoric to be too prescriptive and technical to promote the meaningful and spontaneous public discourse that they believed would facilitate such change. Crowley takes note of this shift, as she argues that in the nineteenth century, the goals of preparing students for participation in civic life are replaced by the goal of cultivating a sensibility that stands apart from rhetorical activity. According to Crowley, nineteenth-century literary study provides the ethical training that had at one time been a feature of rhetorical instruction but focuses on the development of an aesthetic judgment removed from the "ethical subjectivity"[58] that had been a central feature of disciplined training in rhetoric. Thus Crowley maintains that nineteenth-century literature classrooms removed taste from its original grounding in civic negotiation in order to emphasize the purity of subjective aesthetic experience.[59]

The transformation Crowley describes can be seen as both shaping and reflecting cultural change across the nineteenth century. In *Distinction: A Social Critique of the Judgment of Taste,* Pierre Bourdieu characterizes taste not as the product of rhetorical training and civic commitment but as the outward manifestation of a refined internal disposition that is deliberately distanced from the ethical obligations that motivate the average citizen. He discusses at some length the sharp distinction between those whose "popular ethos"[60] leads them to assess art according to "their everyday perception of everyday existence,"[61] an aesthetic sensibility that subordinates form to function and is "necessarily pluralistic and conditional,"[62] and the Kantian aesthetic that privileges the formal representation of art in a manner that willfully "throws the thing itself into the background."[63] Bourdieu identifies the aesthetic disposition as "one dimension of a distant, self-assured relation to the world and to others which presupposes objective assurance and distance,"[64] a distance that is also predicated upon "the suspension and removal of economic necessity"[65] that shapes the daily lives of those without the leisure to invest in the cultural capital guaranteed by the possession of taste. Citing contemporary philosophers of art such as José Ortega y Gasset, Bourdieu depicts the "pure gaze" associated with artistic appreciation as a property that has been methodically removed from the realm of the "ordinary attitude towards the world" associated with "common people."[66] Bourdieu's critique of taste, alongside Crowley's argument concerning its nineteenth-century evolution, provides a useful point of entry for considering the gradual erosion of rhetoric's perceived connection to taste, propriety, sympathy, and sensus communis during the nineteenth century.

The changing practices of public discourse in the nineteenth century, created in large part by the rising prominence of newspapers and periodicals, also called into question many of the presumptions that had previously formed the basis for rhetorical education. Many nineteenth-century writers occupied an ambivalent position toward the innovations in communication, as their essays condemning the rise of the press ironically depended upon the periodicals that they denounced for their publication and dissemination. In his 1828 essay entitled "Rhetoric," Thomas De Quincey insists upon the need for rhetoric to stimulate the intellect in ways that have been stifled by the emphasis on the practical needs of industry.[67] Thomas Carlyle is even more pointed in his critique of the role of print culture in the decline of human society. He notes that the act of writing has become enmeshed in technology, for "books are not only printed, but, in a great measure, written and sold, by machinery."[68] He blames the pervasiveness of machinery in all aspects of life for a fundamental change in the way people view themselves and the world around them, claiming that people have not only been changed in their behavior but have also "grown mechanical in head and in heart" as well.[69] For both Carlyle and De Quincey, then, nineteenth-century developments provided ample evidence that the centrality of written communication had led to a gradual decline in the capacity for sympathy and community that eighteenth-century theorists had worked so hard to protect.

At the same time, the increasing complexity of modern life only intensified the nostalgic longing for shared values that had remained constant throughout the development of British rhetoric. The nineteenth-century interest in the relationships among rhetorical expression, aesthetic experience, and the community in some respects continued the long-standing effort to define the community's identity and preserve sensus communis. However, during the course of the century, the hope for community comes to be attached to the inspired imaginative activity of the exceptional individual who is capable of revitalizing society only through detachment from public life.

The current volume traces the British appropriation of Stoic ideas to devise a role for rhetoric in strengthening the natural order through sensus communis during the eighteenth century and concludes with the nineteenth century's turn away from that goal. Certainly the nineteenth-century turn toward an idealized realm removed from the sordid concerns of daily life is foreshadowed in eighteenth-century rhetorical theories. However, acknowledging the complex influences present within eighteenth-century thought helps to show why those theorists might have perceived themselves as in some respects resistant to modern influences even as they devised theories that ultimately supported the development of a modern division between public and private life. Stephen Engstrom and Jennifer Whiting assert that the Stoic emphasis on moral duty grounded in natural law can be seen as a major influence on Enlightenment thought: "The Stoics thus provide not only a historical link between Aristotle and [Immanuel] Kant, but also an illustration of how putatively ancient and modern thought might be coherently integrated."[70] The effort to achieve this integration posed eighteenth-century theorists with a significant challenge—and offers an intriguing subject of study for contemporary scholarship.

Chapter 1

STOIC ETHICS AND RHETORIC

Stoic thought can be seen as a pervasive yet subtle presence in the development of ideas across centuries far removed from its ancient origins. Precisely locating this presence can be a challenge due to the range of Stoic thought across centuries and to the capacity of central Stoic principles to be integrated with other philosophical systems. A. A. Long argues that "of all the ancient philosophies, Stoicism has probably had the most diffused but also the least explicit and adequately acknowledged influence on western thought."[1] Numerous scholars have identified varied reasons for Stoicism's wide influence and for the subtlety with which that influence is manifested in the thought of subsequent ages. Audrey Chew describes Stoicism as "a good mixer, which means that it is as difficult to find a pure Stoic as to find pure water."[2] Julia Annas describes the holistic Stoic system as one that involves mutually supportive parts that resist the identification of a single controlling idea.[3] The coherence of the Stoic system therefore can be seen as an assembly of supporting ideas that offer several potential points of emphasis during the course of Stoicism's evolution. According to Long, that early Stoicism was exceptionally "systematic, holistic, and formal in methodology"[4] helps to explain the "curiously scattered legacy"[5] of Stoic ideas, as subsequent ages adopted components of Stoic thought without duplicating the system in its entirety. At the same time, ancient Stoic philosophy did evolve with time as the Stoic leaders who followed Zeno introduced variations and as the locus of Stoicism moved from the Stoa in Athens to Rhodes and then to Rome.

These areas of emphasis are particularly subject to interpretation due to the difficulty of gaining direct access to Stoic doctrine. The primary resources for learning about the thought of many major Stoic philosophers, including Zeno, Cleanthes, Chrysippus, Posidonius, and Panaetius, have been the writings of other people. Texts by Roman Stoics constitute the major body of Stoic writings available to later ages; Malcolm Schofield states, "much of the surviving material actually *by* Stoics is what might be called practical ethics, not articulation of doctrine—for which we have to turn to doxographers, anthologists, encyclopedists, and sometimes to hostile or unsympathetic witnesses like Plutarch and Alexander of Aphrodisias."[6] Long comments, "what was most accessible and influential for the Renaissance and Enlightenment were the treatments of Stoic ethics by Cicero, Seneca, Epictetus, and Marcus Aurelius."[7] Stoic ethics has therefore come to be an area of particular interest to thinkers in later eras, even as it has been altered through adaptation to varying social conditions and integration with other philosophical systems and religions, including early Christianity, which "appropriated a great deal of Stoic ethics without acknowledgment."[8]

The Stoic emphasis on the acquisition of an appropriate attitude coupled with their emphasis on the pursuit of ultimate truth has undoubtedly contributed to the lack of attention to Stoicism in traditional accounts of the history of rhetoric, because many of those accounts have defined rhetoric strictly in terms of its role in the production of public discourse responsive to the contingencies that arise in specific public settings such as the courts and legislative assemblies. This omission is understandable, particularly in light of historic assumptions about the gulf between rhetoric and philosophy; however, contemporary efforts to blur disciplinary boundaries, along with the expansion of rhetoric to include uses of symbolic language that fall outside the classical boundaries of forensic and deliberative oratory, open the way to a reconsideration of the place of Stoic thought in the historical evolution of rhetoric. The Stoics explicitly distanced themselves from the formal education in civic discourse that was central to other Greek and Roman rhetorical traditions, but their system included a place for rhetorical action. Their ethical system creates an important role for language and the development of a shared understanding of community values, a view appropriated for a modern context through British rhetorical theories developed in the eighteenth and early nineteenth centuries.

The Stoic understanding of the relationship among language, ethics, and the community begins with the Stoics' belief that virtue entails the recognition that individuals are naturally bound to other people and to the universe as a whole. Virtue requires recognizing the connection between humans and the external world, a view captured in Chrysippus's statement that "our individual natures are part of the nature of the whole universe."[9] This assumed connection between private virtue and a relationship with the external world is also fundamental to the rhetorical theories of both Cicero and Quintilian, which provide a further means by which Stoic thought comes to define the character of eighteenth-century British rhetorics.

Intense interest in Stoic ethical precepts, primarily found in the writings of Cicero, Epictetus, Seneca, and Marcus Aurelius, can be seen as a particularly important feature of the early modern educational environment. These writings reflect different perspectives on Stoicism, shaped in part by the distinct positions of their writers and the diverse genres they represent. Christopher Gill relates that Epictetus, a freed slave who became a Stoic teacher at Nicopolis, presented a technical exposition of Stoic ethics at his school but wrote the *Discourses* to "spell out the core messages of Stoic ethics for a more general audience."[10] Schofield writes, "Much of Epictetus is aptly described as protreptic, summoning his audience as it does to the radical reorientation of their priorities which philosophy entails."[11] Seneca was not a "Stoic teacher" but an aristocrat who wrote essays primarily intended to provide his peers with ethical guidance.[12] Marcus Aurelius's *Meditations* provide the emperor's private reflections on the individual's struggle to pursue a virtuous life. Cicero is not himself a Stoic, but his familiarity with Stoic ideas is evident in a number of treatises; his representation in *De officiis* of Panaetius's thought can be seen as a major resource for the explication of Stoic ethics in subsequent eras.

The writings of these figures can be seen as a foundation for the ongoing vitality of Stoic thought in ages distant from ancient Rome. Brad Inwood describes the influence of Stoicism as experiencing various ebbs and flows through the centuries following Zeno's death, including a decline in the Middle Ages; he concludes that "in the early modern period, Stoicism again became a significant part of the philosophical scene and has remained an influential intellectual force ever since."[13] Inwood acknowledges that Max Pohlenz's depiction of Stoicism as an "intellectual movement" reflects "the longevity and protean variability of Stoicism," but he offers "the metaphor of a special kind of journey"[14] as a term that more aptly describes both the ongoing development of Stoic thought across the centuries and the challenging enterprise of uncovering the threads of that development, which Inwood describes as "an adventure in the history of philosophy . . . a perilous journey for the novice, one requiring guides as varied in their skills and temperaments as was Odysseus."[15] In a sense, Inwood's description of a "perilous journey" can be seen as a valid metaphor for eighteenth-century theorists whose appropriation of Stoicism involved bringing together rhetoric and philosophy, Roman ethics and Christianity, and ancient and modern perspectives. It also effectively anticipates the challenging task of defining the convergence of Stoic ethics and eighteenth-century British rhetorical theories.

Stoic Virtue: Divine Harmony, Providence, and Sensory Experience

One foundation for Stoicism is the premise that each person must see the search for truth as an ultimate concern. This truth is linked to participation in the harmony of the divine order and the development of a mindset focused on spiritual concerns. Epictetus insists that "the true good of man . . . lies in a certain disposition of the will."[16] This disposition involves the development of self-control, which renounces excessive concern with physical circumstances; the Stoic view of negative experience is defined not in terms that would focus on unfortunate material outcomes but in spiritual terms that emphasize the moral fault of allowing such concerns to interfere with the search for truth that should guide each individual's existence. Acquiring the proper ethical orientation, which includes establishing a connection with the divine order that supersedes all human concerns, is therefore of the utmost importance for each person's development. For the Stoics, the individual's central quest therefore lies in the development of an internal ethical sense that cannot be diminished by an excessive concern with external circumstances.

However, the Stoic orientation toward knowledge that transcends the material concerns of the human world is accompanied by a belief they share with Aristotle and with eighteenth-century British rhetoricians—that sensory experience serves as the basis for human knowledge. For the Stoics, the "presentations" that people receive from the external world have the potential to alter the individual mind. Presentations are by definition merely receptive and may be either true or false; the individual has no power over the presentation he or she receives but can choose to accept or reject the mental change that takes place as the result of a presentation. Thus, although experiences inevitably provide people with many presentations, their own assent becomes the basis for determining the place those presentations will ultimately hold in their lives.[17] Whitney J. Oates notes that although the Stoics emphasize the power of fate in each person's life, they provide a certain measure of free will in allowing to individuals the power to determine the correct way their impressions should be used.[18] Different manifestations of this principle are evident across several centuries of Stoicism's development. Zeno holds that the capacity of choice begins with the individual's ability to decide upon which sensory impressions are deserving of mental assent.[19] Epictetus stresses that this is the only measure of control that people do possess, as he states that the gods give humans "the power to deal rightly with our impressions, but everything else they did not put in our hands."[20]

The process of assessing the value of impressions therefore becomes a central source of human knowledge. Over time, presentations leave mental traces that are remembered. The ability to draw upon these traces in order to determine how general principles apply to specific situations enables people to use their sensory knowledge to form ethical judgment. Epictetus writes, "Primary conceptions are common to all men, and one does not conflict with another. Who among us, for instance, does not assume that the good is expedient and desirable and that we ought in all circumstances to follow and pursue it? . . . At what moment then does conflict arise? It arises in the application of primary conceptions to particular facts."[21] The process involved in making such judgments involves the use of a reservoir of assumptions that lie beneath the surface of sensory experiences that individuals have. E. Vernon Arnold points out that these assumptions, or "preconceptions," reflect the view that "not only all practical life, but also all philosophy, takes for granted a great many matters which are either allowed by general consent, or at least assumed by the thinker."[22] Although this term is used in varying ways by different ancient philosophies, Arnold states that "to the Stoics it is one variety of the *ennoia;* it is 'a mental shaping, in accordance with man's nature, of things general.' All such preconceptions are foreshadowings of truth, especially in so far as they correspond to the common judgment of mankind; and the art of life consists in correctly applying these presumptions to the particular circumstances with which each individual man has to deal."[23] Arnold explains that while the Epicureans saw preconceptions as grounded in "memory of a sensation frequently repeated," the Stoics perceive them as "established by the mind, and (so far as they are common to all men) by the universal reason."[24] Thus preconceptions are based in a common reasoning process that enables people to develop a shared understanding of the world, which includes the ability to communicate their insights to each other.

The capacity to explore the relevance of preconceptions in particular cases relies upon an intuitive sense that all humans naturally possess. Because this sense involves making judgments about the world, it has an ethical dimension. Arnold argues that their shared sense also binds people together in a common belief system: "Knowledge cut off from the sense-organs is cut off from all human individuality; it is therefore the expression of the common reason (*koinos logos),* and its parts are 'common notions' (*koinai ennoiai* or *proleipseis*), shared by gods and men, but by men only so far as they are partakers of the divine nature. The principal content of such knowledge is also clear; it includes the conception of what is morally good, and the beliefs that gods exist and that the world is governed by their providence. Lastly, as of all general conceptions, the rudiments or rough outlines only of these beliefs are inborn in men, by virtue of their divine ancestry; whence they are called 'innate notions' (*emfutoi ennoiai notiones*)."[25] Thus, for the Stoics, human knowledge is acquired through both immediate impressions and general assumptions that enable people to make sense of their specific experiences.

The ability to acquire knowledge beyond that which can be seen constitutes an imaginative act, which Dan Flory identifies as an important Stoic contribution to the classical rhetorical tradition and to modern views of the imagination's powerful role in human intellectual development. Countering the tendency of contemporary critics to conceive of the eighteenth century as the period in which imagination's intellectual value first becomes apparent, Flory argues that the Stoic sense of *phantasia* as "the primary source of knowledge and artistic creativity, and as the originator of new ideas for the human mind"[26] offers a classical alternative to the more limited conceptions of the imagination's power found in both Plato and Aristotle. He maintains that the appropriation of Stoic *phantasia* in the rhetorical theories of Cicero, Quintilian, and Longinus[27] becomes a central resource for acknowledging the human capacity to "produce what the senses have never experienced, but the mind has conceived"[28] and recognizing the communicative potential of that ability. He concludes that "for the materialistic Stoics, *phantasia* required an incorporeal mental realm in which to manipulate products of the imagination so that *phantasia's* creative mental dimension could be exercised . . . This view of imagination was a deeply synthetic way of looking at the world, one that emphasized much more strongly than the Platonic or Aristotelian doctrines our active participation over and above our passive presence in acquiring knowledge about the world around us."[29] While impressions provide people with experiences that generate immediate knowledge of the world, the scope of that knowledge expands through their imaginative ability to put those experiences into a framework that makes sense—and to identify possibilities beyond their immediate experiences. Preconceptions therefore enable people not only to acquire knowledge of the world around them but also to engage imaginatively with a world that lies beyond their immediate experience.

This active participation, which puts to use the human capacity to assess the quality of the sensory impressions that form the basis for knowledge, necessarily has ethical implications. Because people have been programmed by nature to acquire and process sensory information, their cultivation of those skills has an important role in fulfilling their spiritual destiny. Epictetus states that "the true nature of good and also of evil depends on how we deal with impressions."[30] The active use of every aspect of human reason ultimately facilitates the cultivation of an innate moral sense, as people develop mental discipline through interpreting their impressions and determining their ethical significance. Epictetus describes this process in detail: "The intellect is so framed that we are not merely the passive subjects of sensations, but select and subtract from them and add to them, and by this means construct particular objects. . . . He brought man into the world to take cognizance of Himself and His works, and not only to take cognizance but also to interpret them."[31] Although the Stoics believe that the material world is not ultimate, they nevertheless maintain that people who are aware of the world around them and attentive to the significance of their experiences in that world are fulfilling their spiritual purpose. In Epictetus's words, "we, to whom He gave also the power of understanding cannot be satisfied without these functions, but, unless we act with method and order and consistently with our respective natures and constitutions, we shall no longer attain to our end."[32]

Sensory Knowledge and Sensus Communis

Their conception that the human capacity for judgment must be seen as an ethical enterprise underscores the Stoic view that the process of acquiring knowledge about the world is both an individual and a collective endeavor. Although an individual's perceptions might appear to exist in isolation from others, the processes people use in interpreting their impressions, including the use of common preconceptions, naturally establish interpersonal connections, because people were naturally created to live as social beings. For this reason, humans who seek to adhere to the natural order must also acknowledge their relationship to each other; Frederick Copleston observes that as Stoic thought evolves, the emphasis on entering into "the natural life or life according to nature" increasingly emphasizes the centrality of human activity, as Stoics interpreted "life according to the nature" as "life according to the principle that is active in nature, *logos,* the principle shared in by the human soul."[33] J. M. Rist characterizes the Stoic optimism emerging from this sense of shared human interest as a central distinction between early Stoicism and Cynicism: "Zeno seems to have thought that it was still worth while talking about communities of men, however much existing cities might need the most radical reform; the Cynics, on the other hand, thought rather in terms of one wise man per generation."[34] The perception that knowledge of the truth inevitably leads to the recognition of one's relationship to other people strengthens throughout Stoicism's evolution, as evident in Seneca's explicit statement that "philosophy's first promise is a sense of participation, of belonging to mankind, being a member of society. Unlikeliness will alienate us from our promise."[35] Thus, becoming a more conscious participant in society refines the individual's virtue and understanding of his or her place in the world.

As people pursue this course of refining their ethical sensibilities, they also strengthen the bonds that naturally exist between them. Because people are universally able to use their senses not only to observe the world but also to interpret the things that they observe,[36] they also develop basic shared assumptions about the world, that is, common sense or "general perception," which Epictetus describes as "certain things which all men who are not utterly perverted can see in virtue of their general faculties."[37] Epictetus anticipates Thomas Reid's eighteenth-century argument against Humean skepticism in insisting that although there may be limits to the knowledge that people can acquire through reason and philosophy, positive action is both necessary and possible for those who "maintain the view of common sense."[38] He eschews what he describes as fallacious technical arguments, adding, "With what argument, then, am I content? With what is appropriate to the subject at hand."[39] For Stoics as for eighteenth-century commonsense philosophers, the use of *common sense* generates practical lines of reasoning that support the social order through reinforcing established beliefs, including religious principles, which the Stoics support through arguments that prove God's existence from design, demonstrate the universality of religion, and refute atheism.[40]

Thus common sense involves a human reasoning capacity that has practical as well as moral significance, because it represents the fulfillment of human nature on individual and social levels. Epictetus notes that although people are not born with innate knowledge of math or music and must be taught those subjects, their moral sense is much more certain, for "every one has come into the world with an innate conception as to good and bad, noble and shameful, becoming and unbecoming, happiness and unhappiness, fitting and inappropriate, what is right to do and what is wrong."[41] However, he also acknowledges that preconceived ideas of abstract terms are not automatically formed into a complete system but become meaningful only when they are actively directed toward the individual's duty to others.[42] Thus sensus communis inevitably directs the individual's reflection outward.

This outward reflection inevitably involves the development of propriety. Although Stoics do not see virtue and propriety as identical, determining appropriate actions in specific situations can be a means toward cultivating the attitude that promotes the development of virtue. Rist explains that the importance of context lies in the fact that "appropriateness cannot be assumed on every individual occasion; rather each individual occasion must be taken on its merits."[43] Gill describes Epictetus's "threefold ethical programme" as enacted in part through guidelines for judging one's impressions and responses in particular contexts: "(1) reexamine the overall goals of his desires; (2) adjust his impulse to action and his view of his social commitments in the light of thought about goals; and (3) aim at complete consistency in belief, attitude, and state of mind."[44] This complex process requires reflection about how one's notion of virtue relates to and can be realized within specific contexts. Rist explains that for Panaetius, "moral goodness is not only the true good; it is also fitting."[45] Although appropriateness does not necessarily encompass virtue, propriety is a natural component of ethical development.

Achieving a harmonious relationship to nature provides the basis for an awareness of that which is appropriate. John M. Cooper argues that the Stoics perceived people as originally guided by instinct but moving gradually through nature's beneficence toward the use of reason in making decisions, which Cicero describes as a process that includes a gradual awareness of "appropriate acts."[46] Cooper draws upon Diogenes Laertius in summarizing Zeno's view of the link between propriety and nature: "What 'comes down on a particular person' to do, what it is your turn or your place to do . . . it is one that it is incumbent upon the one doing it to do, because in those circumstances it is assigned to it by its nature and by the nature of things in general, which made it the way it is. If an act is 'appropriate' to do and fits the circumstances, as indeed it does, that is because not only is it assigned to you by nature to do in those circumstances, but since nature acts to further the life of its creatures, doing whatever it is is 'suitable' from the creature's own point of view."[47]

The process of defining an appropriate response to particular circumstances involves the development of self-control and often begins with internal deliberation, which promotes an individual's awareness of his or her position in the divine order. The Stoics emphasized both the individual's essential unity with the entire universe and the internal unity of each rational soul, a departure from the Platonic and Aristotelian view that people experience conflict between greater and lesser sides of their own natures. Ethical action therefore involves seeking to develop judgments that are in keeping with what the whole person knows to be correct. Epictetus notes that in making correct decisions, "we not only estimate the value of things external, but each one of us considers what is in keeping with his character."[48] For Marcus Aurelius, too, knowledge and virtue are acquired through a process of self-discovery that involves a growing recognition of one's relationship to nature, which can be developed through repeated internal conversations: "Wipe out thy imaginations by often saying to thyself: now it is in my power to let no badness be in this soul, nor desire nor any perturbation at all; but looking at all things I see what is their nature, and I use each according to its value."[49] Such an internal dialogue provides the mechanism for moving the individual from a state dictated by unreasoning passion to one based in reason that encourages recognition of one's proper relationship to others: "When thou art offended with any man's shameless conduct, immediately ask thyself, Is it possible, then, that shameless men should not be in the world? It is not possible. Do not, then, require what is impossible."[50] Seneca advises the reader to avoid anger by achieving distance from the situation and evaluating it from that perspective: "It will be said that some one spoke ill of you; consider whether you spoke ill of him first, consider how many there are of whom you speak ill."[51]

Internal deliberation therefore cultivates the habit of assigning the proper role to external circumstances. Marcus Aurelius advises, "Inquire of thyself as soon as thou wakest from sleep, whether it will make any difference to thee, if another does what is just and right."[52] He goes on to explain that the frequent practice of internal deliberation cultivates a contemplative mindset that enables people to enter fully into the divine order: "Acquire the contemplative way of seeing how all things change into one another, and constantly attend to it, and exercise thyself about this part of philosophy. For nothing is so much adapted to produce magnanimity. Such a man has put off the body, and as he sees that he must, no one knows how soon, go away from among men and leave everything here, he gives himself up entirely to just doing in all his actions, and in everything else that happens he resigns himself to the universal nature."[53]

Such resignation to "the universal nature" entails the recognition that individuals are powerless to control external circumstances. However, learning to accept those situations constitutes an opportunity to develop virtue, a type of personal growth that should not be seen as merely a passive acceptance of fate. Dorothea Frede argues, "Stoic determinism . . . does not lead to resignation, but to a careful study of our capabilities and limitations," which ultimately reflects the Stoic "optimism in the overall causal order."[54] Cultivating the appropriate acceptance of one's external situation therefore provides the means to develop critical judgment that is better attuned to the subtle workings of the cosmic order rather than maintaining a focus on the immediate concerns that tend to distract people from appreciating the deeper significance embedded in the circumstances of their lives. For this reason, Epictetus insists that philosophy has nothing to do with the acquisition of external well-being. He notes that humanity should be elevated by their kinship with God but that people instead tend to focus on "the body which we share with the animals" rather than "the reason and mind which we share with the gods."[55] The goal of humanity must therefore center upon the goal of appreciating the work of Providence and cultivating "a power to see clearly the circumstances of each, and the spirit of gratitude"[56] that enables one to understand God's hand at work in everything that happens, an idea that many eighteenth-century theorists found both reassuring and comfortably compatible with Christian doctrine.

Sensus Communis and Civic Duty

The Stoic appreciation for Providence by no means involves a complete withdrawal from the concerns of social life, however. The Stoics perceived moral development as intrinsically social; in spite of their emphasis on the individual's search for certain truth and their acknowledgment of the uncertainty that surrounds all human affairs, they believed that individual virtue can only be realized through participation in public life. Frede states that the Stoics' "cosmic optimism . . . made the Stoic doctrine attractive to generations of adherents who regarded the faith in an overall divine order as the most plausible explanation of how the world works," adding that Stoic determinism included "good reasons for recommending an active involvement in the world's concerns."[57]

This social dimension assumes particular force in Roman Stoicism. The Stoic emphasis on the individual's responsibility to others appealed to the traditional Roman appreciation for practicality and civic duty, and by the end of the first century B.C.E., Stoicism had become the predominant philosophy among Romans.[58] The Roman appropriation of Stoicism in turn facilitated a stronger emphasis on exploring how the individual's experience with the community might enhance the private search for knowledge of the divine order.

As a result, Stoicism at this point strengthened its earlier conviction that individual virtue develops through civic commitment, a move that builds on Greek views of the relationship between rhetoric and ethics. From the beginning, the Stoic ethical system assumed that the welfare of each individual must be connected to the good that is embedded in the natural world, which leads to the conclusion that ethical action always reflects an awareness of one's relationship to the natural order. Zeno maintains that the wise man will take part in politics if nothing prevents him from doing so, for such activity has the potential to "restrain vice and promote virtue."[59] The consistent Stoic belief that the life of the individual is best understood in its relation to the cosmos provides a natural foundation for the Late Stoic view that sensus communis depends upon the fundamental interdependence between the development of private virtue and the individual's involvement in social concerns. Epictetus argues that the kinship between God and humanity requires the recognition that each person is a "citizen of the universe"[60] and insists that love of oneself inevitably involves acknowledging a connection with others, for the rational person has been so constituted "that he can attain nothing good for himself, unless he contributes some service to the community."[61] Seneca vividly contrasts the vitality and public activity of the virtuous life with the withdrawal from civic life encouraged by the pursuit of pleasure: "Virtue you will find in the temple, in the forum, in the senate-house—you will find her standing in front of the city walls, dusty and stained, and with calloused hands; pleasure you will more often find lurking out of sight, and in search of darkness . . . soft, enervated, reeking with wine and perfume, and pallid, or else painted and made up with cosmetics like a corpse."[62]

Thus the Stoic assumption that each individual must be accountable for pursuing virtue is accompanied by the view that each individual finds the happiness that can only be found in a virtuous life as he or she acknowledges his or her relationships to other people and acts upon that knowledge through ethical public action. Epictetus chastises the Epicureans for their withdrawal from society, noting that "the rest of us are all convinced that we have a natural fellowship with one another and that we are bound by all means to guard it,"[63] and insisting that "You live in an imperial city: you must hold office, judge justly, refrain from other men's property. . . . You must look for judgements that will be in keeping with such conduct."[64]

Basing one's judgments on attention to others also requires that the philosopher recognize his ethical obligation to the concerns of other people; the Stoics anticipated Reid's commonsense argument that philosophy has no value if it is focused on abstract knowledge that has no immediate relevance to human life, which includes the practical application of moral principles. Epictetus's recognition of the importance of human relationships also leads him to acknowledge the importance of human emotion alongside the Stoic emphasis on developing the human capacity for reason, "for I must not be without feeling like a statue, but must maintain my natural and acquired relations, as a religious man, as son, brother, father, citizen."[65]

Marcus Aurelius echoes Epictetus's emphasis on the connections between the individual and the political world. In Marcus Aurelius's view, "rational animals exist for one another,"[66] so people can only fulfill their individual natures through service to others. He advances a carefully reasoned argument that explains the strong social bonds that people acquire through their common capacity to reason and form ethical judgments: "If our intellectual part is common, the reason also, in respect of which we are rational beings, is common: if this is so, common also is the reason which commands us what to do, and what not to do; if this is so, there is a common law also; if this is so, we are fellow-citizens; if this is so, we are members of some political community; if this is so, the world is in a manner a state. For of what other common political community will any one say that the whole human race are members?"[67]

Following this reasoning process means recognizing that the individual's life can never be separated from the existence he or she shares with others. Although people "have their peculiar leading principle and follow their peculiar movement," Marcus Aurelius advocates the pursuit of virtue not in isolation but through "following thy own nature and the common nature; and the way of both is one."[68] This ethical vision leads Marcus Aurelius to define "the proper works of a man" as "to be benevolent to his own kind, to despise the movements of the senses, to form a just judgement of plausible appearances, and to take a survey of the nature of the universe and of the things which happen in it."[69] His identification of these "proper works" leads him to identify three types of human relationships: "the one to the body which surrounds thee; the second to the divine cause from which all things come to all; and the third to those who live with thee."[70] For the Stoics, the ideal realm of the divine order can only be found through the dutiful public conduct that enables individuals to apply their preconceptions to a reasoning process that leads them to understand both the private and social significance of their knowledge.

The Stoic emphasis on civic duty does not entail a wholehearted acceptance of the state's activities, however. For the Stoics, sensus communis entails an intuitive common knowledge of right and wrong that is often removed from a political system characterized by greed and self-interest. With the decline of the Roman Republic and the increasing tyranny of the Roman Emperors, the

Stoics increasingly emphasized the distinction between written civil law, which often becomes corrupted through its connection with material power, and the divinely ordained moral law that humans naturally apprehend and draw upon in forming true communities whose boundaries are not arbitrarily defined by transitory governments. Gill argues that Seneca embodies two distinct features of Stoic thought in the first century C.E.: "a guiding ethical framework for political involvement" and "a theoretical basis for moral disapproval of a specific emperor or his actions."[71] The Stoic distinction between the true human community formed by virtuous individuals and a corrupt and divisive society can be identified as a particularly compelling precept for succeeding generations struggling to maintain some notion of a civic ideal in the midst of social instability. According to this view, the *community* is defined in terms that lie broadly within human nature rather than in the parameters of a particular state. Annas writes, "The Stoics hold that the universe is ruled by divine will, and that it is virtually a single city and state shared by humans and gods. Every one of us is a part of this universe. It follows naturally from this that we value the common good more than our own."[72] The basic value system that ensures social stability therefore transcends the restrictions of formal political systems and consists in those collective ethical principles whose power is reflected in the fact that they usually do not even have to be stated. Johnny Christensen points out that this reservoir of universal ethical principles provides a type of security to those who seek a sense of well-being from a society that is obviously imperfect: "The identification of the supreme moral law with the all-determining law of Nature, is the crowning achievement of the Stoic quest for unity. If the rationality of man, fully expanded in its scope, is the same rationality that governs Nature, man's striving for freedom is no longer senseless. If man may see himself as belonging to a community of rational minds, which is really *one* Universal mind, man is no longer hopelessly alone: he has become a citizen of the Cosmos."[73]

This Stoic assurance has offered comfort and the promise of a transcendent stability to various societies in the midst of change and uncertainty. One illustration of the Stoic opposition to the immediate political views of a particular age can be seen in their opposition to slavery, which is in part a reflection of their refusal to accept materialism. Epictetus, himself a former slave, argues that the kinship of humanity extends to slaves because ownership obtains on earth, rather than reflecting "the laws of the gods."[74] Seneca highlights the distinction between nature and convention: "I smile at those who think it degrading for a man to dine with his slave. . . . It is only because purse-proud etiquette surrounds a householder at his dinner with a mob of standing slaves."[75] In a similar vein, Epictetus asserts that while soldiers swear allegiance to Caesar, the philosopher must swear allegiance to God, in keeping with a commitment to a higher value system: "The soldiers swear to respect no man above Caesar, but we to respect ourselves first of all."[76] Stoic teachings also encouraged greater gender equality than was typical in the ancient world; Epictetus's teacher Musonius Rufus perceived women to be equal to men in their capacity to achieve virtue and accordingly supported women's education.[77] The Stoic contempt for the material world consistently manifests itself in the belief that political power is not as important as the natural moral law that connects humanity to the spiritual world, but adherence to that moral law at the same time places the individual under a social obligation that can be fulfilled only in the domain of the real world of human affairs.

The Stoics therefore anticipate the eighteenth-century search to define a public sphere composed of private citizens united by bonds distinct from those established by an unpredictable state. These bonds originate in the Stoics' view of the connections that exist throughout the universe, which Rist describes as the view that the "cosmos is a living organism whose parts are responsive to one another by 'sympathy.'"[78] According to Annas, this natural connection ensures that the identical bond exists throughout humanity, because nature is the "source of the mutual and natural sympathy between humans, so that the very fact of being human requires that no human be considered a stranger to any other."[79] This Stoic emphasis on sympathy also anticipates an important principle of eighteenth-century moral philosophy and rhetorical theory, which maintains that people have the capacity to communicate in large part through their ability to understand each other sympathetically—a mutual awareness grounded in human nature. This principle supports the Stoic tendency to blur the lines between the individual and humanity as a whole; Rist explains that Panaetius perceived humanity as comprising "two natural 'faces,' one the face of humanity and the second the face of individuality,"[80] which are held together through the active principle that unifies particular people and places with all of nature.[81]

Language and the Negotiation of Sensus Communis

Although sensus communis begins with an intuitive capacity to interpret the world and to make ethical judgments, its vitality comes from the ongoing interactions of individuals, which creates an intersection of Stoic philosophy and rhetoric. The Stoic view that right conduct involves service to the community necessarily requires that people use the gifts of reason and language. Stoic knowledge must be communicable; Annas explains that the Stoics distinguished between simple apprehension and knowledge, the latter of which requires the ability to share one's insights.[82] The emphasis on communication accounts for the Stoic attention to grammar. David Blank and Catherine Atherton explain that "since proper control of assent to one's impressions is essential for building up a system of correct beliefs and for governing correct behaviour, sensitivity to linguistic correctness will be a useful—and may be an essential—asset for the Stoic philosopher."[83] The assumption that knowledge involves examining impressions and communicating about them therefore assigns language a prominent role in Stoic philosophy.

This role involves reflecting the quality of the individual's reasoning processes and enabling people to engage in meaningful interactions, a logical link in view of the Stoic assumption that individuals develop virtue in society. Although the transmission of ideas does not necessarily involve rhetorical negotiation, the Stoics recognize that virtuous individuals are inevitably involved in uncertainty as they begin to communicate about specific situations they encounter in the social world. Arnold notes that from an early period, Stoic teachers "accepted probability as the guide of life in its details,"[84] which reveals their recognition of the contingent nature of human life even as they attempt to integrate their human experiences with the search for absolute truth.

Sensus communis depends upon a type of rhetorical negotiation because the individual's sense of what is right must be constantly refined, and the moral sense is directed toward devising appropriate responses to the issues that arise in community life. Epictetus's emphasis on education's role in guiding people to apply their natural preconceptions to reach judgment about specific cases highlights the Stoic assumption that knowledge is not something that individuals possess in isolation from other people. For Epictetus, education involves "learning to apply the natural primary conceptions to particular occasions in accordance with nature, and further to distinguish between things in our power and things not in our power."[85] Although truth should be the goal every individual seeks to attain, the Stoics acknowledge that the resolution of everyday problems sometimes requires compromise.[86]

Such compromise reflects the Stoic view that the imaginative process of putting impressions and preconceptions to use involves a collective reasoning process. This collaboration is possible because all people share the reasoning skills and common knowledge that enable them to establish meaningful communication. As Cooper explains, "For the Stoics, universal reason is the reason common to all human beings. But it is also, and more fundamentally, the single reason that governs the unified world as a whole. When I consult universal reason in deciding what to do—say, to do an act of justice or humanity—I do of course consult the very same ideas that any other rational human being in my situation would consult, and the very same ones that the recipient of my action, qua rational, will have in mind in considering and assessing what I am doing."[87] The intuitive values and assumptions that people naturally possess become meaningful as applied to particular experiences, measured against common human judgment, and applied to the resolution of concrete problems.

Such a process obviously requires the use of language. However, this appreciation for language is balanced with a suspicion that the Stoics shared with Plato of systematic instruction in rhetoric, as they maintain that rhetoric is often used for display without sufficient attention to the purpose at hand. George A. Kennedy characterizes Stoic rhetoric as emphasizing substance over style, evident in Cato's dictum to "seize the subject, the words will follow."[88] Stoic writings consistently emphasize the importance of pursuing truth without the distraction that potentially comes from undue attention to showy language. Although Zeno endorsed the classical divisions of rhetoric into deliberative, forensic, and panegyric, he clearly emphasizes the importance of content above style in defining rhetoric as the "science of speaking well on matters set forth by plain narrative."[89] Although Epictetus acknowledges the importance of interpreting impressions,[90] he insists that argument involves a straightforward dialectical process of testing true from false.[91] Seneca contrasts the style appropriate to philosophers with that designed to provoke popular appeal: "Speech that deals with the truth should be unadorned and plain. This popular style has nothing to do with the truth; its aim is to impress the common herd, to ravish heedless ears by its speed; it does not offer itself for discussion, but snatches itself away from discussion. But how can that speech govern others which cannot itself be governed?"[92]

Their determination to distinguish the truth from showy expression led the Stoics to place style under narrow boundaries that were frequently criticized by prominent rhetoricians, including Cicero, which has helped to deny them any place in most accounts of rhetoric's history. Diogenes Laertius describes Zeno as "concise in speech,"[93] observing that his preferred style featured clipped syllables, and his guidance on delivery included not opening the mouth too wide.[94] Epictetus insists that disputation should be in service to reason, not the other way around,[95] and maintains that training in argument should be carried out in a way that does not distract people from the central pursuit of truth, an endeavor that will distract people from their proper focus and promote harmful vanity. He acknowledges that skills such as eloquence have some effect but insists that to a philosopher such as Plato, eloquence was incidental to nobler spiritual pursuits.[96] For this reason, Epictetus explains that worthwhile philosophy cannot be found in "syllogisms and shifting terms and hypothetical arguments."[97] Marcus Aurelius begins *Meditations* with a similar claim, as he credits Rusticus with teaching him to avoid all unnecessary display, including "to abstain from rhetoric, and poetry, and fine writing"[98] and instructs those who wish to speak in the political arena and to communicate with other individuals to "speak . . . appropriately, not with any affectation: use plain discourse."[99]

However, even as they insist on the potential harm of emphasizing rhetorical skill at the expense of communicating the truth, the Stoic view of language as a God-given gift did lead them to acknowledge the importance of expression. They support the Ciceronian view that style reveals the character of the speaker and facilitates his or her connection to the audience. In addition to recognizing the value of discursive content in leading people to judgment, Epictetus even goes so far as to acknowledge the importance of the manner in which those ideas are expressed. He admits that "every one can listen more easily to discourse which is expressed in becoming and distinguished language. We must therefore not say that the faculty of expression is nothing."[100] He maintains that ignoring the faculty of expression altogether would be impious, because that ability must be considered a gift of God along with the others that people possess.[101] Moreover, to oppose eloquence too strongly may reflect a certain degree of cowardice, the fear that "if there is a faculty of eloquence, we may not be able to despise it."[102] In Epictetus's view, the danger comes from privileging expression in a way that eclipses the central concern with the cultivation of the will, which ultimately enables people to search for truth. Thus he concludes that he intends not to disparage the power of expression in itself "but only the tendency to dwell unceasingly on such matters and to set your hopes on them."[103] Seneca admits that philosophy should "sometimes take a loftier tone" but adds, "Dignity of character should be preserved. . . . Let philosophy possess great forces, but kept well under control; let her stream flow unceasingly, but never become a torrent."[104] Like Plato, Epictetus and Seneca believe that rhetoric can be valuable—even to the extent of attending to its stylistic quality—when it is employed in the service of a higher good.

This value centers in language's capacity to facilitate sensus communis. Within the Stoic system, the natural gift of speech inevitably becomes one of the means by which human virtue is both reflected and developed through meaningful service to the community. Just as effective rhetoric preserves sensus communis, the judgment of common sense helps to determine the quality of argumentation. Epictetus holds that the ability to construct an argument can be "acquired by him who is to behave with good sense in discussion."[105] Marcus Aurelius emphasizes the need to develop restrained argument that promotes sound judgment; although he acknowledges that a change of opinion in response to a strong argument is acceptable, he adds that "this change of opinion must proceed only from a certain persuasion, as of what is just or of common advantage, and the like, not because it appears pleasant or brings reputation."[106] He also insists that being aware of the state of society is essential: "If he is a stranger to the universe who does not know what is in it, no less is he a stranger who does not know what is going on in it. He is a runaway, who flies from social reason."[107] This principle provides a definite standard by which questions can be measured: "Whatever the rational and political (social) faculty finds to be neither intelligent nor social, it properly judges to be inferior to itself."[108] Thus language for the Stoics becomes the means through which people employ common sense to negotiate the search for truth. While each person possesses preconceptions, those notions can only be realized when they are "articulate and complete."[109] According to Epictetus, "it is impossible to adjust the primary conceptions to the appropriate facts, without making them articulate and without considering just this—what fact must be ranged under each conception."[110] Language should ideally provide the means for people to share their insights with each other, fulfilling the goal of sensus communis that is a central part of the Stoic vision of human nature.

This sharing is possible because language ideally promotes the sympathy that serves as the basis for the social order. For this reason, Epictetus advocates a rhetorical style that supports the ethical purpose of bringing together speaker and audience in a meaningful interaction. He warns against those who use discourse for purposes of display alone, insisting that to be known as a "perfect artist in style"[111] should not be seen as a meaningful compliment. He states that the person who seeks to be heard should place the truth uppermost: "Learn what your words mean, and then speak."[112] This process leads the rhetor to acquire the correct conception of style, which may on occasion include refutation and instruction, but should generally focus on exhortation, which he describes as "the power of showing to one and to many what a sordid struggle they are plunged in, and how they pay regard to everything rather than to what they want."[113] The nature of exhortation demands a heartfelt interaction between the rhetor and audience, for nothing is more effective "than when the speaker makes plain to his hearers that he has need of them."[114] Although the Stoics have generally been assumed to emphasize logos in their rhetorical interactions, Epictetus's description of exhortation actually underscores the importance of ethos as he demonstrates his conviction that rhetoric involves bringing people together into a meaningful relationship. For Marcus Aurelius, such communication places an obligation on the listener as well as the speaker: "Accustom thyself to attend carefully to what is said by another, and as much as it is possible, be in the speaker's mind."[115] The relationship people acquire through language potentially promotes the sympathy that is a necessary function of human society: "All things which participate in anything which is common to them all move towards that which is of the same kind with themselves. . . . In rational animals there are political communities and friendships, and families and meetings of people; and in wars, treaties and armistices. . . . The ascent to the higher degree is able to produce a sympathy even in things which are separated. See, then, what now takes place. For only intelligent animals have now forgotten this mutual desire and inclination, and in them alone the property of flowing together is not seen. But still though men strive to avoid this union, they are caught and held by it, for their nature is too strong for them."[116] Although Epictetus and Marcus Aurelius hold negative views of rhetoric as the empty use of words for show and privilege syllogism as the ideal structure for preserving the necessary emphasis on discursive purpose, it is nevertheless clear that they recognize the importance of argument in fostering sympathy and constructing notions of appropriate conduct as people come together to explore "how the good man may fitly deal with it and fitly behave towards it."[117] Through such interactions, the rhetor and audience may form a bond that promotes the sympathy that is crucial to humanity's fulfillment of its true nature.

Because language has the ethical function of promoting sympathy and community, it also serves as an external manifestation of the individual's character. Seneca's conviction that "man's speech is just like his life"[118] leads him to assign language a prominent role in both reflecting the state of one's character to others: "What is he to think of their souls, when their speech is sent into the charge in utter disorder, and cannot be kept in hand?"[119] In the epistle titled "On Style as a Mirror of Character," he expounds at further length on the connection between style and character: "A man's ability cannot possibly be of one sort and his soul of another. If his soul be wholesome, well-ordered, serious, and restrained, his ability also is sound and sober. Conversely, when the one degenerates, the other is also contaminated."[120] The virtuous individual will fully embody this quality and "will be poised and well ordered, and will show majesty mingled with courtesy in all his actions."[121] In spite of his definite sense of the importance of clarity in philosophical communication, Seneca's sense of the link between style and character leads him to allow for a degree of variation: "These and similar faults, which imitation stamps upon one's style, are not necessarily indications of loose standards or of debased mind; for they are bound to be personal and peculiar to the writer, enabling one to judge thereby of a particular author's temperament."[122] He distinguishes this pattern from those speakers who deliberately create an artificial style so that they can "advertise themselves."[123] Seneca has strong words about such deliberate stylistic corruption: "That is the style of Maecenas and all the others who stray from the path, not by hazard, but consciously and voluntarily. That is the result of great evil in the soul. . . . Therefore, I say, take care of the soul; for from the soul issue our thoughts, from the soul our words, from the soul our dispositions, our expressions, and our very gait. When the soul is sound and strong, the style too is vigorous, energetic, manly; but if the soul lose its balance, down comes all the rest in ruins."[124] In Seneca's view, the reflection of character through style involves a cyclical relationship; a strong character can promote a "vigorous" style, but he suggests that a weak style can also diminish one's character.

Although public service is always desirable, he insists that good citizenship can be enacted in a varied range of actions as well as speech: "If Fortune has removed you from the foremost position in the state, you should, nevertheless, stand your ground and help with the shouting, and if someone stops your throat, you should, nevertheless, stand your ground and help in silence. The service of a good citizen is never useless; by being heard and seen, by his expression, by his gesture, by his silent stubbornness, and by his very walk he helps."[125] Seneca therefore supports Cicero's contention that the individual's ethical sense can be manifested through an "outward, visible propriety" that includes both language and physical appearance. This notion of rhetoric as concerned with the development and manifestation of character and civic virtue also anticipates the emphasis on taste, propriety, and sympathy in eighteenth-century British rhetorical theories.

However, Seneca's emphasis on the integrity of the rhetor's language and disposition does not lead him to a notion of rhetoric that is fixed and static. In concert with the later insights of eighteenth-century rhetoricians, Seneca sees stylistic preference as something that fluctuates according to changing standards in society: "Style has no fixed laws; it is changed by the usage of the people, never the same for any length of time."[126] Although to some extent this is to be expected, Seneca at the same time stresses that particular types of change may also serve as a corrupting influence: "Just as luxurious banquets and elaborate dress are indications of disease in the state, similarly a lax style, if it be popular, shows that the mind (which is the source of the word) has lost its balance."[127] Just as style demonstrates individual character, it also reflects natural language variations and identities: "I suppose that certain styles of speech are more or less suitable to nations also; in a Greek you can put up with the unrestrained style, but we Romans, even when writing, have become accustomed to separate our words."[128] The insight that language reflects the particular circumstances of the individual, alongside the understanding that rhetoric requires a sympathetic exchange between speaker and audience, also suggests that orators must be keenly attuned to the needs of their listeners. This surprisingly leads Seneca to echo Quintilian's endorsement of rhetorical artifice, as he allows for occasions when orators must pretend to be angry even as they inwardly maintain the calm dispositions that are in keeping with the pursuit of wisdom: "'The orator,' you say, 'at times does better when he is angry.' Not so, but when he pretends to be angry. For the actor likewise stirs an audience by his declamation not when he is angry, but when he plays well the role of the angry man; consequently before a jury, in the popular assembly, and wherever we have to force our will upon the minds of other people, we must pretend now anger, now fear, now pity, in order that we may inspire others with the same, and often the feigning of an emotion produces an effect which would not be produced by genuine emotion."[129] The Stoic awareness of language as a social force therefore involves some awareness of the particularity of purpose and context, even as they maintain a strong focus on the role of language in cultivating personal and civic virtue.

The Late Stoic view that civic responsibility both enhances and develops the virtuous individual's adherence to moral law constitutes a historical moment in which extensive attention centers upon the relationship between the way in which experience is interpreted and expressed and the moral status of the community. The Stoic appreciation for reason developed through commitment to civic life inevitably is accompanied by the development of skillful language. The Stoics also conceive of an intrinsic relationship between morality and beauty that foreshadows later versions of rhetoric that focus on the aesthetic effects as well as the reasoned presentation of argument. According to Chrysippus, the influential leader of early Greek Stoicism, perfect good must be assumed to be allied with beauty in a natural and visible sense, because "it has in full all the 'factors' required by nature or has perfect proportion."[130] Through articulating the connection among nature, beauty, and virtue, the Stoics provide a foundation for the eighteenth-century interest in the connections among nature, sensory experience, carefully crafted expression, and moral development.

Oates notes the irony that underlies the situation that the hedonistic Epicureans advocated "withdrawal from the world" and that the "stern and rigid moralism" of the Stoics required that "the peace must be found in the midst of the world's confusions, for after all, all men are brothers."[131] Oates completes his comparison between the two philosophies by noting that its social demands provide Stoicism with greater vitality at different moments in history: "The Stoic doctrine of the universal brotherhood of man has been of incalculable importance in the evolution of democratic theory, particularly in the liberal thought of the French eighteenth century and in the formation of the political institutions of the United States. . . . The purview of Stoicism is the wider, and this accounts undoubtedly for its having exerted a more powerful influence on the subsequent development of Western European thought."[132] The Stoic fusion of individual virtue with a commitment to public life can certainly be seen as a central feature of the development of eighteenth-century British rhetorical theories. Although Stoicism has not previously been assigned a prominent place in rhetoric's history, the Stoic ethical system does play an important role in the evolution of the British rhetorical tradition, beginning with its role in the formation of Cicero's notion of the ethical function of expression and Quintilian's conception of a rhetoric that "is appropriate only to a good man and is itself a virtue."[133]

Cicero and Quintilian: Applying Stoic Ethics to Rhetoric

Cicero's relationship to the Stoics is complicated. It would certainly not be accurate to refer to him as a Stoic rhetorician because he was not an avowed Stoic and was strongly critical of the Stoic approach to rhetorical style. Although he exempts Panaetius from his harshest criticisms of Stoic rhetoric, noting that "in doctrine he was mellower, and in style more lucid,"[134] he makes it clear elsewhere that these qualities are not always found in Stoic rhetoric. In *De finibus bonorum et malorum,* he complains of the Stoic resistance to addressing matters of rhetorical skill: Stoic rhetorical treatises "furnish a complete manual for anyone whose ambition is to hold his tongue."[135] Such passages clearly establish Cicero's opposition to some aspects of the Stoic approach to rhetoric.

At the same time, Cicero exhibits a strong interest in Stoic ethics, which becomes increasingly evident in his later writings. His integration of Stoic ethics with his own philosophical approach to rhetoric provides a major avenue through which Stoic thought achieves a place in eighteenth-century British rhetorical theories. Although Cicero's philosophical views tend to be less absolute than those of the Stoics, he generally shares the Stoic view that the world functions in keeping with a divine order. His own appreciation for such order is reflected in his exposition of Stoic thought in *De finibus,* which contains a criticism of the Epicurean belief that the universe came into being through the random swerving and colliding of atoms, for it "is the capital offense in a natural philosopher, to speak of something taking place uncaused."[136] He goes on to explain that this Stoic insistence upon agency in the creation of the cosmos derives from their emphasis on the presence of a divine order: "This riotous hurly-burly of atoms could not possibly result in the ordered beauty of the world we know."[137]

Cicero demonstrates that this line of reasoning supports a theological argument from design; he cites Cleanthes in outlining the evidence that supports God's existence: "When a man goes into a house, a wrestling-school or a public assembly and observes in all that goes on arrangement, regularity and system, he cannot possibly suppose that these things come about without a cause: he realizes that there is someone who presides and controls. Far more therefore with the vast movements and phases of the heavenly bodies, and these ordered processes of a multitude of enormous masses of matter, which throughout the countless ages of the infinite past have never in the smallest degree played false, is he compelled to infer that these mighty world-motions are regulated by some Mind."[138]

Cicero also articulates the Stoic belief that virtue is immediately connected with participation in the natural order. He identifies justice as based in nature in *De legibus*[139] and in *De finibus* eloquently expresses the Stoic view that "the

Chief Good consists in applying to the conduct of life a knowledge of the working of natural causes, choosing what is in accordance with nature and rejecting what is contrary to it; in other words, the Chief Good is to live in agreement and in harmony with nature."[140] To accept this natural order ultimately contributes to the good of humanity, because people were designed to live in harmony with nature and consequently with each other: "We perceive the very system of the universe and of nature to be constituted with a view to the safety and preservation of the whole."[141] He also follows the Stoics in linking this assumption to the view that nature has an intricate role in determining the character of human virtue and guiding people toward an understanding of appropriate conduct. Cicero expresses the Stoic link among human reason, morality, and the natural law in *De legibus,* "for virtue is reason completely developed; and this is certainly natural; therefore everything honourable is likewise natural."[142]

Because nature has an ultimate role in assigning value, people must by virtue of their participation in the natural order discover guiding principles both in nature and in the social relationships that are ordained by nature. Cicero explains that Stoics see propriety not as identical with virtue but as a step in cultivating virtue, as "appropriate actions" exemplify "choice fully rationalized and in harmony with nature."[143] Those who develop the habit of acting appropriately will gradually develop a stronger sense of natural and right conduct. Thus practicing and developing propriety can be seen as a means to acquire virtue.

Cicero strongly adheres to the Stoic view that the quest for virtue takes place in communities. He demonstrates how the Stoic perspective counters the Epicurean emphasis on pleasure in *De finibus,* as he explains, "It is Reason moreover that has inspired man with a relish for his kind; she has produced conformity of character, of language and of habit; she has prompted the individual, starting from friendship and from family affection, to expand his interests, forming social ties first with his fellow-citizens and later with all mankind."[144] He also shares the Stoic belief that the natural moral law that governs humanity has precedence over any political system in binding people together, as he distinguishes between this natural moral sense and the customary practices that form the basis for human society. Like Seneca and Epictetus, Cicero understands the value of informal consensus in forming the fabric of society; he states that "no rules need to be given about what is done in accordance with the established customs and conventions of a community; for these are in themselves rules."[145] Even in times when the structures of society seem to be on the verge of collapse, Cicero is nevertheless confident that the moral law that provides the basis for human understanding is still in effect: "For there is a bond of fellowship—although I have often made this statement, I must still repeat it again and again—which has the very widest application, uniting all men together and each to each."[146] In spite of his own struggles to protect the stability of the Roman Republic against the encroachment of the Triumvirate's autocratic rule, Cicero maintains an optimistic view that people possess an inherent sense of right that cannot be completely eradicated even by the most corrupt political system.

However, Cicero's role as an important public figure and his extensive education in rhetoric enabled him to explain how a stronger emphasis on rhetorical training could foster the ethical community the Stoics envisioned. He shares the Stoic sense that education refines the individual's ability to make judgments about the world, a process that promotes the development of virtue. Because language is a natural component of human life, both Cicero and the Stoics perceive its proper cultivation as an inherently virtuous endeavor that involves people in assuming their rightful position in the natural order.

Cicero also shares the Stoics' sense that the moral dimension of language comes about through its ability to strengthen the bond of fellowship that binds people together, as he maintains that people "are by nature fitted to form unions, societies, and states."[147] He cites the Stoics in describing the human community as one that transcends any artificial boundaries and instead can be seen as "a city or state of which both men and gods are members, and each one of us is a part of this universe; from which it is a natural consequence that we should prefer the common advantage to our own."[148] In Cicero's view, individuals skilled in communication ensure the creation of strong communities. He maintains that the origin of eloquence makes community possible:

> If we wish to consider the origin of this thing we call eloquence . . . we shall find that it arose from most honourable causes and continued on its way from the best of reasons. For there was a time when men wandered at large in the fields like animals and lived on wild fare; they did nothing by the guidance of reason, but relied chiefly on physical strength. . . . And so through their ignorance and error blind and unreasoning passion satisfied itself by misuse of bodily strength, which is a very dangerous servant.
>
> At this juncture a man—great and wise I am sure—became aware of the power latent in man and the wide field offered by his mind for great achievements if one could develop this power and improve it by instruction. . . . He introduced them to every useful and honourable occupation, though they cried out against it at first because of its novelty, and then when through reason and eloquence they had listened with greater attention, he transformed them from wild savages into a kind and gentle folk.[149]

For Cicero, as for Isocrates, the "civilization myth" provides a powerful statement about the capacity of eloquence to construct a stable community. Without language, humanity would exist on the level of beasts. The gift of language

46

helps to define humanity itself, and the link between language and the formation of a community reinforces the underlying assumption that people are social by nature. Eloquence serves as a vital force in the process by which people "learn to keep faith and observe justice and become accustomed to obey others voluntarily and believe not only that they must work for the common good but even sacrifice life itself."[150] Unlike the Stoics, he emphasizes rhetorical education as a vital component in the development of a strong society, perceiving this educational focus to be a natural outgrowth of language's recognized intellectual and social function. Cicero asserts, "nature inspires us with the desire to benefit as many people as we can, and especially by imparting information and the principles of wisdom. Hence it would be hard to discover anyone who will not impart to another any knowledge that he may himself possess; so strong is our propensity not only to learn but also to teach."[151] Those who teach and use eloquence to bring moral judgment to bear on the law that governs society are achieving the ultimate goal of virtue, as they use their own wisdom and eloquence to enact the ethical potential that is latent in others. Eloquence must be considered "one of the most eminent virtues,"[152] because it potentially promotes the good in all aspects of human life.

The assumption that language is a civilizing force creates a cyclical relationship between the development of the individual and the welfare of society, a notion that mirrors the Stoic concept of sensus communis. People who are trained to use language appropriately are first of all equipped to strengthen the public standards that ensure stability. Although Cicero is a well-known proponent of stylistic flexibility and strongly opposes what he describes as the unnecessarily narrow boundaries of Stoic style, he adheres to their belief in the centrality of reasoned discourse: "As we have a most excellent rule for every phase of life, to avoid exhibitions of passion, that is, mental excitement that is excessive and uncontrolled by reason; so our conversation ought to be free from such emotions."[153] Rhetors and audiences who work together to enact this principle form the type of community whose members appreciate each other and are able to work together toward common goals.

For Cicero, then, any opportunity to learn appropriate language use encourages the development of good judgment. In *De officiis*, Cicero's final work and that which most strongly reflects his interest in Stoic philosophy, he links propriety, a term commonly identified as a stylistic feature of rhetoric, to virtue: "Under this head is further included what, in Latin, may be called *decorum* [propriety]; for in Greek it is called *prepon*. Such is its essential nature, that it is inseparable from moral goodness; for what is proper is morally right, and what is morally right is proper."[154] The social dimension of language ensures that language does not simply reflect the sense of propriety an individual already possesses but serves as a great aid in "the attainment of propriety."[155] He points out that no single type of style can be assumed to be appropriate for every cause; achieving propriety therefore means determining the nature and the needs of the audience that will be addressed.[156] Rhetoric therefore instantiates a notion of propriety that creates a dynamic relationship between the orator and the public; the orator's central concern is with "language of power and elegance accommodated to the feelings and understandings of mankind."[157] Propriety therefore becomes concrete and actually visible through the interaction between the orator and the audience: "The propriety to which I refer shows itself also in every deed, in every word, even in every movement and attitude of the body. And in outward, visible propriety there are three elements—beauty, tact, and taste. . . . In these three elements is included also our concern for the good opinion of those with whom and amongst whom we live."[158] Cicero perceives ethos as deriving from the orator's skillful use of style that will create meaningful communication with a specific audience—an echo of Epictetus's injunction that the rhetor must develop a connection to the audience through demonstrating that he has "need of them."

Cicero's consistent view that the validity of any argument rests with the audience relates to his belief that style has an ethical function in establishing a relationship between speaker and listeners. His belief that language externally demonstrates an individual's reasoning capacity leads him to the view that rhetorical style becomes one means for revealing the orator's character. This revelation is made possible because nature has ordained that "the mere fact of their common humanity requires that one man should feel another man to be akin to him."[159] The audience's natural moral and aesthetic sense provides the means for an immediate sympathetic response to the skillful expression of the virtuous orator: "And because that very quality which we term moral goodness and propriety is pleasing to us by and of itself and touches all our hearts both by its inward essence and its outward aspect and shines forth with most lustre through those virtues named above, we are, therefore, compelled by Nature herself to love those in whom we believe those virtues to reside."[160] Because of the natural sympathy between the rhetor and audience, expression becomes an important means by which the community validates an individual's conduct: "As, therefore, a musical ear detects even the slightest falsity of tone in a harp, so we, if we wish to be keen and careful observers of moral faults, shall often draw important conclusions from trifles. We observe others and from a glance of the eyes, from a contracting or relaxing of the brows . . . and the like, we shall easily judge which of our actions is proper, and which is out of accord with duty and Nature."[161]

Cicero's belief that an individual's moral judgment must manifest itself externally through language that reflects public values provides the link between style and ethos. People are naturally drawn toward the orator whose language touches them, and the virtue of the orator only becomes real through devising language that appropriately meets the needs of the audience. Well-formed language actually possesses the same characteristics that are considered the ideal for human behavior: "Such orderliness of conduct is, therefore, to be observed, that everything in the conduct of our life shall balance and harmonize, as in a finished speech."[162] Like Seneca, Cicero identifies style as that which conveys the orator's character to the audience in a tangible form: "Such influence, indeed, is produced by a certain feeling and art in speaking, that the speech seems to represent, as it were, the character of the speaker; for, by adopting a peculiar mode of thought and expression, united with action that is gentle and indicative of amiableness, such an effect is produced that the speaker seems to be a man of probity, integrity, and virtue."[163] Rhetorical excellence both develops and demonstrates the rhetor's merit in a manner that potentially extends beyond the immediate exigence of the situation at hand in order to benefit the individual and the community at large. For Cicero, rhetorical training becomes the vehicle through which individuals cultivate the mental discipline and social sensibility that lie at the heart of the Stoic ethical system.

Stoic principles also subtly infuse Cicero's treatment of the canon of delivery, as he again emphasizes delivery that attends to nature, propriety, and the external control that reflects harmony with nature: "Nature has given eyes to us, to declare our internal emotions, as she has bestowed a mane, tail, and ears on the horse and the lion. For these reasons, in our oratorical action, the countenance is next in power to the voice, and is influenced by the motion of the eyes."[164] Although rhetorical action is inevitably bound to specific contexts, he perceives the natural force of delivery as possessing a certain universal quality, "for words move none but those who are associated in a participation of the same language; and sensible thoughts often escape the understandings of senseless men; but action, which by its own powers displays the movements of the soul, affects all mankind; for the minds of all men are excited by the same emotions which they recognize in others, and indicate in themselves by the same tokens."[165] In Cicero's view, disciplined rhetorical training therefore establishes connections among people, sharpens the reason that enhances virtue, and affords the ethical individual the practical application that is a necessary element in achieving virtue. To develop skill in the appropriate use of language is inherently good, because language is the natural and external embodiment of human reason.

Although Cicero's career in rhetoric revolved around public address, he also expresses an interest in the modes of private discourse that demonstrates an awareness that he shares with the Stoics and eighteenth-century British rhetoricians—that even private modes of reflection can have a direct connection to public life. He observes that conversation has the same power to cultivate virtue as the more traditional rhetorical form of oratory: "The power of speech in the attainment of propriety is great, and its function is twofold: the first is oratory, the second, conversation. . . . There are rules for oratory laid down by rhetoricians; there are none for conversation; and yet I do not know why there should not be. . . . The same rules that we have for words and sentences in rhetoric will apply also to conversation."[166] Later in the same passage, Cicero proceeds to provide more detailed guidelines about the correct subject matter and conduct that should guide the development of conversation. His willingness to expand the consideration of rhetoric to include conversation derives from his conviction that the private world of discourse also provides people with the opportunity to develop the sense of propriety that comes from speaking to public audiences.

Cicero's philosophical approach to rhetoric enables him to expand upon the Stoic notion that language instills virtue in people who use it to achieve practical civic goals. For Cicero, as for the Stoics, there is an important correlation among expression, the development of an individual's moral sense, and civic responsibility. Cicero's use of the Stoics in developing his rhetorical theory probably began early in his career; Kennedy claims that although Cicero does not name the philosophical source that complements his rhetorical theory in *De inventione,* "there is no reasonable doubt that it is Stoic."[167] Flory suggests that Cicero's reading of the Stoics could have led him to draw upon Stoic as well as Platonic notions of *phantasia,* "for his description in the *Orator,* book 7, of mental capacities needed by the perfect orator."[168] His use of Stoic thought in articulating the links between language and virtue is also apparent in *De oratore* but is most fully evident in *De officiis,* a text frequently cited by eighteenth-century language theorists. Through this range of texts, Cicero's application of Stoic ethics to rhetoric becomes a driving force behind the presence of Stoic ethics in eighteenth-century British rhetorical theories.

The links between Stoic thought and rhetoric are further developed in what Arthur E. Walzer describes as Quintilian's careful fusion of Stoic philosophy with Ciceronian eloquence. Walzer sees Roman Stoicism as "an important hermeneutical key to the *Institutes,*"[169] and his argument that the *Institutes* can be seen as "a synthesis of Cicero's ideal of the liberally educated orator with the Stoic ideal of the Wise Man"[170] is amply borne out through Quintilian's systematic explication of the necessary integration of rhetorical expression with the pursuit of virtue. Quintilian begins the *Institutes* with the insistence that the "the perfect orator . . . cannot exist except in the person of a good man"[171] and goes on to list specific virtues, such as "justice, courage, and temperance," that are integral to every rhetorical situation. He also shares the Stoic assumption that the orator's development of virtue and rhetorical skill must be grounded in social life, as he asks, "Where will he learn what we call common feeling if he shuts himself off from society, which is natural not only to humans but to the dumb animals?"[172]

The cultivation of this "common feeling" offers an alternative to developing rhetorical practice directed by the "sort of rules that most writers of textbooks have handed down."[173] In keeping with other classical rhetoricians, Quintilian insists that rhetoric inevitably requires sensitivity to particular situations. However, the orator's attention to "what is becoming and what is expedient"[174] acknowledges rhetoric's role in preserving the integrity of the individual in addition to facilitating an appropriate response to specific and immediate contexts. Quintilian cites the Stoics in acknowledging that there are occasions when orators may not be completely honest if such a step is necessary in order to promote what they understand to be the greater good,[175] a perspective that reveals the awareness of both Quintilian and the Stoics that enacting an ethical position in the world of human affairs involves a complex array of choices. Walzer notes that Quintilian's ethical system is "situational (and therefore appropriately rhetorical) but suggests a hierarchy of values."[176] He goes on to argue that Quintilian's values acknowledge both "general propriety at the species level" and conduct deemed appropriate to specific circumstances.[177] At the same time, the individual's carefully cultivated ethical character must remain constant. Walzer maintains that Quintilian's integration of philosophy with rhetoric "allowed rhetoric, in the context of offering practical training in public speaking, to take on responsibility for character formation."[178] This synthesis provides a central foundation for eighteenth-century British articulations of rhetoric as practically useful but more significantly connected to the development of public and private virtue. Thus George Campbell's recognition of the rhetor's need to consider both "men in general" and "men in particular" can be seen as grounded in Quintilian's attempt to acknowledge language's significance in strengthening the human relationships established by nature alongside rhetoric's function in resolving immediate practical problems that arise within specific contexts.

In keeping with Stoic insights, Quintilian perceives both the universal and practical functions of rhetoric as elements that contribute to its ethical potential. Because people have been ordained to use language, their cultivation of that gift necessarily has an ethical dimension. At the same time, the requirement that people live in communities places a high value on rhetoric's function in resolving problems and promoting a harmonious social environment.

Quintilian's discussion of "what is becoming and what is expedient" is soon followed by his reiteration of earlier themes related to rhetoric's ethical potential. While he notes that rhetoric may be used for good or evil purposes, he focuses on its capacity to reinforce virtue through fostering the sense of community that is the ideal. He echoes Cicero's description of the role of eloquence in the formation of communities[179] and expresses his agreement with what he identifies as the Stoic belief in the virtuous potential of rhetoric applied to the pursuit of wisdom.[180] His insistence that eloquence touches a natural aesthetic sense aligned with virtue, as the "brilliance of eloquence illumines the beauty of the subject,"[181] resonates with Chrysippus's connection between virtue and the beauty of language. This concept leads to his assertion that rhetoric should be seen as an art that cultivates qualities originally found in nature,[182] a claim that he supports with references to Cicero, the Peripatetics, and the Stoics. Although this outlook allows for rhetoric's practical function in the world of human affairs, it nevertheless promotes Quintilian's consistent emphasis on rhetoric's ethical function, as he insists that this art depends on the value of the activity, not on the outcome.[183] Defining rhetoric in terms of ethical outlook rather than immediate effects reflects Quintilian's orientation toward rhetoric's role in promoting sensus communis, as it plays an instrumental role in developing the shared understanding that people have been granted by nature.

This understanding, for Quintilian, as for Cicero, both depends upon and fosters the sympathy that makes communication possible. His discussion of forensic oratory lends an immediate practical value to the strategy of objective introspection, as he advises the orator to put himself in the position of "a third person, namely the judge"[184] as part of his thorough examination of the case at hand. Thus rhetoric exemplifies the potential people naturally possess to acquire true understanding of each other, and its practice encourages the development of the shared sensitivity toward others that people must cultivate in order to become truly virtuous. For Quintilian, as for the Stoics, language's central function involves developing virtue and strong social relationships, which emerge as people are able to imagine how their actions would appear to others.

As both Kennedy and Walzer have pointed out, Quintilian's repeated references to Stoicism and his appropriation of Cato's "good man" reveal the importance of Stoic philosophy in the development of Quintilian's thinking about language and virtue.[185] Quintilian follows and expands Cicero's enactment of Stoic principles through methodically fusing Stoicism with rhetorical precepts. In bringing the Stoic associations among nature, language, propriety, and the community to bear on their understanding of rhetoric and its ethical impact, Cicero and Quintilian further develop the relationship between individual expression and the community's moral identity in a way that will directly influence the development of British rhetorical theory.

■

The exact nature of the Stoic influence on subsequent thought is difficult to determine. Stoic concepts can be seen as informing developments in Western thought at numerous points in history. However, while the assessments of scholars such as R. M. Wenley provide evidence of the link between Stoicism and the changing cultural climates that shaped the evolution of British intellectual history at key moments, the long evolution of Stoic philosophy, the flexibility of its central precepts, and the widespread assimilation of Stoic thought into various areas of British cultural life complicate any effort to define exactly how the Stoic influence manifests itself in later times. Wenley describes the process of recognizing the presence of Stoic philosophy in subsequent ages as the discovery of "resemblance of mood or outlook rather than discipleship to a system."[186] Evelyn A. Hanley echoes this view, stating that "Stoicism reveals itself as a prevailing attitude or temper of mind."[187] Because of the complexity of Stoic ideals and the diverse ways in which those perspectives are interpreted and appropriated at different historical moments, exploring the relationship between Stoic philosophy and the later development of rhetoric relies upon first identifying intersections between Stoic ethics and rhetoric and then considering how those philosophical convergences contribute to the formation of British rhetorical theories and illuminate the deeper assumptions that undergird those theories.

Such an undertaking has important implications. Stoic philosophy provides a useful framework for understanding the varied and persistent manifestations in British rhetoric of the belief in language's vital role in cultivating individual integrity and pursuing social cohesion in a changing and unstable world. This insight is in keeping with the observation of a number of scholars that the pervasive influence of Stoicism is most evident in British culture during periods when significant change leads to instability and anxiety. Wenley explains that the Stoic outlook typically manifests itself in historical periods in which there is a particularly acute need for assurance that "men dwell together in political communities and, given due fortune, may contrive a union able to preserve and enlist their best qualities."[188] The eighteenth century was just such a moment. The development of an industrial economy, the accompanying evolution of new class structures, and expanded access to print created an atmosphere of excitement and fear about the rapid transformation of British culture. Both sentiments shaped the work of British rhetorical theorists who sought to delineate the role of communication in the formation of a public that maintained stability even as it inevitably reflected the dramatic social changes that were taking place.

Although Stoic writings often minimize the importance of rhetorical training in ethical development, they describe language as integral to the human effort to discover truth through harmony with a natural order that encompasses human society. Eighteenth-century British rhetorical theorists built on this insight with the hope that rhetoric can play a role in bringing new vitality to public life. While their interest in science might have led them to appreciate a portion of what Quentin Skinner describes as Hobbes's effort "to convert the study of moral and political theory into a scientific discipline,"[189] many of them resisted what they saw as his pessimistic assumption that people are essentially motivated by self-interest. These thinkers found value in the optimism of Stoic claims concerning sensus communis and the connection between reason and the natural human capacity for virtue. Their conservative impulse to maintain social order drew them to the Stoic notion of self-control as the means to culti-vate a virtuous disposition, and the Stoic strictures against excessive emotion corresponded to a growing eighteenth-century concern about party politics and the way in which unbridled emotion might corrupt public judgment. Eighteenth-century theorists found in the work of Cicero and Quintilian addi-tional resources for applying insights about the Stoics' imaginative enterprise of promoting sensus communis to rhetorical training aimed at the cultivation of a virtuous character. These theorists adapted Stoic views to the vocabulary and concerns of their own day but devised an intellectual framework that maintains a striking connection to their ancient philosophical ancestors.

This connection begins to develop through the concept of common sense. Because historic notions of common sense, originating in the Stoic notion of sensus communis, posited a link between private and public moral judgment and knowledge, these ideas were particularly useful in eighteenth-century efforts to negotiate the changing relationships between individuals and society. They provide a useful starting point for tracing the infusion of Stoic principles into eighteenth-century language theories.

Chapter 2

EIGHTEENTH-CENTURY COMMON SENSE AND SENSUS COMMUNIS

The ideal of sensus communis provides a central framework for understanding the workings of Stoic thought in eighteenth-century British rhetorics. The term *sensus communis* is given an incarnation that reflects eighteenth-century concerns in the writings of Anthony Ashley Cooper, Third Earl of Shaftesbury, which have a major influence on both Francis Hutcheson's exposition of the moral sense and on the subsequent development of Scottish commonsense philosophy. Many influential eighteenth-century theories of language, rhetoric, and aesthetics were in turn directly or indirectly informed by Shaftesbury, Hutcheson, and Scottish commonsense philosophy, founded by Thomas Reid, so their appropriation of Stoic thought emerges both through these philosophical systems and through the writings of Roman Stoics, Cicero, and Quintilian. Although the Stoics, Shaftesbury, Hutcheson, and Reid all have distinct ways of articulating what sensus communis, the moral sense, or common sense entails, they share the basic premise that nature should be seen as a positive force that provides human life with order and meaning. The beneficence of nature includes the human ability to process sensory experiences and to make reasoned judgments. People participate in the natural order through using and developing these gifts and through participating in the formation of orderly societies that mirror the harmony they experience in the natural world. For the Stoics, Shaftesbury, and Reid, sensus communis, or common sense, therefore becomes both a description of the human ability to make judgments about the world and a shared capacity to develop individual and civic virtue through discovering and promoting shared understanding. These ideas become integral to eighteenth-century British rhetorical theorists dedicated to ensuring that rhetoric contributes to the type of understanding that will foster the virtuous society they hope to preserve.

Although Shaftesbury, Hutcheson, and Reid hold different philosophical and religious beliefs, all of them share an optimistic perspective that leads them to challenge what they conceive to be the skepticism and pessimism embedded in modern science and philosophy. Shaftesbury expresses respect for John Locke's intellectual contributions but counters the image of the human mind as a tabula rasa, insisting that nature provides everyone with instinctive knowledge that establishes a foundation for moral judgment. His emphasis on the civility of sensus communis and insistence on the natural social impulse represent an explicit challenge to Hobbes. Hutcheson's moral sense builds on this principle, offering a vision of an internal attraction to virtue that promotes public and private happiness, in contrast with what he perceived to be Bernard Mandeville's destructive exploration of the potential practical ends of undesirable actions. Scottish common sense constitutes an immediate response to the skeptical philosophy of David Hume, which raised questions about people's ability to apprehend a reality outside of their own perception. Reid insistently argues that the reality of the material world is immediately accessible to human experience but distinct from that experience and that the ability to interpret external reality is available through common sense. The parameters of this debate are distinct to this eighteenth-century incarnation of the notion of common sense, and Reid's insights are indebted in many respects to Enlightenment ideas about knowledge and sensory perception developed by Locke and even by Hume himself; however, Reid's work represents a fusion of these contemporary ideas with ancient commonsense traditions, as he sustains the Stoic views that an internal sense provides immediate knowledge of the world, that this shared sense establishes natural connections among people, and that the process of working with this knowledge has ethical implications. Considering the philosophical links between eighteenth-century British conversations about common sense and Stoic sensus communis helps to illuminate the ancient assumptions that inform many of the "new rhetorics."

Aristotle, the Stoics, and Eighteenth-Century Common Sense

Scottish commonsense philosophers share with the Stoics, as well as Aristotle, the view that human knowledge begins with sensory experience and develops through the innate ability to apply general knowledge to the resolution of specific questions. Aristotle's notion of common sense primarily involves internally coordinating the workings of the senses in order to arrive at knowledge of the external world;[1] the Stoics endorse the view that common sense involves sensory knowledge of the external world, but they move the work of common sense outward in order to demonstrate its capacity to promote shared collective understanding. Much of the scholarship that has placed Scottish common sense within a historic tradition of common sense has aligned it more closely with

Aristotle's position than with the Stoics. John D. Schaeffer argues that "what Giambattista Vico did was synthesize the Greek and Roman ideas of sensus communis,"[2] but he includes Reid among Enlightenment philosophers who "returned to the Greek tradition of sensus communis and invoked common sense as a first principle on which the reflective and judging actions of the mind were based."[3] This statement accurately reflects the starting point for the Scottish exposition of common sense, the relationship between perception through the physical senses and the beliefs about the world that those sensations inspire in the individual. Scottish commonsense philosophers, like Aristotle and the Stoics, understand these beliefs to be central to human nature, and they insist that human happiness depends upon the ability to appreciate the power that people possess through their intuitive understanding of the world. However, they also share the Stoic conclusion that this understanding becomes fully realized only when common sense is seen as an ethical endeavor that strengthens the community. Beginning with Shaftesbury, British philosophers and rhetoricians also fuse Greek and Roman conceptions of common sense in ways that significantly shape their perspectives on rhetoric's function in building individual character and civic virtue.

Common Sense: A Philosophy for the Common Good

Both Stoicism and Scottish common sense begin with the assumption that their philosophical approaches address the genuine needs of humanity, while other philosophies construct artificial systems that harm people's ability to live constructively. Various iterations of this theme occur at different historical moments, as illustrated by Epictetus's charge that the Epicureans contradicted themselves by demonstrating a philanthropic concern with others that lies at the heart of all teaching, even as they advance a philosophy grounded in self-interest. Shaftesbury similarly acknowledges that contemporary philosophical skepticism denies the possibility of "common sense" but insists that even those thinkers such as Thomas Hobbes who deny the existence of an innate moral sense are, through the very act of writing treatises that are intended to enlighten people, demonstrating the basic concern for others that their philosophies attempt to deny.[4] In his view, engaging in abstract philosophical disputation can itself serve as an influence that corrupts the natural moral sense with which people are born: "For a common honest Man, whilst left to himself, and undisturb'd by Philosophy and subtle Reasonings about his Interest, gives no other Answer to the Thought of Villany, than that *he can't possibly find in his heart* to set about it, or conquer the natural Aversion he has to it. And this is *natural,* and *just.* . . . The Truth is; as Notions stand now in the World, with respect to Morals; Honesty is like to gain little by Philosophy, or deep Speculations of any kind."[5] Shaftesbury calls into question the view that reason can be taught by the philosophical treatises that have come to dominate public discourse, as he claims that "'Tis the Habit alone of Reasoning, which can make *a Reasoner.* And Men can never be better invited to the Habit, than when they find Pleasure in it."[6] He carefully distances himself from those appeals to the passions that undermine the reasoned judgment upon which society's stability depends, but he believes that the imagination works in concert with reason to promote virtue through common sense, which stands in opposition to the artificial philosophical systems that define public morality in strictly pragmatic terms: "According to common Speech, as well as common Sense, *Honesty is the best Policy:* But according to refin'd Sense, the only *well-advis'd* Persons, as to this World, are *errant Knaves;* and they alone are thought to serve themselves, who serve their Passions, and indulge their loosest Appetites and Desires.—Such, it seems, are *the Wise,* and such *the Wisdom of this World!*"[7]

Reid similarly charges Hume with developing a skeptical philosophy that he cannot in reality believe, because to do so would prevent him from being able to function effectively in daily life. He identifies Aristotle as an ancient exemplar of rescuing the principles of common sense from destructive philosophical trends: "In the first Ages of the World when Common Sense reigned uncontrouled by the Subtleties of Philosophy, Primary and Secondary Qualities dealt peaceably under the same Roof and were joynt Proprietors of the same Subject, Body. Democritus and Epicurus set them at variance. And pretending to find out that secondary Qualities were mere Spectres and Illusions of Sense they banished them to Fairy land. Aristotle took compassion upon them, recalled them and restored them to their former Inheritance."[8] Reid's proclamation, "I despise Philosophy, and renounce its guidance—let my soul dwell with Common Sense,"[9] is implicitly endorsed by George Campbell's insistence that relying upon common sense is preferable to philosophical wrangling: "No person who is influenced in his judgment of things, not by philosophical subtleties, but by common sense, a much surer guide, will hesitate to declare, that in such a testimony I have probable evidence of the fact asserted."[10] Common sense, for Scottish philosophers as well as for the Stoics and Shaftesbury, serves as an internal mechanism for discovering truth that becomes meaningful through its engagement with genuine material concerns that bring people together.

Of course, the fact that these individuals are philosophers suggests that they are not in principle entirely opposed to all philosophy. Shaftesbury draws distinctions between philosophical systems that advance views that benefit humanity and those that instead have a destructive influence. His philosophical alliance with Stoicism leads him to the step of positioning himself in opposition to a common enemy, Epicureanism. In *Second Characters,* he argues that "one may divide the moral philosophy into three sorts; one that establishes a Providence disposing all things in the most beautiful order, and giving to man a capacity to attend to its laws and to follow them; another that attributes the disposition of things to atoms and chance and that makes the pursuit of pleasure its end; and the third that takes part neither way, but judges things not to be at all comprehensible, and therefore suspends opinion entirely. Socrates and the branch derived from Chrysippus were of the first sort, Aristippus and Epicurus of the second, and Pyrrho of the third."[11] Clearly Shaftesbury chooses to align himself in the first school with Socrates and the Stoics, and he undoubtedly could have named contemporary parallels for both the Epicureans and Skeptics. Reid follows this example, occasionally casting Epicureanism as an ongoing philosophical evil, as in the following passage of a letter to Kames: "I am not much surprised that your Lordship has found little Entertainment in a late French Writer on Human Nature. From what I learn they are all become rank Epicureans."[12] Thus both Shaftesbury and Reid not only appropriate Stoic thought in developing their philosophies but also adopt Stoic enemies in describing the positions they choose to refute.

The challenge to what they see as the destructive nature of philosophical skepticism can be seen as a central feature that eighteenth-century British commonsense philosophers share with Stoics. In countering this perspective, they articulate a philosophy that explains how people understand the world and offer guidance in refining that natural understanding in ways that will help people lead meaningful lives. This goal, in both versions of common sense, involves developing an internal consciousness that connects with broad human concerns and in the process facilitates a more skillful engagement with particular civic issues. Eighteenth-century British theorists therefore share with the Stoics the assumption that the individual's internal judgment must inevitably develop through social contact. Hans-Georg Gadamer identifies Shaftesbury as the eighteenth-century thinker whose influence established a place for Vico's notion of sensus communis, which Gadamer describes as defined by "the sense of the right and the general good that is to be found in all men, moreover, a sense that is acquired through living in the community and is determined by its structures and aims."[13] He contrasts this social orientation with the scholastic notion of sensus communis as "the common root of the outer senses, ie the faculty that combines them, that makes judgments about what is given, a faculty that is given to all men."[14] While Gadamer acknowledges that Vico had negligible influence on eighteenth-century thought, he goes on to argue that Shaftesbury was a much more significant influence in bringing to the eighteenth century the Latin Stoic view that sensus communis "is not so much a feature given to all men, part of the natural law, as a social virtue, a virtue of the heart more than of the head."[15] In Gadamer's view, the philosophical heritage for this view is reflected in Vico's appeal to a classical tradition that contrasts the scholar and the wise man, phronesis versus sophia, as well as in his appeal to public knowledge. He argues that both strains can also be traced through Shaftesbury to Scottish commonsense philosophy.

> The idea of "common sense" acquired a quite central systematic function in Scottish philosophy, which was directed polemically against metaphysics and against its dissolution in skepticism, and built up its new system on the basis of original and natural judgments of common sense (Thomas Reid). Doubtless this was influenced by the Aristotelian-scholastic tradition of the concept of sensus communis. The enquiry into the senses and their capacity to provide knowledge comes from this tradition and is intended ultimately to correct the exaggerations of philosophical speculation. At the same time, however, the connection between common sense and society is preserved. . . . In their eyes, the philosophy of sound understanding, of "good sense," is not only a cure for the "moon-sickness" of metaphysics, but also contains the basis of a moral philosophy that really does justice to the life of society.[16]

For Gadamer, Scottish common sense therefore combines Aristotelian notions of the role of the senses in the human acquisition of knowledge with the social awareness assumed and developed in Roman Stoicism's sensus communis. This synthesis begins with the rejection of esoteric philosophical systems that isolate people and inhibit the development of a common understanding of the world, a concern that Reid and his colleagues share with the Roman Stoics, and develops through the eighteenth-century integration of Stoic sensus communis with rhetoric.

The Stoic objective of "universal brotherhood" ironically serves as the driving force for what some people have perceived as eighteenth-century rhetoric's "inward turn." Although Thomas Miller acknowledges common sense's social function[17] and even allows for the "democratic potential" of "commonsense moral philosophy,"[18] he concludes that "in rhetoric, as in moral philosophy, commonsense philosophy helped shift the focus from the sociological to the psychological, and rhetoric became more concerned with the workings of the individual consciousness than with the practical art of drawing on common beliefs to speak to public issues."[19] The presence of Stoic thought in eighteenth-century iterations of common sense complicates this division between the social and psychological. Exploring the implications of this presence can help to illuminate specific ways in which eighteenth-century rhetoricians connect the power of internal deliberation to the development of community. Such a goal can be seen as particularly relevant in addressing the concerns of eighteenth-century thinkers whose perception of the rapidly changing nature of "the public" un-doubtedly made the Stoic promise of stability particularly appealing.

Language, Literacy, and Cultural Instability

Many eighteenth-century British theorists center their concern about social sta-bility in language, specifically in the transition from an oral to a literate culture. In their study of the nineteenth-century American shift from an oratorical to a literary culture, Gregory Clark and S. Michael Halloran argue that an oratori-cal culture is primarily oriented toward consensus, while a literary culture tends to the view that "the locus of public morality is the expert and autonomous individual."[20] This cultural transition had begun to be evident in Britain dur-ing the latter half of the eighteenth century and was due to the expansion of industrialization and the increasing dependence on a mercantile economy. The consequences of social change were apparent in Scotland, where a rapidly expanding population and opportunities for social mobility placed pressure on a number of institutions, including the educational system, which, as Winifred Bryan Horner notes, had traditionally offered a more democratic approach to education than universities in England.[21]

The effects of this democratic impulse were certainly noted by educators. In a letter to Andrew Skene written in November of 1764, Reid articulates the connection between economics and enrollment patterns in describing the envi-ronment he has encountered as part of his new appointment as professor of moral philosophy at the University of Glasgow: "Many of the Irish as well as Scotch are poor and come up late to save money, so that we are not yet fully conveened although I have been teaching ever since the 10 of October."[22] While his tone in this passage is matter of fact and generally supportive of the univer-sity's attempt to diversify its population, Reid occasionally reveals a less-sanguine outlook in discussing his attitude toward the students with whom he deals: "The most disagreeable thing in the teaching part is to have a great Number of stupid Irish teagues who attend classes for two or three years to qualify them for teaching Schools or being dissenting teachers. I preach to these as St Fran-cis did to the fishes."[23] The concerns Reid expresses in this passage are also evi-dent in the New Rhetorics, which reveal in more subtle ways the tensions embedded in a culture that is in the midst of educational change and techno-logical transition. These theories reflect the anxiety that arose in the midst of a transformation from a rural society in which oral discourse formed the public consciousness, characterized by at least an apparently manageable relationship between speaker and audience, to an industrial society being transformed by the mass distribution of printed material, which offered increasing numbers of individuals a new sense of private authority based on the solitary act of reading.

In spite of the anxiety they express about ways in which mechanical forms of literary production might jeopardize the dynamic quality of language and the shared understanding that had been assumed as a goal of an oratorical culture, eighteenth-century British thinkers acknowledged that the widespread distribution of printed texts constituted an unstoppable force. As a result, new interest emerges in how language use might be shaped in a manner that links earlier forms of communication, which relied upon the optimistic pursuit of public consensus, with a literate British society that promoted the development of a more individualistic moral sense. Common sense provided a vocabulary for creating such a bridge, as it posited a shared knowledge of the world that united people in spite of their isolated experiences, a process of discovering common social ground that promised to restore discipline and order to a world on the verge of chaos. Integrating notions of common sense with rhetorical theory and promoting the affective potential of written language constitute strategies that eighteenth-century theorists developed in order to preserve the oratorical power and sense of collective identity that they were afraid might be subsumed by the private world of the written text.

Imagination and the Revitalization of Common Sense

Many eighteenth-century theorists believed that the language of modern science and philosophy contributed to this isolated privacy, and they sought to explore imaginative ways in which language might be used in order to reflect the range of human experience that could ultimately restore social harmony. This perception is in some respects ironic in view of the tremendous influence that the scientific and philosophical writings of thinkers such as Francis Bacon and Locke had in forming some of the fundamental principles of eighteenth-century rhetorical theories: the belief that different types of discourse appeal to different mental faculties; the appreciation for the value of empirical evidence and inductive reasoning; the assumed validity of the association of ideas; and the perception at least partially inherited from Bacon that the imagination plays a vital role in mediating between the reason and the will.[24]

However, in spite of their interest in drawing upon the insights of science to develop a modern rhetoric, eighteenth-century British rhetoricians consistently express their desire to preserve the traditional ethical and social function of rhetoric. This ethical concern prevents them from fully embracing the strictly factual orientation of scientific discourse exemplified in Thomas Sprat's 1667 *History of the Royal Society.* Although Sprat's depiction of the Royal Society's mission in some ways anticipates Shaftesbury's opposition to philosophical disputations that fail to advance human knowledge, Sprat, differing significantly from Shaftesbury, insists that the remedy lies not in an imaginative vision that touches an innate moral sense but in "the *solid substance of Science* itself."[25] In

Sprat's view, correct action is assured not through the cultivation of virtuous sentiment but through objective observation of the external world, and it is in this area that ancient philosophy has gone wrong: "There can never be found, in the breast of any particular *Philosopher,* as much wariness, and coldness of thinking, and rigorous examination; as is needful, to a solid *assent,* and to a lasting *conclusion,* on the whole frame of *Nature.*"[26] Perceiving the "coldness" of objective observation as a desirable attribute leads Sprat to denigrate ancient philosophers on general principle, a view that contrasts with Shaftesbury's later claims concerning the restorative power of the imagination; Sprat states that Plato, Aristotle, Zeno, and Epicurus would be better respected in later ages "if they had only set things in a way of propagating Experiences down to us; and not impos'd their *imaginations* on us, as the only *Truths.*"[27] In spite of their respect for the advances of science and their willingness to use scientific insights to shape their theories, many of the New Rhetoricians follow Shaftesbury and the Stoics in rejecting the scientific materialism that forms the basis for the Royal Society's conception of knowledge, as represented by Sprat, in favor of exploring the diverse factors, including intuition, imagination, and social interaction, that serve as important resources in people's efforts to acquire knowledge of the world around them.

The prominence of scientific writing oriented strictly toward "the things themselves"[28] throughout the late seventeenth century, along with the cynical doctrines of philosophers such as Hobbes, led many eighteenth-century thinkers to express their general distrust of learned writing. Shaftesbury cites Hobbes's view that humans are motivated strictly by self-interest in juxtaposing the formal writings of philosophers against the heartfelt extrarational perceptions of those whose common sense enables them to follow the more important moral course of action.[29] Hutcheson, whose challenge to Mandeville in *Inquiry Concerning Beauty, Order, Harmony, Design* significantly begins with an epigram from *De officiis,* argues that philosophers who ignore the finer pleasures discovered through the internal sense fail to recognize the true spiritual quality that undergirds human life.[30] Reid describes the philosophies of René Descartes, Nicolas Malebranche, and Locke as "very fruitful in creating doubts, but very unhappy in resolving them."[31]

The suspicion that writing has in some cases fostered a philosophical community removed from the concerns of real life has widespread consequences for rhetorical theory in the eighteenth century because those concerned with preserving the traditional ethical function of rhetoric consciously attempt to maintain the power of oral discourse even in a society that is increasingly dependent upon literacy. The rise of the elocutionary movement late in the eighteenth century reflects the concerns of theorists such as Thomas Sheridan about the growing dominance of writing at the expense of oral discourse.

Eighteenth-century theorists outside the elocutionary movement shared Sheridan's concern about the artificiality and isolation promoted by scientific and philosophical writings, but their alternative rested not in a style of delivery that could transcend the barriers erected through written discourse. Instead, many of them returned to ancient notions of common sense in order to explore the possibility that a shared human capacity could overcome the diffusion of thought and intellectual isolation that seemed to be outgrowths of science and technology. These writers found in Stoicism a framework for explaining the natural connections among sensory knowledge, the shared intuitive and intellectual processes involved in interpreting experiences, the individual's moral development, and the well-being of society—a constellation of relationships that seemed to promise stability in spite of evidence that their world was going through the type of change that could radically alter the nature of human communication and social relationships.

Shaftesbury and Eighteenth-Century Stoicism

Shaftesbury's work provides an example of an early and direct manifestation of the tie between Stoicism and eighteenth-century language theories, and his exploration of the potential of an intuitive inner sense to inspire a search for collective harmony influenced much eighteenth-century thought. Most notable among Shaftesbury's influences are Hutcheson's characterization of the different senses, which James McCosh[32] places under the categories of sensory experiences, the public sense captured in the idea of sensus communis, and the moral sense[33] and Scottish commonsense philosophy, both of which were in turn highly influential in subsequent developments in eighteenth- and nineteenth-century thought.

Shaftesbury's preoccupation with Stoicism is apparent in several of his works. Benjamin Rand observes that "the study . . . of the ancient classics, and more especially of the works of Horace, Epictetus, and Marcus Aurelius, had the profoundest bearing upon Shaftesbury's own philosophy."[34] As Rand notes, that Shaftesbury "was most thoroughly saturated"[35] with the philosophies of Epictetus and Marcus Aurelius is evident in the *Philosophical Regimen,* where "almost every page . . . demonstrates that the philosophy of Shaftesbury belongs to what . . . he calls the civil, social and theistic, derivable from the Stoics."[36] In "Shaftesbury as Stoic," Esther A. Tiffany argues that in the years leading up to his death, "the chief food for Shaftesbury's personal philosophical reflection came from the Stoic philosophers."[37] Although she concedes that Shaftesbury shares with his contemporaries the tendency to blend a variety of philosophical influences, Tiffany notes that Shaftesbury's uniqueness resides in his departure from the neo-Platonic belief that individuals must accept their subordination to "the One." In place of this view, Tiffany asserts, Shaftesbury's "prevailing

symbolism . . . is that of the Stoic whole, and of harmony, in the sense of cooperation of the individual with the whole."[38] Shaftesbury's exploration of the
individual's self-realization as the means to collective harmony creates a system
that Rand describes as grounded in Stoic thought but representing "a new and
brilliant presentation of that moral system."[39] McCosh also describes Shaftesbury as endorsing basic principles of Stoicism but creating a variation that
modifies those principles in order to reflect his own particular disposition and
cultural environment: "He shows that virtue, as consisting in these affections,
is natural to man, and that he who practices it is obeying the ancient Stoic
maxim, and living according to nature. The virtues which he recommends fall
far beneath the stern standard of the stoics, and leave out all the peculiar graces
of Christianity: they consist of,—'a mind subordinate to reason, a temper
humanized and fitted to all natural affection, an exercise of friendship uninter-
rupted, thorough candor, benignity, and good-nature, with constant security,
tranquillity, equanimity.'"[40] Shaftesbury's appropriation of Stoic ethics for his
contemporary philosophical system therefore represents an attempt to infuse
modern life with ancient wisdom that asserts the individual's intrinsic relationships to nature and society—a goal that assumed great urgency in a world in
which scientific and philosophical theories about the nature of human knowledge had raised questions about those relationships. At the same time, this
infusion translates Stoic self-discipline into the modern values of gentility and
politeness in response to the demands of mercantile society and concerns about
the social discord that could result from the modern emphasis on competition
captured in the term *party spirit*.

Although Shaftesbury modifies Stoic philosophy to suit the modern objectives of a polite society, his fundamental belief in the importance of a harmonious society is grounded in Stoic thought about the natural harmony that
governs the universe. A central feature of Shaftesbury's philosophy lies in his
insistence that nature provides an organizing principle for human life. The
Philosophical Regimen begins with the claim that "the only means and rule of
happiness (even amongst these other creatures, as far as they are capable of happiness) is *to follow nature,* and . . . to act in pursuance of this design."[41] This
pursuit inevitably places constraints on individuals who must subordinate themselves to an external system, a notion he emphasizes by citing Epictetus's dictum, "Of things that are, some are of our own power and jurisdiction, some
not."[42] Shaftesbury also shares the Stoic belief that recognizing the limits of
one's power facilitates an acceptance of Providence; he again quotes Epictetus,
"But am always content with that which happens, for I think what God chooses
is better than what I choose,"[43] adding, "Such is the harmony of Providence
with one who has harmony in himself, and knows wherein Providence has
placed his good and ill; wherein not."[44] Wisdom is available to the person who

learns "how to submit all of his affections to the rule and government of the whole; how to accompany with his whole mind that supreme and perfect mind and reason of the universe."[45]

For Shaftesbury, as for the Stoics, participating in the "mind and reason of the universe" immediately places people in relationship to all of nature and to each other. In *Philosophical Regimen,* he notes that "all things in this world are united, for as the branch is united and is as one with the tree, so is the tree with the earth, air, and water which feed it, and with the flies, worms, and insects which it feeds."[46] This unity creates a common nature that ensures understanding among those who pursue it: "All things stand together or exist together by one necessity, one reason, one law: therefore there is one nature of all things, or common to all. Nothing is out of the whole, nor nothing happens but according to the laws of the whole."[47] Like the Stoics, Shaftesbury uses the term *pre-conception* to describe the collected assumptions that enable people to make sense of the world, which he connects to a moral and aesthetic sense: "Preconceptions of a higher kind have place in human kind, preconceptions of the 'fair and beautiful.'"[48] Thus Shaftesbury's affinity with Stoic thought leads him to make similar connections among common sense, aesthetic judgment, and ethical commitments.

Accepting the laws of the whole entails an awareness of the common nature that promotes shared understanding. He explains that "to sympathize" means "to feel together, or be united in one sense or feeling."[49] Because this endeavor can be seen throughout nature and within humanity, people can be assured of "one all-knowing and all-intelligent nature" that participates in the "sympathizing of the whole."[50] He shares the Stoic assumption that to recognize the relationship of part to whole naturally leads to awareness of the common bond that unites people to nature and to each other. Because this bond represents an embodiment of the natural order that appropriately structures the existence of all of creation, the recognition of a common nature constitutes an ethical act. Through this line of reasoning, Shaftesbury duplicates the Stoic understanding that common sense not only reflects a fact about human perception but also has a moral dimension.

This notion is further developed in Shaftesbury's treatise, *Sensus Communis: An Essay on the Freedom of Wit and Humour.* In this treatise, Shaftesbury cites Stoic philosophy in arguing that people are appropriately guided through an intuitive moral sense that they share with others, which counters his interpretation of the Hobbesian view that people learn about the world independently and are primarily motivated to act through self-interest. Shaftesbury's distaste for contemporary public discourse is grounded in his belief that it has been appropriated for the presentation of such skeptical and cynical views that appear to challenge "common sense." He echoes the Stoic contention that sensus communis does in fact exist and is a fundamental facet of human life that cannot be circumvented even by those who most stridently deny its validity. Both Shaftesbury and the Stoics attempt to locate a human essence grounded in nature and superior to philosophical abstraction; Shaftesbury therefore appropriates Stoic philosophy in order to argue that the realm of polite society, the evolving "public sphere," can be shaped as a resource for recapturing and developing that human essence.

Like the Stoics, Shaftesbury argues that individuals possess an innate ethical sense that makes them aware of their obligation to each other. This sense of responsibility cannot be imposed from outside through the agency of political systems but is instead a fact of nature deriving from "a social Feeling or *Sense of Partnership* with Human Kind."[51] He denies the need for the notion of a social contract based in government, for the preservation of human rights comes from a higher source, a "*Promise*—made in the *State of Nature:* And that which cou'd make *a Promise* obligatory in the State of Nature, must make *all* other Acts of Humanity as much our real Duty, and natural Part."[52] Although a virtuous community usefully supports the ethical orientation of its citizens, Shaftesbury argues that the natural ties that bind people are so strong that they can even withstand a corrupt environment: "They who live under *a Tyranny*, and have learnt to admire its Power as Sacred and Divine, are debauch'd as much in their Religion, as in their Morals. *Publick Good,* according to their apprehension, is as little the Measure or Rule of Government in *the Universe,* as in *the State.* They have scarce a Notion of what is good or just, other than as mere *Will* and *Power* have determin'd. . . . But notwithstanding the Prejudices and Corruptions of this kind, 'tis plain there is something still of a *publick Principle,* even where it is most perverted and depress'd."[53]

Internal deliberation and private conversation can serve as the means for promoting sensus communis, but Shaftesbury stresses that this goal must never be subsumed by factionalism or self-interest. The tendency to acquire power through the formation of localized factions derives from the misuse of the "*associating Genius*"[54] that is an inherent part of human nature; people who sense their need to establish communities with others can be misguided in their attempts to fulfill that instinct and place their hopes in the small groups within their immediate sight in a way that jeopardizes "the *close sympathy*"[55] and broader concern for humanity that should be every person's ultimate goal.

Thus Shaftesbury invokes Stoic ethics and the model of Stoic deliberation in identifying the natural law as an alternative to the tyranny of mechanization that inevitably challenges the individual's innate sense of morality. Like the Stoics, Shaftesbury describes this morality as beginning with internal dialogue that enables the individual to develop self-awareness: "This Operation is for no inconsiderable End: since 'tis to gain him *a Will,* and ensure him *a certain*

Resolution; by which he shall know where to find himself; be sure of his own Meaning and Design; and as to all his Desires, Opinions, and Inclinations, be warranted *one and the same* Person to day as yesterday, and to morrow as to day."[56] The internal conversation Shaftesbury advocates naturally leads the individual to a clearer understanding of his or her objectives, because it facilitates a process of reason that is removed from the conflict that pervades everyday life.

Shaftesbury believes that such detachment facilitates a perspective that avoids falling prey to the frivolity and capriciousness of the world. In his notes titled "Moral and Theological Maxims," published in *Second Characters,* he writes, "Extemporary life miserable. Better the settled miser or covetous passion (when attended with thought of name, family, etc.), than the full, easy, contented, but uncertain floating. . . . But 'what shall I do next?' . . . The collector of a cabinet and intent virtuoso, still more secure as nearer order, virtue, beauty."[57] Avoiding an obsession with the whims of the moment can provide the individual with the grounding necessary to appreciate the types of qualities that the Stoics also upheld: order, virtue, and beauty. For Shaftesbury, as for the Stoics, the true merits of restraint and virtue are set in opposition to material contentment that people are inclined to pursue without reflection.

Yet, even as he emphasizes the individual's need to avoid placing an undue emphasis on the immediate urgings of a materialistic society, Shaftesbury shares the Stoic view that developing rational knowledge of the self ultimately works against the individual's isolation from others. The process of internal reflection, manifested in both the individual's thought processes and in the privacy of polite conversation, simultaneously promotes individual virtue and sensus communis, the "*Sense* of *Publick Weal,* and of the *Common Interest;* Love of the *Community* or *Society,* natural Affection, Humanity, Obligingness, or that sort of *Civility* which rises from a just *Sense* of the *common Rights* of Mankind, and the *natural Equality* there is amongst those of the same Species."[58] In Shaftesbury's view, philosophical treatises obstruct collective harmony through engaging in emotion-filled wrangling. Polite conversation, in contrast, gently engages the reason and imagination and ultimately promotes the awareness of common interests that ultimately enhances sensus communis. He asserts that "if any thing be *natural,* in any Creature, or any Kind; 'tis that which is *preservative* of the Kind it-self, and conducing to its Welfare and Support."[59] In *Philosophical Regimen,* he echoes the Stoic opposition between nature and convention in arguing that to preserve social affection necessarily entails the rejection of the vain pursuits the world might encourage: "Is it not better to be *truly sociable,* retaining true simplicity and gravity, than, by being what the world calls sociable, to give up these and live a stranger to social affection?"[60] Yet, for Shaftesbury, as for the Stoics, the recognition that society can sometimes corrupt people's natural impulses in no way threatens the central assumption that people can only develop their moral sense through an awareness of their relationship to the human community to which they have been assigned by nature. He insists that "the end or design of nature in man is society"[61] and advises the reader to be concerned not with "what relates to thy body, and the satisfaction of those desires which have nothing in common with virtue"[62] but instead to be concerned with "what is of a generous kind and relates to virtue and common good."[63] Thus, for Shaftesbury and the Stoics, the private and public are inevitably fused together, as the individual's discovery of his or her natural place in the world inevitably entails recognizing his or her ties to the human community.

While the skeptical systems of philosophers such as Hobbes attempt to subvert the true practice of reason through questioning the moral intuition that forms the basis for human society, Shaftesbury argues that true wisdom lies in using the dictates of common sense to restore society to its natural state of morality and cooperation. Jean Nienkamp describes Shaftesbury as "a Platonist who believes that people are endowed with an innate capacity for virtue that must be developed in accordance with a 'fixed standard' of virtue and reason,"[64] but it is important to recognize the difference that the Stoic influence makes in understanding Shaftesbury's understanding of how people define and locate virtue.[65] Plato's idealism places the discovery of truth in a cloistered realm; while the Stoics agree that an absolute truth lies outside human control or knowledge, their understanding of humans as naturally ordained to live in society leads them to perceive virtue as something that can only be fully realized within the social context embodied in the ideal of sensus communis. While Plato and the Stoics certainly share the conviction that each individual must ultimately pursue truth, then, the perceived role of community in that pursuit creates a crucial distinction between the two—and illustrates the importance of understanding the lineage of Stoic thought in both Shaftesbury and the New Rhetoricians.

Thomas Reid and the Development of Scottish Common Sense

Reid, whose writings provided the central core of what soon came to be known as Scottish commonsense philosophy, also has connections to Stoic thought. The precise nature of those connections is more elusive than in the case of Shaftesbury because of gaps in recorded information concerning the influences that shaped his thought—and perhaps because he, like many other eighteenth-century thinkers, was so fully immersed in classical thought that those ideas became seamlessly embedded in his own philosophical position.[66] Reid's reading notes from Arrian's arrangement of Epictetus certainly demonstrate his thorough familiarity with Stoic ideas, and this knowledge can be seen as significantly shaping Reid's view of common sense as a fundamental capacity that guides human life. In his 1753 *Philosophical Orations,* Reid restates his charge that philosophical systems that obscure the simple reality of human experience fail to accomplish the essential goal of providing helpful guidance to humanity: "Those, either among the ancient or the modern writers, who have tried to philosophise about the causes, origins and nature of virtue . . . beyond the common sense of mankind in general, have made little progress and rather have rendered a subject, clear and obvious to the multitude, obscure and doubtful by their philosophical subtleties."[67] Haakonssen notes that Reid goes on to advise that more useful guidance in morality can be found in Socrates and in Stoicism, including Cicero's *De officiis,* "both of which apparently manifest the moral essence of Christianity."[68] According to Haakonssen, Reid maintained his connection to Stoic thought as his philosophical ideas continued to develop at Glasgow: "Once Reid had, with Hutcheson's help, mastered natural jurisprudence, he clearly took to it and made it his own, recognizing its congruence with his own theological ideas, and the adaptability of the Stoic-Christian doctrine of virtue to a theory of duty consistent with both his notion of divine law and his theory of moral judgment."[69]

Because Reid's "Stoic-Christian doctrine" exists alongside a strong interest in science, the intricate fusion of ancient and modern sources that can be found throughout his work has not been uniformly acknowledged. Alexander Broadie acknowledges that Reid was "steeped in the old rhetoric no less than in the old logic," but he goes on to characterize Reid as one who was "among the modernisers" in both disciplines, adding that "their attitude to science made it difficult to be a moderniser in one discipline and a traditionalist in the other."[70] Even if establishing such clear categories is a legitimate practice in characterizing particular aspects of the thought of certain theorists, Reid's ideas about the workings of language fuse ancient and modern principles in ways that cannot be easily divided. Although Reid was clearly attentive to modern ideas, to identify him as strictly creating new insights in rhetoric and logic obscures the thorough grounding in ancient ideas that drives his views of language and society.

Although Reid does not cite the Stoics with the same consistency Shaftesbury does, his familiarity with Stoic thought and with Shaftesbury's adaptation of Stoic principles can be seen as a guiding presence in his explication of his philosophical system. He repeatedly echoes the Stoic emphasis on sensory experience as the basis of all knowledge, as in a 1780 letter to Kames: "All that we know of the material World must be grounded upon the testimony of our Senses."[71] His detailed explanation of the workings of the five senses emphasizes the stability that the intuitive capacity of common sense provides in an individual's experience with the everyday world. His views parallel Aristotle in perceiving common sense as having a certain coordinating function; he characterizes the evidence people receive from the senses and from memory as "distinct and original kinds of evidence," adding that such evidence should be classified as "first principles; and such fall not within the province of Reason, but of Common Sense."[72] He emphasizes interpretation as the key to the individual's attempt to acquire knowledge from experience, a feature that corresponds to both Stoic and Aristotelian common sense. He painstakingly defines perception as a starting point, "that immediate Knowledge which we have of eternal Objects by our Senses"[73] but adds that developing knowledge requires the individual to use common sense to make judgments about his or her perceptions. Such judgment comes about naturally and should be seen as a fundamental feature of human experience: "If there are certain principles, as I think there are, which the constitution of our nature leads us to believe, and which we are under a necessity to take for granted in the common concerns of life, without being able to give a reason for them; these are what we call the principles of common sense; and what is manifestly contrary to them, is what we call absurd."[74] Yet the fact that sensation is a natural feature of human experience does not mean that sense perception should be seen as a passive enterprise. Reid explicitly addresses this question in *Inquiry:* "Although the Peripatetics had no good reason to suppose an active and a passive intellect, since attention may be well enough accounted an act of the will; yet I think they came nearer to the truth, in holding the mind to be in sensation partly passive and partly active, than the moderns, in affirming it to be purely passive. Sensation, imagination, memory, and judgment, have, by the vulgar, in all ages, been considered as acts of the mind."[75] Haakonssen notes that according to Reid's system, the mind is not the "passive recipient of ideas causally implanted by sense perception" but constitutes a "highly active cognitive agency" that constantly engages in judgments of experience.[76]

While Locke's theories certainly influenced their notion that human knowledge develops through sense perception, Scottish commonsense philosophers are indebted both to Aristotle and the Stoics in their description of the mental process involved in interpreting those perceptions, in their assumption that this interpretive process connects with an intuitive moral sense, and in the related view that this link ensures a connection between private reflection and civic responsibility. Eighteenth-century commonsense philosophers also share the Stoic view that the moral reasoning processes available through common sense promote arguments from design that confirm God's existence through pointing toward a natural connection between the order found in nature and the existence of an intelligent creator. Reid criticizes the Stoics for lacking a sufficient emphasis on God's central role in guiding people's moral development.[77] At the same time, he praises the nobility of the Stoic notion of duty and argues that a sense of duty to others is part of the natural order that is accessible to everyone through common sense: "As the duty we owe to the Supreme Being results from the Natures of God and of Man, and from the Relation we stand in to him as our Creator Benefactor and Moral Governour and Judge, So all the Duties we owe to Men result from the common Nature of Men and the Relations they stand in to one another, and the same thing may be said of the Rights."[78]

Thus the order that exists in the universe provides the structure through which individuals discover the order that governs their individual lives, gain an awareness of the divine intelligence that brought this order into being, and determine how their interactions with other people can facilitate their constructive participation in the harmonious system they are destined to support. Reid cites *De officiis* in advancing the view that all virtues are connected, which means that individuals who pursue virtuous qualities acquire an internal harmony that intimately connects them with the unity and harmony of the divine order. For Reid, as for the Stoics, the processes through which people develop internal discipline inevitably bind people to each other through their shared sense of humanity and also "continue to bind them as Citizens."[79] He also shares the Stoic sense that language is central to human experience, as it both embodies the natural order and supports the preservation of that order through human society: "The signs by which objects are presented to us in perception, are the language of Nature to man; and as, in many respects, it hath great affinity with the language of man to man; so particularly in this, that both are partly natural and original, partly acquired by custom. Our original or natural perceptions are analogous to the natural language of man to man . . . and our acquired perceptions are analogous to artificial language, which, in our mother-tongue, is got very much in the same manner with our acquired perceptions."[80] Like language, perception is simultaneously natural and cultivated through practice; the common nature of both ensures that individuals are developing their own knowledge of the world in concert with others through passively and actively processing their perceptions. Thus Reid sets out to overcome the potential isolation of the individual implicit in contemporary philosophical thought through developing a new iteration of the Stoic connections among private reflection, shared human experiences, and the duties of citizenship, all manifested in and strengthened by language. This awareness of the intrinsically social nature of humanity contributes to the commonsense emphasis on the value of testimony for human knowledge, which both Reid and Campbell use as a foundation for Christian belief. In expounding on the subject of testimony, Reid again maintains the links among nature, common sense, and human society: "The wise and beneficent Author of Nature, who intended that we should be social creatures, and that we should receive the greatest and most important part of our knowledge by the information of others, hath, for these purposes, implanted in our natures two principles that tally with each other. The first of these principles is, a propensity to speak truth, and to use the signs of language, so as to convey our real sentiments. . . . Another original principle implanted in us by the Supreme Being, is a disposition to confide in the veracity of others, and to believe what they tell us."[81]

Reid's explication of common sense has unique features, but his view that common sense is simultaneously an internal mechanism for apprehending the world and a moral force that binds people together has important ties to notions of sensus communis found in both the Stoics and Shaftesbury. Numerous commentators have traced Reid's use of the term *common sense* immediately to Shaftesbury, whose translation of that concept into eighteenth-century discourse was widely influential. Reid's own influence was broad as well, extending well into the nineteenth century and expanding to North America as well as to other European countries. This influence was certainly significant in the work of contemporary rhetorical theorists. One of Reid's closest friends was Henry Home, Lord Kames, whose aesthetic theories played a pivotal role in the development of criticism; his colleagues in the Aberdeen Philosophical Society, where Reid initially presented many of the ideas that he later published, included prominent theorists such as George Campbell, Alexander Gerard, and James Beattie. Common sense also became a guiding principle in the rhetorical theories of both Hugh Blair and Richard Whately. Through both Shaftesbury and Reid, the pursuit of sensus communis became an important force in the development of eighteenth-century British theories of language and rhetoric.

Scottish Common Sense and British Rhetorical Theories

Many of these rhetorical theories begin with the Stoic premise that sensory experiences shape people's understanding of the natural world, and that the interpretation of these experiences involves the use of an intuitive sense that everyone shares. Reid's version of common sense shares the Stoic assumption that although common sense is not rational, it works in concert with reason. He notes that the first principles recognized by common sense are fundamental to the exercise of reason, adding that "reason can neither make nor destroy them; nor can it do any thing without them: it is like a telescope, which may help a man to see farther, who hath eyes; but without eyes, a telescope shews nothing at all."[82] While common sense and reason ideally complement each other, Reid's opposition to contemporary philosophy leads him to emphasize the primacy of common sense above a notion of reason that has come to be associated with an abstruse logic that questions the reality that is readily accessible to all of humanity. He complains that in modern philosophy, "the wisdom of *philosophy* is set in opposition to the *common sense* of mankind. The first pretends to demonstrate *a priori*, that there can be no such thing as a material world; that sun, moon, stars, and earth, vegetable and animal bodies, are, and can be nothing else, but sensations in the mind, or images of those sensations in the memory and imagination. . . . The last can conceive no otherwise of this opinion, than as a kind of metaphysical lunacy."[83] Reid's position in this opposition is clearly on the side of common sense: "If this is wisdom, let me be deluded with the vulgar. . . . It were better to make a virtue of necessity; and, since we cannot get rid of the vulgar notion and belief of an external world, to reconcile our reason to it as well as we can: for if Reason should stomach and fret ever so much at this yoke, she cannot throw it off; if she will not be the servant of Common Sense, she must be her slave."[84] Although Reid generally supports the Stoic belief in the value of reasoned judgment, his cultural environment leads him to adjust the parameters of reason's domain, as he counters what he sees as a philosophical threat to common sense by strengthening the emphasis on social knowledge.

Reid's philosophy therefore both alters and sustains the Stoic perception that common sense provides stability not only through enabling individuals to apprehend the self-evident reality of the physical world but also through facilitating the reasoning process that brings people together in seeking judgments about the difficult questions that arise within the life of the community—a process that, for eighteenth-century rhetoricians as well as the Stoics, has moral implications because it involves the use of natural gifts that people have been given. Kames goes so far as to argue, "Man is superior to the brute, not more by his rational faculties, than by his senses."[85] The sensory knowledge that people acquire puts them immediately in touch with the natural order, for "the most wonderful connection of all . . . is that of our internal frame with the works of nature."[86]

For Reid, Campbell, and other commonsense philosophers, language, another ability that is part of the natural framework of human life, constitutes an essential component in acquiring the knowledge that common sense makes available to everyone. Thus commonsense philosophers join Sheridan in attempting to counter the mechanical corruption of language that has taken place through dry, philosophical disputations, but they depart from his methods in favor of theories that seek to capture the internal vitality of human nature that was so forcefully invoked in Shaftesbury's writings. Because people possess common sense, they have the natural ability to make the mental connections that are required for the discovery of the truth. However, the inborn function of common sense is fully activated through language and develops as people work together to apply what they have experienced as fundamental truths (in Epictetus's terms, preconceptions) to particular situations. Reid defends this connection by explaining that the process of using language reinforces the general way in which people acquire knowledge of the world around them through the senses: "If we compare the general principles of our constitution, which fit us for receiving information from our fellow-creatures by language, with the general principles which fit us for acquiring the perception of things by our senses, we shall find them to be very similar in their nature and manner of operation."[87] Just as people develop judgment through processing their sensory experiences, they develop greater proficiency with language, even though language is an innate gift that everyone possesses: "The seed of language is the natural signs of our thoughts, which nature has taught all men to use, and all men to understand. But its growth is the effect of the united energy of all who do or ever did use it. . . . Grammarians have, without doubt, contributed much to its regularity and beauty; and philosophers, by increasing our knowledge, have added many a fair branch to it; but it would have been a tree without the aid of either."[88] Like the moral and aesthetic senses, people are born with the ability to use language, but this ability is enhanced through cultivation that can be seen as a collective effort. Teaching people to use language more effectively simultaneously enacts common sense and promotes an ethical engagement with the community.

One of the most complete theories linking this intuitive sense to rhetoric can be found in George Campbell's *Philosophy of Rhetoric.* Arthur Walzer aptly argues that Campbell's rhetorical theory must be viewed as "a merging of ancient and modern perspectives,"[89] which for Walzer centers upon Campbell's integration of classical rhetorics and Enlightenment psychological theories. This integration can also be seen in Campbell's fusion of Stoic ideas of common sense, developed in concert with Reid and other colleagues, with contemporary views of the role of sense perception in the acquisition of human knowledge. Campbell begins his discussion of common sense in *Philosophy of Rhetoric* with a definition that focuses on its presence as an intuitive sense that enables people to be confident that their perceptions of the world are real and meaningful. In introducing the form of "intuitive evidence" that he labels "common sense," Campbell stresses the way in which common sense facilitates the apprehension of certain "primary principles"[90] that he perceives to be fundamental truths that everyone must accept. Common sense in this passage seems to be limited to an internal apprehension of reality as the individual experiences the world. Such statements might suggest that Scottish common sense, as articulated by Reid and applied in the work of colleagues such as Campbell, must be viewed only as an ability to interpret those sensory experiences that fall completely outside the rational realm, an intuitive capacity that would hold little benefit to rhetoric. However, the orator's participation in common sense will also facilitate the type of connection with others that creates a successful argument. Early in *Philosophy of Rhetoric,* Campbell expresses his intention to identify the way in which language may "operate on the soul of the hearer,"[91] with the implicit recognition that such interpersonal interactions have broader significance to the quality of public communication.

Whately also articulates the connections among individual deliberation, common sense, and language in his discussion of the internalized debates that enhance the individual's ability to make sound arguments. Although Whately's neo-Aristotelian rhetorical theory differs in important respects from that of belletristic theorists such as Blair and Kames and from Campbell's attempt to integrate contemporary insights about psychology with rhetorical theory, his incorporation of commonsense principles in his rhetorical theory also includes an assumed connection between the individual's internal perceptions of the world and his or her ethical communication with others. For Whately, human language does more than simply transmit ideas from one person to another. He notes that animals are able to communicate with each other but adds that the distinctive characteristic of human language is its use as an "instrument of thought" integral to the reasoning process.[92] He therefore stresses that rhetoric must not be conceived merely as a tool for passing along accumulated information but must be assessed in light of "accuracy in the logical processes."[93] In Whately's view, language must begin with internal reasoning that provides the foundation for this type of meaningful communication with others.

Whately's emphasis on effective argumentation consistently leads him to link the way in which common processes of reasoning connect people to each other. Like the Stoics and other commonsense adherents, Whately insists that argument must be assessed through the reservoir of common assumptions that guide people's interpretations of specific circumstances, and these assumptions change gradually over time in response to public discourse. His extensive treatment of the burden of proof provides a thorough accounting of how argument functions in new situations in order to build on current communal beliefs. Those presenting arguments must be aware of the way in which their evidence must respond to the audience's unstated understanding of the world around them—an awareness that comes through "common sense."[94] Thus Whately's notion of presumptions formed through internal perception and developed through common sense parallels Stoic discussions of preconceptions.

Like Campbell, Whately endorses the proper use of emotion in order to prompt correct action, and he recognizes that the orator must personally enter into the emotion of a situation in order to communicate a sense of urgency to the audience: "Now in any process such as this, (which is exactly analogous to that of taking a medicine that is to operate on the involuntary bodily organs,) a process to which a man of well-regulated mind continually finds occasion to resort, he is precisely acting the skillful orator, to himself; and that too, in respect of the very point to which the most invidious names are usually given, 'the appeal to the feelings.'"[95] That it is possible for people to practice skillful oratory on themselves leads Whately to caution that just as orators are capable of misleading the public, the orator may at times mislead him/herself: "A man is in danger—the more, in proportion to his abilities—of exercising on himself, when under the influence of some passion, a most pernicious oratorical power, by pleading the cause as it were, before himself, of that passion."[96] Yet, he adds that people are unduly fearful of emotional appeals, for it is flawed reasoning that has the most dangerous effect both on the orator and the audience: "Most persons are fearful, even to excess, of being misled by the eloquence of another: but an ingenious reasoner ought to be especially fearful of his own. There is no one whom he is likely so much, and so hurtfully, to mislead as himself, if he be not sedulously on his guard against this self-deceit."[97] Thus Whately asserts that the common sense that connects the individual to the audience naturally creates a bond between private deliberation and public discourse. Those who work to develop an ethical mode of communication with themselves are better equipped to communicate with others in a way that does not mislead.

Nienkamp's discussion of internal rhetorics includes Whately but excludes eighteenth-century theorists such as Reid, Campbell, and Kames due to Nienkamp's definition of internal rhetoric as the explicit description of the rhetorical interactions among the internal faculties of the individual. While this distinction is valid for the purposes of Nienkamp's study, placing Reid, Campbell, Kames, and Whately within the Stoic model of private deliberation illuminates assumptions that are shared by a broader range of language theorists influenced by notions of common sense. The Stoic model of private deliberation offers a pattern that puts private perceptions to use in creating self-knowledge that ultimately leads to productive social interactions.

Common Sense, Sensus Communis, and Eighteenth-Century Society

Like the Stoics and Shaftesbury, language theorists of the latter part of the eighteenth century believe that a shared common sense makes self-knowledge possible but that the proper pursuit of such knowledge in turn inevitably strengthens ties among members of the human community. The very nature of common sense entails the development of knowledge that is both public and private, for people learn through their senses but are encouraged through society to develop trust in what they learn about others' experiences.[98] Reid acknowledges that people do not always act in ways that fulfill their responsibility to the common good, but he insists that this reflects their failure to understand that their fate is intricately bound to that of others: "God Almighty has made it the Interest as well as the duty of every Man to promote the good of Society. But such is the folly of Many that they act against the Interest of Society wherein their own chief Interest in this World is Included."[99] Reid, Campbell, and Whately implicitly reinforce the Stoic appreciation for truth apprehended through private deliberation rather than through an agonistic public forum. However, for these theorists, as for the Stoics, common sense provides the means for individuals to deliberate and come to judgment in a manner that inevitably strengthens their connections to others and ultimately facilitates their participation in civic life.

Numerous scholars have questioned this link, pointing out that the awareness of audience found in Campbell and Whately does not necessarily lead to discourse that does more than transmit the rhetor's predetermined communicative goals. Joel Weinsheimer notes that Campbell may be viewed as encouraging a monological approach to rhetoric through depicting "the end of rhetoric as an effect."[100] Thomas Miller depicts Campbell's notion of common sense as redefining rhetoric through relying upon an innate sense of judgment rather than common opinion, ultimately becoming "more concerned with the workings of the individual consciousness than with the practical art of drawing on common beliefs to speak to public issues."[101] However, reading Campbell's conception of common sense through a Stoic lens modifies this interpretation, offering as an alternative the possibility that Campbell, like Reid and the Stoics, deliberately blurs the apparent boundary between the workings of the individual mind and the formation and application of shared public beliefs.

Although Campbell's faith in government reflects a departure from the Stoics' determination to resist political tyranny through seeking the transcendent harmony of the divine order, he nevertheless shares their basic impulse to sublimate the individual's authority both to a broader public good and to a higher authority. He insists that the purpose of government is based upon the "principle of common sense, that a less evil should be borne to prevent a greater" and adds that within government, "whose end is common utility . . . private interest should give place to public."[102] For the circle of commonsense philosophers, as for the Stoics, the internal process of common sense given to humans as a fundamental part of their nature can be separated neither from the need to share information with others through language nor from the social obligation that constitutes the best part of human nature. Campbell identifies sensitivity to audience as the means not only for achieving immediate rhetorical success but also for putting common sense to use through language that effectively establishes a bond with others.

For commonsense theorists, learning to articulate knowledge effectively and appropriately inevitably promotes this bond, which ultimately strengthens the community. Reid invokes Stoic philosophy in his own endorsement of the relationships among individual virtue, moral development, and the community: "The Stoics defined Virtue to be a life according to nature. . . . The life of a moral agent cannot be according to his nature, unless it be virtuous. That conscience which is in every man's breast, is the law of God written in his heart, which he can not disobey without acting unnaturally. . . . No man is born for himself only. Every man, therefore, ought to consider himself as a member of the common society of mankind, and of those subordinate societies to which he belongs."[103] Campbell joins Reid in insisting that common sense includes a natural tie that creates a bond throughout humanity. For Campbell, as for the Stoics and Reid, common sense provides the basis for a bond that exists between the individual and the natural world, which includes the social order that people have created to fulfill their human need for connections with others. Echoing Epictetus's claim that common sense is possessed by all those who are "not altogether perverted,"[104] Campbell states that everyone has common sense "who is not accounted a monster in his own kind."[105]

Scottish commonsense theorists consistently emphasize the link between the personal virtue acquired through common sense and the social knowledge that emerges through the common capacity to interpret the world. Campbell insists that social relationships are reciprocal. He perceives that religion has a social obligation of its own and insists that religion, whose truths he also holds to be supported by "the common sense of mankind,"[106] should not only address the private concerns of the individual soul but "must, wheresoever it is believed, conduce greatly even to the temporal happiness and flourishing state of the community."[107] In connecting common sense to the formation of a religious community, Campbell also implicitly highlights the role of religion in solidifying the social function of common sense, as he argues that religion clarifies those principles which, "giving additional strength to social duties, bind men more closely to one another."[108] In Campbell's view, common sense therefore simultaneously supports religious insight and facilitates the process by which people share their insights with each other and express their concern for others within the community.

Campbell's rhetorical theory explicitly builds upon his insights concerning the reciprocal relationship between the community and the individual. Campbell's interest in testimony represents a resistance to skeptical arguments for rational religion, which were also sometimes supported by Stoicism,[109] but testimony for Campbell interestingly supports links among the natural function of common sense, language, and the social interactions that promote new understanding. His discussion of the way testimony works is based on the view that common sense provides people with a shared basis for perceiving reality and enables them to reason together in resolving the questions that arise in public life. He begins his *Dissertation on Miracles* by asserting that "the gospel, as well as common sense"[110] support the notion that Christian doctrine can and should be supported by rational argument.[111] Campbell's concern with contemporary debates leads him to emphasize the connection between common sense and testimony, because he relies upon evidence provided by the apostles to demonstrate the reality of miracles. Although common sense partially depends upon the insights gained through experience, he supports Reid's contention that humanity is uniquely endowed with the ability to benefit from the experience of others, in the form of testimony.[112] Campbell maintains that the ability to acquire knowledge from testimony constitutes a natural and divinely ordained human quality; although even animals are capable of learning from their own experiences, testimony leads people to benefit from "the attested experiences and observations of others."[113] This commonsense reliance upon testimony helps human affairs function effectively; Campbell claims that testimony not only provides people with a greater understanding of all aspects of human society but also offers the means for "our acquaintance with Nature and her works."[114] Thus the acceptance of testimony becomes a natural outgrowth of common sense.[115] Campbell, like his Stoic predecessors, argues that common sense enables people to escape from the confusion imposed upon them by a complex and at times false social order in order to identify the truth that lies at the heart of human existence. As in the case of the Stoics, Campbell's perception of the way in which common sense leads people to know each other and to appreciate their relationship with nature is based on religious principles; he adapts this perspective for Christian purposes in arguing that people are naturally drawn toward the rational argument derived from testimony because "God has neither in natural nor in revealed religion *left himself without witness.*"[116] Thus Campbell maintains that God has determined that people will attain their understanding of truth not simply through immediate personal revelation but through reasoned consultation with each other.

Campbell therefore follows the Stoics, Cicero, and Quintilian in emphasizing rhetoric's capacity to promote the development of social relationships. This function means that the audience's power not only resides in its immediate judgment of the effects of the discourse but also in its ability to offer judgment on the speaker's authority to speak for them. He warns the rhetor that it is necessary to reflect upon his character not as he sees himself but based on an estimate "which is obtained reflexively from the opinion entertained of him by the hearers, or the character which he bears with them."[117] Campbell's vision of rhetoric not only portrays the psychological process through which a speaker reveals his message to the audience but also describes the process by which rhetoric draws people together in anticipating their responses to each other. As Weinsheimer points out, "once a speaker begins thinking about addressing a particular audience and adapting himself to it, then it becomes clear that along with the speaker's effect on the audience, the audience is likewise exercising an influence on the speaker."[118] Stuart C. Brown and Thomas Willard argue that although critics such as James Berlin and Chaim Perelman have characterized Campbell as a pioneer in current-traditional rhetoric and list him among those who "emphasize product rather than process, abandon invention, and prescribe forms of expression,"[119] Campbell's theory represents "one of the first modern instances of audience awareness."[120] They point out that in spite of Campbell's apparent belief that rhetoric transmits truth that is self-evident, he insists that rhetoric "not only considers the subject, but also the hearers and the speaker,"[121] and they suggest that Campbell's emphasis on the speaker's relationship with the audience leads him to restore indirectly the function of invention to rhetoric as he stresses the importance of assessing the audience's needs in order to create discourse that responds appropriately to a given situation. Such a view is consistent with the Stoic understanding that people's initial experiences of reality must acquire meaning through a process of interpretation that has social implications; Campbell's insistence that rhetoric unites the hearers and speaker in a shared enterprise resonates in significant ways with Epictetus's assessment that the most effective communication comes about "when the speaker makes plain to his hearers that he has need of them."[122]

Campbell's first advice to the rhetor about audience adaptation concerns "men in general,"[123] a category constituted by the characteristics that the rhetor can assume are shared by humanity at large. In summarizing the human faculties that must be engaged in order to ensure an audience's conviction, Campbell stresses the need to support rational argument with the tools that will satisfy not only the intellect but also the imagination, the memory, and the passions.[124] While he never wavers from insisting that rhetoric must be rationally grounded, Campbell ultimately recognizes that in matters involving rhetoric, "it is not therefore the understanding alone that is here concerned."[125] Although Campbell's discussion of audience contains insights he has gleaned from his interest in faculty psychology, his assumption that people possess certain common ways of interpreting the world leads him to begin with principles pertinent to all audiences, "men in general," which corresponds to the Stoic view that nature provides people with basic shared assumptions.

However, Campbell's subsequent discussion of the need to consider the needs of specific audiences and contexts also shares the Stoic recognition of the particularity of human experience, as he acknowledges that contingencies of time and place are important elements in the rhetorical context. Just as common sense enables Campbell to articulate the connection between the fundamental potential inherent in human nature and the reasoning process that constitutes the dynamic reality of rhetorical interactions, common sense similarly provides a foundation for understanding human nature that establishes the basis for using a broad knowledge of "men in general" in order to understand the needs of a specific audience, "men in particular."[126] In the section devoted to this category, Campbell cautions the rhetor to be aware of "the special character of the audience, as composed of such individuals."[127] Campbell includes among the differences that can define an audience's particular personality the level of education and cultural training, habits, occupations, and temperament.[128] In spite of the fact that Campbell believes religious oratory offers the most powerful subject matter of any form of discourse, he points out that even in this context, speakers such as ministers are faced with the greatest challenges in developing discourse that will be meaningful to as many people as possible, because they regularly address diverse audiences.[129] For Campbell, the nature of the audience inevitably shapes the type of discourse that is produced in response to a given situation. Thus Campbell's rhetoric shares with Stoic philosophy the effort to achieve an intricate balance between common and particular, social and individual. For both Campbell and the Stoics, the link that enacts the cyclical relationship between the speaker and the audience, the individual and the community, is common sense, the shared understanding of the world that enables people to come together and arrive at social understanding.

While commonsense philosophers believe that common sense begins with the individual's mental processes, they also believe that common sense ultimately serves the epistemic function of making knowledge meaningful in specific situations. As Lloyd F. Bitzer points out in "A Re-Evaluation of Campbell's Doctrine of Evidence," commonsense principles provide for an understanding of "an intelligible universe in which rhetoric may be both useful and sound";[130] however, it is equally worthwhile to note that rhetoric also provides a forum within which common sense achieves a sense of purpose. Through using common sense as a basis for rhetoric, Campbell and Whately identify common sense as a faculty that provides individuals with the means for understanding the world around them *and* as the force that enables the rhetor and audience to engage in a mutual process of applying shared fundamental precepts to those circumstances of life that are not only "real" but also "often changeable and contingent."[131] Campbell maintains the Stoic links among common sense, language, and the formation of social relationships. He also follows the Stoics in recognizing that while the human mind possesses the potential for knowledge in the form of sensations and remembered experiences, common sense provides the foundation through which the significance of those experiences becomes apparent. However, like other eighteenth-century theorists, he applies general Stoic principles in ways that are unique. Campbell's version of rhetoric enacts the potential of common sense in a new way through enabling the rhetor and the audience to join in determining how the pressing needs of a particular moment can best be interpreted in light of their shared experiences and assumptions about the world. Commonsense philosophy tells people that they know something; Campbell reveals rhetoric's role in helping them discover just what it is that they know and how to articulate that knowledge.

Campbell's perception that common sense maintains an inherent connection with "the common society of mankind" can be seen as a foundation for his statement that without common sense, it would be impossible "to advance a single step in the acquisition of knowledge, especially in all that regards mankind, life, and conduct."[132] Because common sense enables people to grasp certain principles fundamental to their existence, it also functions as a starting point in achieving consensus in a world in which not all truths are self-evident. Scottish commonsense philosophers maintain the strong interest in the individual's moral sense that is central to Stoic philosophy and at the same time share the Stoic conviction that such a sense cannot be detached from the tie with other people that is an endemic feature of human life.

■

Critics have rightly noted ways in which "common sense" theories rest on notions of consensus that can become an oppressive force; however, eighteenth-century British theorists at least perceived themselves to be engaged in upholding the value of common knowledge against the esoteric extremes found in modern science and philosophy. Clearly eighteenth-century commonsense theories failed to reconcile their assertion of universal principles with the diversity of experiences and social practices that surrounded them. However, this failure emerged as part of their focus on challenging what they perceived to be the dangers of philosophical skepticism and pessimism. For Shaftesbury and Scottish commonsense theorists, as for the Stoics, the value of common sense for collective deliberation follows naturally from the assumption that common sense is a divine gift granted to people for the purpose of achieving the social harmony that must be the ideal for which people were created. Shaftesbury, Reid, and the rhetorical theorists they influenced drew upon an optimistic Stoic vision of humanity's natural capacity for sociability, benevolence, and shared understanding in order to challenge images of a world governed by competition and self-interest. Such optimism inevitably overlooks the reality that underlies the ideal of consensus. However, tracing the Stoic roots underlying their thought at least helps to illuminate the idealistic vision of language's role in society that theorists such as Shaftesbury, Reid, Campbell, Blair, and Whately pursued through the notion of common sense and its promise of universal harmony.

Like the Stoics, the eighteenth-century British theorists' search for tangible ways of promoting that harmony ultimately leads them to explore connections among aesthetics, ethics, and language. These eighteenth-century theorists built on the Stoic view that language has a part to play in ensuring the preservation of sensus communis, and their concerns about factionalism and party spirit ensured their appreciation for the Stoic emphasis on the role of language in promoting harmonious social relationships rather than achieving victory in debate. Their interest in taste and sympathy, like their engagement with commonsense philosophy, can be more fully understood against the backdrop of their appropriation of the ancient principles of Stoic philosophy as they seek to respond to contemporary concerns.

Chapter 3

TASTE AND SENSUS COMMUNIS

The Stoic union among sensus communis, sensory experience, and aesthetic judgment provides a foundation for eighteenth-century conversations about taste. Although Stoic philosophers do not use the term *taste,* this important eighteenth-century concept exemplifies how a distinctly modern vocabulary emerges from Stoic foundations. Both ancient and modern theorists assert that learning by sense is a natural process for everyone; the notion of common sense both presumes and enacts a bridge among sensory experience, the individual's innate search for virtue, and the development of an ethical community. Although the meaning of sensory experience is immediately apprehended and requires no rational activity, judgment of those experiences and the determination of how common knowledge can be applied to particular circumstances do connect with reason. Reasoning requires an awareness of one's place in the natural order, which includes a connection with others. This connection entails both an awareness of one's natural relationship to others who experience the world in a similar way and a commitment to fulfill one's responsibility to society, both of which provide common sense with a strong ethical component.

Their conviction that common sense serves as a natural means by which people mutually process their experiences also leads eighteenth-century theorists to share the Stoic view that common sense connects to aesthetic judgment. If people are indeed programmed to respond positively to the harmony that they encounter in the world around them, this shared aesthetic response must be part of the common judgment that common sense offers. It can therefore be seen as one aspect of the ethical framework that people draw upon in order to become abler participants in society. This insight is particularly important with respect to language, which the Stoics perceived as potentially conveying truth, promoting strong social relationships, and offering a window into the character. Refining the ability to make judgments about language therefore becomes a vehicle through which people simultaneously develop their reasoning ability and strengthen their natural sense of duty toward their community.

This insight provides a foundation for eighteenth-century theories of taste, which eighteenth-century theorists use to reinforce the links they construct between sensory experience and virtue. According to Diogenes Laertius, the Stoics describe beauty as one component of goodness. This involves the perception that goodness "has in full all the 'factors' required by nature or has perfect proportion."[1] The accompanying view that beauty consists of "four species, namely, what is just, courageous, orderly, and wise"[2] further delineates the link between ethics and aesthetics. Cicero's subsequent identification of "beauty, tact, and taste" as components of "outward, visible propriety"[3] also assumes that the qualities that people naturally appreciate are visible and available to the entire community—and elements in the development of virtue. Through uniting his ideas about language, including the aesthetic features of "beauty, tact, and taste," with Stoic notions of a virtuous community inscribed by nature, Cicero provides eighteenth-century rhetoricians with a model for explaining the connections among the human appreciation for the harmony and order found in nature, the development of individual virtue, and the strength of the community. His insistence that nature ordains an appreciation for the "inward essence and outward aspect" of "moral goodness and propriety"[4] establishes an early philosophical foundation for eighteenth-century notions of taste and its role in the development of the moral sense.

Hugh Blair's adaptation of eighteenth-century notions of taste regarding rhetoric integrates Stoic principles with both modern aesthetic and rhetorical theories. Blair's notion of taste, like common sense, resides between sense and intellect, facilitates the development of reason, and is innate but developed through cultivation. Moreover, aesthetic judgment, like sensus communis, serves both a private function and social one, as it begins with personal experience, is refined through contact with others, and in the process ultimately strengthens the natural bonds that provide social stability.

The negative connotations that have come to be associated with the language of the aesthetic, particularly terms such as *taste,* have led in recent times to their general dismissal, without a full recognition of the philosophical principles that initially surrounded such terms. Many contemporary critiques of eighteenth-century British rhetorics focus on Blair as the figure who has been assigned primary responsibility for rhetoric's shift during that period toward what has been seen as a belletristic appreciation for reception over production, form over substance, and the private over the social. Linda Ferreira-Buckley notes that "in popular lore, the belletristic system ranks at the nadir of language theory";[5] she adds that as early as the mid-nineteenth century, the adjective *belletristic* began to be viewed in a negative light, as "it became associated with a dilettantesque interest in the fine arts."[6] The widespread view of taste as a vehicle for codifying cultural norms through fixed literary texts has generated much criticism of Blair's theory, as a number of scholars have characterized Blair's departure from central rhetorical principles as a catalyst for the demise of traditional rhetorical training and the accompanying emphasis on the study of literature.[7]

The foundation for these negative characterizations of belletristic theories often depends upon emphasizing those elements of ancient rhetorical theory that are grounded in agonistic oratory aimed at resolving immediate public problems and then sharply juxtaposing those elements with the eighteenth century's interest in cultivating an internal sensibility. This approach is exemplified in Thomas Miller's charge that "from the outset, the paradigm of rhetoric and belles lettres emphasized polite taste and deemphasized rhetoric's traditional concern for civic discourse."[8] Miller contends that the ancient ideals of civic oratory are threatened as rhetoric is appropriated by a polite society directed toward mercantile aims; he charges that while Blair "valorized the civic ideals and practical essentials of classical rhetoric, he did not discuss the political oratory of his own era because he was far more concerned with instilling polite sentiments than in teaching students how to speak to public controversies."[9] However, the recognition that Blair's interest in classical thought incorporates Stoic concepts as well as classical rhetorical theories complicates the implicit binary this statement assumes. While using oratory and the resolution of immediate public issues as the emblem of ancient rhetorical theory seems to establish a clear demarcation between ancient and modern rhetoric, it does so at the expense of accounting for those ancient strains that emphasize rhetoric's role in cultivating character, responsible discursive practices, and strong social relationships—strains found not only in Stoic philosophy but also in portions of the rhetorical adaptations of Stoicism found in *De officiis* and Quintilian's *Institutes*. While Cicero certainly embodies the interest in oratory and democratic practice Miller identifies with "classical ideals,"[10] his interest in Stoic ethics leads him to articulate additional ways of conceiving rhetoric, which include the pursuit of public and private virtue through the cultivation of an array of skills including an aesthetic sensibility. Cicero's interest in ethical concerns and the expansive knowledge of the orator are often discussed, but his fame as an orator and his stature in representing the classical sites for rhetorical practice have in some respects overshadowed the presence of Stoic themes in his writings —themes that become an important link between classical thought and evolving modern theories that emphasize rhetoric's role in the cultivation of character. The Stoics, Cicero, and Quintilian therefore provide models for theories that fuse private and public, an internal aesthetic sense with virtuous civic discourse. Tracking these strains in eighteenth-century rhetorical theories can illuminate ways in which eighteenth-century theorists conceived of their work as having a rhetorical function, even as it adopted approaches distinct from the civic ideal represented in particular elements of the Greco-Roman rhetorical tradition.

Eighteenth-century theorists found the cultivation of character to be a rhetorical model particularly relevant to the demands of their era. The theories of rhetoricians such as Blair connected the goal of preparing students for entry into "polite society" with an array of ancient assumptions about language's role in promoting civic virtue. Nan Johnson acknowledges that Blair's notion of taste is tied to his civic commitments: "Blair's regard for the edifying function of taste goes beyond an argument for its influence on the powers of reason to include an advocacy for its impact on the development of moral character and civil commitment."[11] For Blair, as for other eighteenth-century theorists, Stoic thought provides a vocabulary for demonstrating how individual character and civic virtue unite in aesthetic experience.

A number of scholars argue that Blair's willingness to connect refined aesthetic judgment with moral character underscores the problematic assumptions that pervade his lectures.[12] Without question, Blair and his contemporaries were driven by the immediate political concerns of their own day, and their appropriation of the Stoic emphasis on harmony and order creates a framework that supports a conservative social agenda. In describing the perspectives of Edinburgh's "Moderate literati," Sher describes Blair and his colleagues as participating in a collective enterprise that sought to outline a moderate position in the midst of religious extremes, as they occupied a position between strict Calvinists and more radical challenges to "the political and religious status quo."[13] This group can therefore be seen as engaged in arguing for moderation and order in ways that affect developments both within the Church of Scotland and in a larger political environment, including "efforts to resolve, or at least ease . . . tension between British patriotism and Scottish nationalism."[14] Sher identifies Stoic thought as an important element of the Moderates' ideology, as they built on Hutcheson's fusion of Stoic thought with Christian images concerning God's beneficent Providence. In arguing for the cultivation of a refined taste that promotes public and private virtue, Blair, whom Sher describes as "the greatest Moderate preacher of Christian Stoicism,"[15] applies Stoic principles to demonstrate how rhetorical education can prepare individuals to support a harmonious society and to enact their appropriate positions within that society.

The goal of examining the presence of Stoic principles in Blair's notions of taste and rhetoric can therefore be seen not as calling into question the elitist tendencies in Blair's lectures but instead as acquiring a more complete understanding of the philosophical premises that might have provided Blair and his colleagues with a sense of the deeper significance of their work, an understanding that complicates contemporary interpretations of the implications surrounding the work of earlier theorists. Thomas Miller argues, "By emphasizing stylistic niceties and romanticizing natural genius, Blair alienated provincial students from their own traditions, and from the dialectical potential of their experience as outsiders."[16] While this critique may accurately describe what Blair's theory does, it is nevertheless worthwhile to recognize that Blair's philosophical assumptions would probably have led him to conceive of his work in very different terms. Blair's Christian-Stoic perspective creates a rationale for teaching taste that goes beyond the material aims of indoctrinating students into the demands of polite society. This philosophical orientation also resists the notion of cultural insider and outsider that seems so evident to us in retrospect, as it seeks common ground that provides the basis for a community that transcends division. While the intervening centuries have convinced most people that such a community is an untenable (and even undesirable) goal, Blair and his contemporaries clung to the hope that it might be achieved, although their tenacity in holding to this view was more pronounced in part because of their fears that such a unified and virtuous society might be on the verge of obsolescence.

Placing taste within a Stoic framework involves using nature both to reinscribe order and to challenge the established social system to the extent that society creates false standards that corrupt natural judgment. Just as Thomas Reid expresses concern that the elaborate reasoning of philosophers might overwhelm the natural insights of ordinary people, eighteenth-century theorists attempt to define taste as reflecting a natural sensibility that counters the false refinement of modern society. In doing so, they follow Seneca's explanation of how the pursuit of virtue leads people to pursue moderation in the possessions they acquire: "Our motto, as you know, is 'Live according to Nature'; but it is quite contrary to nature to torture the body, to hate unlaboured elegance, to be dirty on purpose, to eat food that is not only plain, but disgusting and forbidding. Just as it is a sign of luxury to seek out dainties, so it is madness to avoid that which is customary and can be purchased at no great price."[17] Such advice was still compelling to eighteenth-century theorists seeking to preserve order in the midst of increasing consumption. While the idealistic framework of eighteenth-century taste over time did accommodate the goals of emerging capitalism, that goal was integrated with the loftier goals of theorists whose classical training encouraged them to attempt a reinscription of an earlier notion of civic unity for their rapidly changing society. Blair's rhetorical theory can be interpreted as indoctrination into "polite society," and an awareness of this theory's connection to Stoic thought does not directly challenge that interpretation. However, an exploration of Blair's Stoic affiliation does provide a more complete grasp of the broader system within which he perceived himself to function and a more nuanced understanding of how a church leader and educator could have conceived of himself as devising a rhetorical theory that advanced a substantial ethical and pedagogical agenda even as it appeared to support more immediate material aims.

The transitional character of eighteenth-century society, along with the complexity underlying ancient theories of language, also complicates contemporary characterizations of belletristic rhetoric, specifically as represented in notions of taste, as deliberately shifting rhetorical training from a classical emphasis on agonistic public discourse to the pursuit of heightened critical perception and personal autonomy. For eighteenth-century theorists, as for the Stoics and other classical thinkers, this apparent opposition between the internal and external worlds is not as sharply defined as it might appear to be. The Stoic fusion of private and civic virtue can be seen as a significant influence on even the traditionally oratorical theories of Cicero and Quintilian; the recognition that internal standards of judgment inevitably develop through engagement with the external world also shapes belletristic theories. As Ferreira-Buckley and Halloran note, Blair's interest in style and individual identity signals the eighteenth-century shift toward a consciousness of individuality as a component of style, but this shift toward genius continued to exist in tension with notions of correctness and public standards that had existed for centuries.[18] Blair's theory, then, represents neither the wholesale appropriation of classical rhetorical models nor their complete rejection in favor of a modern turn toward individualism.

The Stoic bridge between public and private represents one way in which eighteenth-century theorists such as Blair negotiated the tensions that emerge at their historical moment. Eighteenth-century theorists share with the Stoics the understanding that taste and style have both a personal and social function. Hans-Georg Gadamer argues that "taste was originally more a moral than an aesthetic idea. It describes an ideal of genuine humanity."[19] In his view, critical judgment for eighteenth-century British theorists, as for Vico, connects with sensus communis: "The sensus communis is an element of social and moral being. Even when, as in pietism or in Scottish philosophy, this concept was associated with a polemical attack on metaphysics, it still retained its original critical function."[20] This interpretation suggests that Ulman's interpretation that Blair's oral and written language operate in "fixed systems"[21] must be qualified by the recognition that Blair's commonsense orientation does ascribe to language a character that is to a certain degree fixed by nature but also develops through ongoing social interaction that inevitably involves fluctuation as it participates in social change. In seeking this balance, Blair adheres to Seneca's view that language reflects not only individual dispositions but also "that certain styles of speech are more or less suitable to nations also."[22]

Taste and Sensus Communis:
Cultivating Appreciation for the Natural Order

The discussions of taste and aesthetic judgment found in the writings of Blair, Shaftesbury, and Kames, participate in a broader cultural conversation that consistently explores the role of taste in promoting natural judgment and a moral sensibility. Herman Cohen notes that Blair's originality lies not in his subject matter alone but in his systematic application of principles of taste to rhetoric.[23] The Stoic influences that permeate Blair's treatment of taste can also be seen in early eighteenth-century essays on taste, which reveal key principles that eighteenth-century theorists draw upon in adapting the Stoic emphasis on natural harmony and community sensibility to an eighteenth-century environment.

For writers in the early decades of the century, as for the Stoics and Scottish commonsense philosophers, an awareness of nature necessarily entails a recognition of the divine order that undergirds creation. Many eighteenth-century writers describe the proper cultivation of taste as an endeavor that encourages people to develop preferences that ultimately support notions of virtue that strongly resonate with Stoic prescriptions. The anonymous writer of a 1739 essay on taste describes taste as "a perfect representation"[24] of nature, which encourages restrained and moderate language use: "In the midst of riches and plenty, it is sober and reserved, dispensing duly and prudently all the beauties and graces of Discourse; never suffering itself to be dazzled by what is false, how gla[r]ing soever it be."[25] Citing Quintilian, the writer goes on to observe, "It is the want of this quality which occasions the fault of all corrupt stiles, such as bombast, false wit and point, when, as Quintilian observes, the genius wanteth judgment, and is deceived by the appearance of excellence."[26] Such moderation connects to the eighteenth-century ideal of politeness, which is often described in terms that resonate with the Stoic goal of moderation, as when the author of "Of Politeness" describes politeness as maintaining "the *golden Mean*" in the midst of extremes that inevitably promote "Vice or Folly."[27]

In concert with other early eighteenth-century writers, Shaftesbury assumes an ethical function for aesthetic judgment. Esther A. Tiffany comments that Shaftesbury's taste "operates both in the field of art and in the field of morals."[28] Gadamer insists that this notion of taste is distinct from Immanuel Kant's aesthetic because of Shaftesbury's insistence that aesthetic encounters provide a vehicle through which people develop their ongoing ethical engagement with the world. Echoing Gadamer, Benjamin Rand states, "Shaftesbury's theory of ethics may be readily transformed into a theory of aesthetics."[29] He further emphasizes the civic commitment this entails: "Philosophy and aesthetics . . . meant more to him than mere theoretical systems. They must be carried over into the life of the community."[30] Shaftesbury clearly articulates his own lofty sense of these connections in a letter to Sir John Cropley dated February 16, 1712: "My own designs . . . you know run all on moral emblems and what relates to ancient Roman and Greek history, philosophy and virtue. Of this the modern painters have but little taste. If anything be stirred, or any studies turned this way, it must be I that must set the wheel a going and help to raise the spirit. . . . My changes turn wholly, as you see, towards the raising of art and the improvement of virtue in the living, and in posterity to come."[31] Shaftesbury maintains that aesthetic experience may help to promote virtue first through its capacity to touch the heart of the observer in a manner that more aptly carries forth the goals of philosophical disputation: "This Lesson of Philosophy, even a Romance, a Poem, or a Play may teach us; whilst the fabulous Author leads us with such Pleasure thro the Labyrinth of the Affections, and interests us, whether we will or no, in the Passions of his Heros and Heroines."[32]

However, Shaftesbury's description of the character of aesthetic experience extends beyond an immediate emotional reaction to the plight of the heroes represented in a literary text. Shaftesbury believes that regular encounters with beauty initiate a methodical process by which the individual becomes attuned to the higher reality that beauty reflects. He departs subtly from the Platonic notion that beauty in the material world guides the individual toward a spiritual realm that is ultimately separate. Tiffany maintains that this distinction reveals the Stoic foundation that underlies Shaftesbury's theory of aesthetic perception, as he describes experiences of beauty not as pure intellectual exercises removed from the sensory realm but as a social and functional enterprise that requires thorough engagement with "the whole, including and dominating in perfect harmony of mutual adjustment all its parts."[33] She maintains that this emphasis on the Stoic whole shapes Shaftesbury's perception that beauty lies in "the oneness and the rightness of the universe, for the good of which all the parts, including man, exist."[34]

Like Shaftesbury, Reid grounds aesthetic appreciation in the intersection between common sense and beauty defined in terms that correspond to the laws of nature. Reid, like the Stoics, believes that people have access to the divine mind through developing an appreciation for the order that governs nature. In a lecture on the culture of the mind delivered at the University of Glasgow, Reid explains, "Every Law of Our Nature that can be discovered by us deserves our Serious Attention. Because the Laws of Nature are in Reality nothing else but the Rules according to which God Governs the World."[35] Those who study the uniformity that can be found in nature "will see farthest into the intention of their great Author."[36] He also shares with the Stoics and Shaftesbury the conviction that all beauty approximates the order found in nature, which means that those who methodically come to appreciate that beauty are in touch with the order that God has intended to be delightful to humanity.

Reid's contemporary Alexander Gerard echoes these themes in his *Essay on Taste,* in which he cites *De officiis* in describing the necessary connection between beauty and the natural order: "We pay a very great regard to fitness and utility, in establishing the standard of beauty and proportion in the several kinds. And, though the most perfect art falls infinitely short of nature, in combining the useful with the regular; yet none of its productions is reckoned a masterpiece, in which these excellencies do not meet."[37] Gerard's view that beauty can be defined according to fitness and order parallels not only Shaftesbury and Kames but also draws directly upon Cicero's appropriation of Stoic thought and resonates with Chrysippus's definition of beauty's visible inscription in nature.

Cultivating Taste: The Artistic Development of Nature's Gifts

Because Shaftesbury and other eighteenth-century writers adhere to the Stoic belief that nature provides the basis for human knowledge, they also share the Stoic view that human learning entails the development of inborn talents that have been given to everyone. These views are articulated in discussions of taste early in the century, as in the 1739 "Taste: An Essay," which anticipates Blair's integration of taste with rhetoric. The writer argues that "all men bring this first principle of Taste with them into the world, as well as those of Rhetorick and Logick."[38] He cites Cicero in arguing that the universal appreciation of good oratory illustrates this point and claims that Seneca supports the view that "the Taste which we here speak of, almost every-body have in themselves the first principles of it, altho' in the greater part of mankind they are less clear for want of instruction and reflection."[39] Thus eighteenth-century conversations predating Blair describe taste as involving both feeling and judgment, sense and reason. These early writers share the conviction of Shaftesbury and later theorists that the cultivation of taste strengthens the intellect and ultimately benefits an individual's ethical development. Like the Stoics, Shaftesbury perceives varied outcomes as available to those who engage in a disciplined encounter with all of the components that contribute to aesthetic experience. Tiffany notes that for Shaftesbury, "This sense in the original form is finally represented as no more than a blindly-held, groping ideal, at the first incorrectly applied, and only rightly applied after vigorous training. Its characterization in this aspect bears a marked resemblance to the precognitions of Epictetus, who, like Shaftesbury, places his principal emphasis not on the rudimentary state of the faculty, but on the purification and development of it into what shall become the eye of vision as well as the motive of right choice, or will."[40] For Shaftesbury, practice in judgment therefore becomes the means to strengthen the aesthetic and ethical sense that he believed to be inborn.

> 'Twere to be wish'd we had the same regard to *a right* TASTE in Life and Manners. What Mortal, being once convinc'd of a difference in *inward Character,* and of a Preference due to *one* Kind above *another;* wou'd not be concern'd to make *his own* the best? If *Civility* and *Humanity* be a TASTE; if *Brutality, Insolence, Riot,* be in the same manner a TASTE; who, if he cou'd reflect, wou'd not chuse to form himself on the amiable and agreeable, rather than the odious and perverse Model? Who wou'd not endeavour to *force* NATURE as well in this respect, as in what relates to a *Taste* or *Judgment* in other Arts and Sciences? For in each place the *Force on* NATURE is us'd only for its Redress. If a natural *good* TASTE be not already form'd in us; why shou'd not we endeavour to form it, and become *natural?*[41]

Shaftesbury encourages people to make careful assessments of the vital quality of "unity of design," adding that "nothing is more fatal . . . than this false relish, which is governed rather by what immediately strikes the sense, than by what consequentially and by reflection pleases the mind, and satisfies the thought and reason."[42] Avoiding the "false relish" that comes from inadequate reflection concerning sensory experience helps to promote the mental control that is so important to moral development: "Concerning freedom see a moral explanation: The same doctrine and explanation of liberty and freedom in true moral philosophy as in painting, viz. 'That the truly austere, severe, and self-severe, regular, restraintive, character and regimen corresponds (not fights or thwarts) with the free, the easy, the secure, the bold.' . . . *Sibi qui imperiosus* [who controls himself]."[43] The Stoic goal of self-control therefore develops as people understand the connections between their internal states and the noble qualities that reside in the world around them; their awareness of these connections helps them to cultivate good judgment. Shaftesbury writes that the goal of cultivating taste can be identified "the same here as in life and true wisdom in order to avoid deceit and imposture."[44] Practicing aesthetic judgment holds the potential to develop strengths in areas that humans have naturally been given, which includes both the intellect and the moral sense. This enterprise is valuable first because it cultivates habits of reflection in people who otherwise might carelessly make judgments based on initial impressions.

For Shaftesbury, the connection between the process people use in developing taste and the natural refinement of reason reinforces the cyclical relationship between beauty and virtue. That which is beautiful points toward a deeper truth; learning to appreciate the beautiful inevitably cultivates a virtuous disposition. Tiffany argues that Shaftesbury, like the Stoics, describes the process of refining aesthetic judgment as one that involves an "ascent . . . to higher and yet higher forms of beauty—to a 'coalition of beauties which form a beautiful society,' from 'public good in one community' to 'the good of mankind,' and finally to the 'universal mind' presiding over all."[45] He repeatedly refers to beauty as a quality that is intricately connected to morality, as in the *Second Characters,* where he refers to "the unity and equality of life, made by unity of object."[46] Ultimately, then, the moral function of taste resides in its requirement that people actively engage with the intersections among beauty, the natural world, and human society: "And thus, after all, the most natural Beauty in the World is *Honesty,* and *moral Truth.* For all *Beauty is* TRUTH."[47] Aesthetic experience represents not only the internal appreciation of standards of beauty but an ethical encounter with the community that embodies the ideal of "the Stoic whole, and of harmony, in the sense of cooperation of the individual with the whole."[48] Such an encounter begins with the individual's perceptions of the world, but those perceptions naturally require development through acknowledging the shared experiences that bind the individual to the community.

Kames shares Shaftesbury's belief that people are naturally drawn to order. He insists that "we are framed by nature to relish order and connection."[49] Cultivating this natural appreciation for order elevates the mind. However, he also adheres to the view that this instinct may sometimes be overpowered by external concerns that debilitate the spirit. Criticism can, in Kames's view, provide people with opportunities to reflect on the fine arts in ways that will bring them pleasure and mental discipline, as well as employing the reasoning processes that can promote ethical behavior.[50] Ultimately, Kames echoes Stoic arguments for internal reflection in promising that criticism can support morality through the search for "a principle of order"[51] that will instill in people a habit of adhering to their sense of duty. Kames explains that the mental discipline required in appreciating art draws upon a reasoning process that prepares the individual "for acting in the social state with dignity and propriety."[52] Such a venture requires that people cultivate the habit not only of perception but of reflecting constructively upon their perceptions, for "as *intention,* a capital circumstance in human actions, is not visible, it requires reflection to discover their true character."[53] For Kames, then, criticism serves as a deliberative faculty that refines the common sense of taste and in the process facilitates sensus communis.

Taste and Common Sense: The Social Character of Beauty

This belief that internal refinement ultimately connects to social understanding is an important dimension that connects eighteenth-century thought to Stoic ethics. Shaftesbury has been widely acknowledged to have a Stoic orientation toward the individual's necessary relationship to the community; it is important to take note of the fact that other early eighteenth-century writers share this perspective, as they persistently assert the connection between the interests of individuals and their communities. Although the emphasis on the cultivation of taste has been one of the chief examples used by those who argue for belletristic rhetoric's inward, critical turn, discussions of taste can be seen as an application of Stoic ideas concerning the way in which the cultivation of individual perceptions facilitates a constructive participation in the larger community. To be sure, this participation is framed in ways that replace the agonistic discourse associated with major strains of classical rhetoric with the harmonious society envisioned as a feature of Stoic sensus communis. At the same time, many eighteenth-century writers explicitly emphasize ways in which the proper cultivation of taste and politeness can help to preserve the strains of public spirit that they interpret as part of their inheritance from the classical world. The 1733 epistle titled "The Happy Life" juxtaposes the sound moral sense of modern rural life with the corruption of the city and concludes with a decision to replace the heated biases of eighteenth-century society with a spirit of Stoic calm: "No Party Factions should my Mind engage. . . . I'd serve my Country with a Roman Soul."[54] The impartial judgment of the "Roman Soul" strips away the external concerns that prohibit true agreement among people who pursue the standards of judgment that are naturally given to them. At the same time, the fact that taste is socially cultivated means that it may become corrupted as well as strengthened through contact with others. Although the writer of *An Essay on Taste* stresses that taste is an inborn capacity, he extensively cites Seneca's account of the process by which taste may gradually "degenerate into excess and luxury"[55] rather than promoting the personal and civic virtue toward which it should be naturally directed.

Thus theorists throughout the century advocate taste's capacity to promote genuine public spiritedness against the corruption that comes about through false priorities that interfere with sensus communis. Writers across the eighteenth century adhere to the Stoic view that cultivating the taste that is grounded in common sense inevitably has ethical significance. In the charge that concludes the 1738 poem titled "Of Politeness," the writer asserts the intrinsic connections among the divine order represented in nature, the individual, and social commitments, advising the reader to "plough your Course, thus steer between the Shelves / *Polite* to Heav'n, your Neighbour, and Yourselves."[56] The writer of the 1739 essay on taste asserts that "Taste in Literature communicates itself both to publick behaviour, and our manner of living."[57] Early conversations about taste can therefore be seen to link aesthetic judgment, individual virtue, and the community in ways that parallel the relationships outlined in Stoic thought.

Shaftesbury, too, assumes that the formation of taste is visibly manifested in the individual's character. In a passage of *Soliloquy* that resonates with Cicero's description of "outward, visible propriety," Shaftesbury writes, "In the very nature of Things there must of necessity be the Foundation of a right and wrong TASTE, as well in respect of inward Characters and Features, as of outward Person, Behaviour, and Action."[58] Shaftesbury's assumed union among aesthetic experience, character, and social order illustrates what Gadamer refers to as "the great moral and political tradition of the concept of sensus communis,"[59] which grounds aesthetic experience not in what Gadamer characterizes as the more subjective realm of Kant but "positively by what grounds communicability and creates community."[60] This quality of a communicable taste, refined not in isolation but in collaboration with community, ensures the utility of Shaftesbury's appropriation of Stoic thought for rhetoricians later in the century.

Reid assumes that because human society is a part of this order, people who develop a tasteful appreciation for beauty and the natural order are in turn equipping themselves for meaningful participation in the human community. In his lecture notes for the "Culture of the Mind" course delivered annually at Glasgow, Reid expresses the view that individuals are uniquely equipped to fulfill their potential in the community, as he defines "Society as the chief Mean of raising the human Mind to that degree of Illumination and that use of its rational and Moral Powers which is necessary in order to our being capable either of Virtue or Vice."[61] For Reid, as for Shaftesbury and the Stoics, aesthetic judgment, personal development, and society's well-being are all intricately connected.

Gerard's conviction that beauty is naturally ordained also leads him to insist that individuals must reflect thoughtfully upon the harmony that underlies the divinely ordained system in order to cultivate the moral sense that lies within. Gerard also shares the view that this internal process has significant social implications: "But what extensive influence the moral sense has on taste of every kind, it will be unnecessary particularly to describe, if we only recollect the various perceptions which it conveys. To it belongs our perception of the fairness, beauty, and loveliness of virtue; of the ugliness, deformity, and hatefulness of vice; produced by the native qualities of each considered simply."[62] Thus, like Shaftesbury, Gerard fuses aesthetics and ethics and explains how both are refined through their mutual interactions.

Kames also perceives the development of an aesthetic sense that comes about through the refinement of language use as a socially significant act. He explains in detail the way in which not only feeling the passions available through art but also reflecting on those passions enables people to develop discernment about the issues that guide their lives.[63] In his view, the senses of sight and hearing provide a middle ground between external reality and an individual's purely internal intellectual pursuits. The physical tie to the organic pleasures—touch, taste, and smell—makes them eventually exhausting, but the "finer pleasures" associated with sight and hearing revive people gently through leading their intellects toward constructive engagement with the world. According to Kames, this process of engaging the senses and intellect in reflecting on the external world is intrinsic to human nature and provides the foundation for criticism.[64] The practice of criticism therefore enables people to develop a critical awareness of the external forces that shape their inner lives; this function means that the practice of criticism enhances human life through simultaneously developing an individual's internal artistic taste and moral sense. Adam Smith also links the natural appreciation for beauty to the individual's social awareness: "The same principle, the same love of system, the same regard to the beauty of order, of art and contrivance, frequently serves to recommend those institutions which tend to promote the public welfare."[65] Thus both Smith and Kames assert that the perspective cultivated in criticism readily translates to greater facility in grasping and enacting an individual's civic commitments.

Eighteenth-century attempts to translate Stoic notions of sensus communis in terms that acknowledge the distinct features of eighteenth-century society clearly face many challenges. Like the Stoics, Kames assumes that sensus communis involves a universal brotherhood, in spite of the fact that such a vision ignores the reality of the emerging class system that surrounds him. On this point, Kames demonstrates an interesting ambiguity that reveals the tension underlying the use of internal aesthetic judgment as a resource accessible across social boundaries. Clearly Kames adheres to the view that although the principles of taste are established by nature, their refinement has been perfected by civilized society. In describing the superiority of civilized taste as compared with that of "savages," he insists that "men, originally savage and brutal, acquire not rationality nor delicacy of taste till they be long disciplined in society."[66] For this reason, he suggests that there may be a slight distinction between common sense related to morality and common sense related to aesthetic judgment: "However languid and cloudy the common sense of mankind may be as to the fine arts, it is notwithstanding the only standard in these as well as in morals. True it is indeed, that in gathering the common sense of mankind, more circumspection is requisite with respect to the fine arts than with respect to morals: upon the latter, any person may be consulted: but in the former, a wary choice is necessary, for to collect votes indifferently would certainly mislead us."[67] Yet, the connection between aesthetic judgment and morality continues to inspire Kames to the belief that artistic experience provides certain opportunities for creating a universal brotherhood in spite of the barriers that exist among classes in society: "The separation of men into different classes, by birth, office, or occupation, however necessary, tends to relax the connection that ought to be among members of the same state; which bad effect is in some measure prevented by the access all ranks of people have to public spectacles, and to amusements that are best enjoyed in company. Such meetings, where every one partakes of the same pleasures in common, are of no slight support to the social affections."[68]

Thus Kames asserts that cultivating internal perceptions could have the potential to heighten the common sense that unites people even across the class lines that are becoming increasingly apparent in the eighteenth century. People who cultivate aesthetic sensitivity soon realize that "in point of dignity, the social emotions rise above the selfish, and much above those of the eye and ear: man is by his nature a social being; and to qualify him for society, it is wisely contrived that he should value himself more for being social than selfish."[69] While Kames never denies that self-interest, including a natural desire for property, plays a significant role in society, he, like Smith, assumes that even this self-interest is one dimension of a broader natural bond that enables people to live cooperatively in communities—an inclination fostered through cultivated critical judgment.

Blair, Taste, and Common Sense

Hugh Blair's development of taste as a rhetorical concept also reflects the Stoic assumption that people's shared ability to interpret and reflect upon sensory experiences provides them with the potential for a common experience of the world that can be individually and collectively meaningful. The Stoic link between private insight and the external world can therefore be seen as a force that draws Blair's notion of taste into the realm of public discourse. Blair's definition of taste as "the power of receiving pleasure from the beauties of nature and of art"[70] seems to focus on taste as an internal process, but his decision to incorporate taste into a theory of rhetoric reflects his assumption that taste serves as a vehicle that promotes collective understanding. It is this perspective that creates a rationale for Blair's view that taste has a part to play in his rhetorical theory.

Blair's notion of taste therefore connects with Stoic sensus communis in creating an opportunity for individuals simultaneously to refine their internal aesthetic judgment and to participate in the formation of community values. At the same time, Blair's Stoic orientation assumes that the entire process of negotiating taste exists within a framework geared toward acquiring a stronger appreciation for the natural order, a perspective that supports Blair's broader political goals. His appreciation for moderation and order certainly contributes to his depiction of taste as grounded in nature but developed through ongoing interaction with the surrounding community, which provides taste with a function in prodding human society to reflect more fully the orderly system found in nature. In keeping with Stoic views concerning the common human experience of interpreting sensory impressions, Blair also maintains that taste involves both reason and the "sentiments and perceptions which belong to our nature."[71] The notion that taste possesses an intuitive quality has often led to the assumption that belletristic rhetoricians such as Blair advocate an individual's cultivation of a sensibility that removes him or her from the mundane realm of daily life. However, Blair's discussion of taste reflects a deliberate counterbalancing of private and public concerns that parallels Stoic thought. He perceives criticism to rely upon experience and observation,[72] and he maintains that the standards of taste reside with the public and evolve through a dynamic interplay of judgments. Public judgment is the final arbiter in matters of taste, but it cannot be too hastily determined, for true public judgment evolves gradually and in concert with true criticism.[73] His view that rhetors and audiences must work together to determine the "fitness and design"[74] that reflect propriety and constitute beauty strikingly parallels Stoic injunctions concerning the need to align oneself with the harmony that exists in the universe.

Thus, for Blair, as for other commonsense rhetoricians, taste does not emerge as a feeling individuals possess and develop in isolation from others. This line of thought begins with the premise that communication inevitably both reflects and cultivates reason. He explains that "the study of eloquence and composition . . . is intimately connected with the improvement of our intellectual powers."[75] Blair shares the view of the Stoics, Cicero, and Quintilian that human knowledge in all areas, including communication, may be refined through instruction; while people naturally possess varying degrees of talent for eloquence, he insists that nature "has left much to be wrought out by every man's own industry."[76] Although taste exists as "a certain natural and instinctive sensibility to beauty,"[77] reason has a role to play in guiding and strengthening taste. This means that taste, like the use of language itself, is "a most improveable faculty,"[78] which can be refined through systematic training.

Training in taste enables people to become more conscious of ways in which language helps to enact a bridge between nature and human society. Blair insists that even the arrangement of a speech "is not a rhetorical invention. It is founded upon nature, and suggested by common sense."[79] While some commentators have argued that such passages illustrate Blair's rejection of classical models of rhetorical instruction, examining Blair's thought through a Stoic lens complicates this view. Blair does maintain that much about human language is grounded in nature and can be revealed through common sense, a position that does involve a rejection of the classical canons. At the same time, Blair's awareness of Stoic thought can be seen as aligning his notion of common sense with ancient goals involving the formation of character and civic virtue. Thus

Blair's notion of arrangement as something available through nature and common sense can ultimately be expressed as an approach to language use that alters traditional rhetorical instruction but maintains the commitment to personal development through language use that can be found in many classical theories.

Even the traditional rhetorical influences that are acknowledged to be present in Blair's theory can be better understood through recognizing the Stoic influence that permeates both classical and modern rhetorical theories. Halloran effectively argues that Quintilian can be seen as a significant classical influence on Blair's theory,[80] although Ferreira-Buckley and Halloran elsewhere note that Blair's emphasis on moral development through eloquence goes beyond Quintilian's claims.[81] This emphasis in itself reflects the fact that Blair not only builds on Quintilian's rhetorical theory but also participates in sustaining and developing Quintilian's fusion of Stoic ethics with rhetorical theory. Blair believes that an individual's encounters with skillful language use, which inevitably help to refine taste, can be included "among the means of disposing the heart to virtue."[82] He further maintains that "moral beauties" are of the highest quality and therefore "are not only in themselves superiour to all others, but they exert an influence, either more near or more remote, on a great variety of other objects of Taste."[83]

Throughout his lectures, Blair appropriates and subtly alters Stoic connections among beauty, nature, ethics, reason, and social life in order to address the demands of his cultural context. His interest in preserving rhetoric's role in the developing social order leads him to resist the scientific turn toward an individualistic language use that privileges empirical observation. Unlike Locke, who suggests that rhetoric may confuse the individual's immediate apprehension of experience, Blair insists that without communication, "Reason would be a solitary, and, in some measure, an unavailing principle."[84] He therefore insists that even the individual's use of reason must be informed by contact and communication with others: "What we call human reason, is not the effort or ability of one, so much as it is the result of the reason of many, arising from lights mutually communicated, in consequence of discourse and writing."[85] Communication therefore plays a fundamental role in developing the society that people were naturally ordained to construct: "For, by what bond could any multitude of men be kept together, or be made to join in the prosecution of any common interest, until once, by the intervention of Speech, they could communicate their wants and intentions to one another?"[86]

Blair's endorsement of rhetoric's role in preserving community shares common ground with the classical rhetorical theories of Isocrates and Cicero, but his Stoic perspective shapes his rationale for connecting rhetoric, aesthetics, and ethics with the goals of individual virtue and the pursuit of an orderly society. In keeping with Stoic insights and their subsequent appropriation by Shaftesbury, Blair defines beauty in ethical terms; while he acknowledges that it may not always be the case that taste and virtue are connected, he insists that "the exercise of taste is, in its native tendency, moral and purifying."[87] The moral dimension of taste comes from its ability to bring people into a strong connection with the types of judgments that they are naturally programmed to develop. He locates sublimity "in the nature of the object described"[88] and argues that assessments of beauty are inevitably grounded in the external world, which promotes an awareness of natural harmony and a correspondence between the object and its external function: "Although each of these produce a separate agreeable sensation, yet they are of such a similar nature, as readily to mix and blend in one general perception of Beauty, which we ascribe to the whole object as its cause: for Beauty is always conceived by us, as something residing in the object which raises the pleasant sensation; a sort of glory which dwells upon, and invests it."[89] Melissa Ianetta takes note of Blair's consistent connection between aesthetic judgment and the community, as she contrasts the social orientation found in Blair's concept of sublimity with well-known eighteenth-century statesman and orator Edmund Burke's use of that term: "Rather than presenting the spectator with an object whose sublimity is based in Burkean asocial feelings of self-preservation and fear, this Blairian sublime is overtly social. Its power over the spectator comes from a sort of excessive ethos, a superabundant appeal to community values of goodness that separates the Blairian sublime from Burke's aesthetically oriented counterpart."[90] Blair's notion of rhetoric's role in forming an aesthetic sensibility consistently reflects his attempt to assert and strengthen the ethical connections among beauty, the natural order, and human society.

Blair's Christian Stoic outlook contributes to this assumption that the individual's cultivation of taste and development of a stronger moral sense has automatic implications for the community. In Blair's view, the cultivation of taste never stops with the individual, as it requires ongoing sensitivity to the judgments and concerns of others: "It is from consulting our own imagination and heart, and from attending to the feelings of others, that any principles are formed which acquire authority in matters of Taste."[91] Ferreira-Buckley and Halloran suggest that Blair's view of taste cannot be seen as hedonistic due to its tie to nature,[92] a characteristic that also applies to Stoic aesthetics. For Blair, human society represents a part of the natural order, which means that people's engagement with each other becomes the basis for reinforcing their appreciation for the harmony that exists throughout the world around them[93]—a principle he shares with the Stoics.

The relationship between taste and the broader community therefore provides the basis for the type of negotiation that cultivates sensus communis. Blair articulates the process of arriving at judgments concerning taste in a way that mirrors the Stoic process of internal and collective deliberation about the significance of preconceptions.

> Now, were there any one person who possessed in full perfection all the powers of human nature, whose internal senses were in every instance exquisite and just, and whose reason was unerring and sure, the determinations of such a person concerning beauty, would, beyond doubt, be a perfect standard for the Taste of all others. Wherever their Taste differed from his, it could be imputed only to some imperfection in their natural powers. But as there is no such living standard, no one person to whom all mankind will allow such submission to be due, what is there of sufficient authority to be the standard of the various and opposite Tastes of men? Most certainly there is nothing but the Taste, as far as it can be gathered, of human nature. . . . With regard to the objects of sentiment or internal Taste, the common feelings of men carry the same authority, and have a title to regulate the taste of every individual.[94]

As numerous critics have noted, the authority Blair assigns to "common feelings" against "the taste of every individual" presents a number of serious problems, particularly given that many parts of his discussion reveal the limitations he places on which groups should be included in the range of those whose "common feelings" have merit. The recognition that Blair's notion of taste at least in part reflects his broader interest in Stoic thought by no means addresses those problems. However, understanding the philosophical basis for Blair's thought does offer insight into his rationale for assuming that emphasizing aesthetic judgment as a feature of rhetorical training could ultimately bring a new vitality to rhetoric's civic mission. This assumption goes beyond the practical goal of preparing individuals to be socially successful, as Blair connects standards of taste not only with the immediate community but also with a Stoic vision of humanity's higher nature: "The public is the supreme judge to whom the last appeal must be made in every work of Taste; as the standard of Taste is founded on the sentiments that are natural and common to all men. But with respect to this we are to observe, that the sense of the Public is often too hastily judged of. The genuine public Taste does not always appear in the first applause given upon the publication of any new work."[95] He translates particular Stoic principles into an eighteenth-century vocabulary as he argues that public standards may be temporarily corrupted by "passions or prejudices, with the party-spirit or superstitious notions, that may chance to rule for a time almost a whole nation."[96] Like the Stoics, however, he remains optimistic that the judgments inscribed in nature will ultimately foster the type of collective reasoning that will ensure the proper balance between ethics and aesthetics, "for the judgment of true Criticism, and the voice of the Public, when once become unprejudiced and dispassionate, will ever coincide at last."[97] Blair therefore reinforces both the Stoic view that human perception is refined through encounters with the external world and the Stoic distinction between the true insight available through common sense and the corrupt influences that arise when particular societies pursue materialistic goals at the expense of a higher good.

This social vision unquestionably includes a bias for European culture. Like Kames, Blair's attribution of taste to the judgments of particular societies and contexts reveals what appears to be a certain desire to cross social barriers, but this opportunity is repeatedly undermined by his own immersion in the standards of his day. There is no doubt that Blair participates in the modern narrative of progress common to eighteenth-century intellectuals, a view that has the unfortunate potential of supporting the notion that the British Empire serves as a civilizing presence for the rest of the world. Although Blair discusses at length his belief that taste evolves in local and immediate contexts, a view that corresponds to the Stoic view that individuals learn through their direct encounters with the physical world, his belief that all standards for human judgment and conduct are grounded in nature also participates in the Stoic search for a universal truth. Thus Blair's belief that standards of taste to a certain extent evolve in particular times and places exists alongside statements that seem to contradict that view, as when he asserts that the foundation for all feelings about taste can be found in "what has been found from experience to please mankind universally"[98] and his insistence that "in every composition what interests the imagination, and touches the heart, pleases all ages and all nations."[99] The uneasy tension that resides in Blair's thought, which can also be identified as a dynamic of Stoic ethics, manifests itself in various ways throughout his lectures. Although everyone has the capacity for taste, that taste improves through education and develops through civic interactions ultimately suggests that societies that have reached a certain level of sophistication, "men placed in such situations as are favourable to the proper exertions of Taste,"[100] will come closer to discovering that "universal standard" that lies beneath the surface of Blair's theory. The connection between taste and morality in turn means that such societies ultimately have the capacity to attain a degree of moral superiority not available to those who fail to study and discuss standards of taste. Blair's discussion of the history of language reveals his assumption that civilized societies have achieved levels of proficiency not available to "savages," as when he maintains that Europeans are "of more correct imagination."[101] His frequent repetition of such radical generalizations about various cultures is certain to baffle, perplex, and at times outrage contemporary readers.

Appreciating the influence of Stoic thought upon Blair and his contemporaries helps to reveal the complexity that underlies the internal tensions that pervade their thought. While this does not justify an attitude that must be described as elitist by today's standards, there is value in recognizing that their endorsement of hierarchical order emerges from a philosophy that advances complex ideas concerning the relationship between public and private virtue and the broader concerns of humanity. This complexity challenges the suggestion that Blair and his colleagues were simply promoting the development of a polite society with purely material aims in mind. While Blair acknowledges that the study of criticism may facilitate an individual's ability to speak about "fashionable topics" and "to support a proper rank in social life," he adds, "But I should be sorry if we could not rest the merit of such studies on somewhat of solid and intrinsical use, independent, of appearance and show."[102] His circumstances made it impossible for him, as it is for most of us, to depart entirely from concerns with "appearance and show," but careful study of his thought can at least promote a more complete understanding of the ways in which his stated intentions of providing individuals access to community participation fall short of achieving that goal. Such an understanding is particularly important in light of the fact that the tensions between intention and reality in the work of Blair and other eighteenth-century theorists exemplify the complexity that generally surrounds language instruction—and that continues to be a tension in our teaching and scholarship today. Examined through one lens, Blair's insistence upon a universal order can be seen as a tool of oppression; however, it also needs to be understood as an attempt to offer education as the means through which people might participate in the development of sensus communis. Clearly this version of common sense becomes oppressive as soon as eighteenth-century theorists begin distinguishing those who are "civilized" from those who are not. However, their imperfect enactment of Stoic thought involves at least an attempt to allow people the opportunity to pursue a good that lies beyond the immediate limitations of their experience—and to assert a connection across humanity that could provide the basis for mutual understanding.

Blair builds on the work of other theorists in arguing that taste enacts in a particular way common sense's role in facilitating social interaction that strengthens society through refining judgment. Blair's oratorical outlook ensured that he did not fully conceive of taste as a literary property or of words as fixed and static entities. When it is viewed as a vital force primarily realized and reinforced through oral discourse, taste can be seen to benefit society through creating the reservoir of public knowledge that Lloyd F. Bitzer defines as the often unstated "truths, values, interests, and principles located in the public's tradition and experience."[103] The explicit limitations that Blair imposes on rhetoric are therefore subtly expanded through his vision of rhetoric's power to mediate a society's struggle to define itself. Blair follows the Stoics, Cicero, and Quintilian in perceiving that language not only serves as a tool through which specific thoughts are communicated but more significantly embodies the community's very identity and defines its course for the future. While his stated view that rhetoric simply transmits ideas formed and organized elsewhere limits the role of invention in his theory, Blair's doctrine of taste provides rhetoric with another social role in negotiating meaning between the rhetor and audience, which ultimately builds individual character and contributes to the development of civic virtue.

Taste and Rhetoric's Social Function

Undoubtedly Blair's sense of social propriety was grounded in a conservative impulse to support a value system that was essentially hierarchical, and to say that Blair was influenced by Stoicism is not to suggest that this philosophical foundation counterbalanced Blair's immediate concerns with the material circumstances of his own society. However, acknowledging the ancient roots that define the theories of Blair and his contemporaries at least helps to illuminate the complexity with which they viewed their educational mission. Blair's conviction that taste is available to everyone and his endorsement of education as a resource for developing both taste and civic commitment provides rhetorical education with a potentially expansive role. At the same time, his view of taste can be seen as a particular representation of a Moderate opposition between virtue and material success, which Sher describes as "a profoundly conservative doctrine, in that it emphasizes the limited extent of human control over the world, the desirability of total resignation to the will of God, and the insignificance of one's social 'station' for the attainment of true happiness."[104] Blair's cultivation of the inborn capacity of taste can therefore be seen as a type of rhetorical enterprise but one that assumes from the outset that the cultivation of virtue will lead to participation in civic life that simultaneously reflects civic commitment and social restraint.

Delineating the ancient roots of eighteenth-century theories of taste counters current scholarship that grounds the origins of those theories entirely in the intellectual environment of an emerging bourgeois society. Of course eighteenth-century theories of taste are undoubtedly firmly situated in the culture that surrounds them. At the same time, their unique character can only be understood through acknowledging how eighteenth-century theorists employ ancient thought in attempting to make sense of their world. The widespread perception that the "new" rhetorics of the eighteenth century are defined by their departure from classical principles becomes more complicated through detecting Stoic thought as an alternative ancient strain that can be seen as an important presence in the classical theories of Cicero and Quintilian and in the new rhetorics of the eighteenth century.

This strain is clearly delineated in the notion of a "new" rhetoric founded upon ancient principles outlined in the 1739 "Taste: An Essay": "A Rhetorician who, perhaps, is very learned, will run into a long train of precepts, defining very exactly every trope and figure, justly remarking the distinction, and very tediously treating of parallel questions, which were formerly banded about very briskly by the ancient Rhetoricians, and thus resembling that Rhetorician who Cicero tells us, was only capable of teaching people not to speak at all, or to speak ill. . . . In one word, the most necessary quality, not only in relation to the art of Speaking, and the Sciences, but also for the conduct of Life, is this Taste, this Prudence, this Discernment, which teaches us in every particular, and on every occasion, what ought to be done, and how it is to be done."[105] While the writer of this essay conveys the modern resistance to defining rhetoric according to the technical features of language use, a frequent characterization of certain strands of classical rhetoric, the writer cannot be seen as advancing an argument for an entirely new rhetoric, given the reference to Cicero in the first section and citation of Quintilian in the last. What he advocates is not a wholesale rejection of classical rhetoric but a renewed emphasis on a notion of taste that involves the values of prudence and discernment— dimensions of a Stoic ethical strain that, at least in part, informs the rhetorical theories of Cicero and Quintilian. Although this strain departs from the negotiation of immediate public issues that is typically found in classical rhetorical theories, it creates an alternative civic function for rhetoric—one grounded in the cultivation of character and the development of sensus communis.

This writer reflects the widespread eighteenth-century view that taste provides one avenue through which people may fulfill rhetoric's potential of speaking to "the conduct of Life." Eighteenth-century theorists borrow other concepts from Stoicism, including propriety and sympathy, in shifting rhetoric's focus to "the conduct of Life." These ancient Stoic principles are adapted and deployed in the formation of new rhetorics that reflect concerns of a time and place far distant from those in which they originated.

Chapter 4

PROPRIETY, SYMPATHY, AND STYLE—
FUSING THE INDIVIDUAL AND SOCIAL

Stoic philosophy provides a model for explaining how the individual's pursuit of excellence naturally connects to the welfare of society—an idea that was particularly compelling for eighteenth-century theorists who were both interested in the workings of the mind and concerned about the social instability that seemed inevitable if individuals pursued their own interests without regard for others. Fundamental to this connection are eighteenth-century notions of common sense, which provide a bridge between the individual and the social that is very much in keeping with the Stoic concept of *sensus communis*. Scottish common sense describes an innate human ability to understand the world, which ultimately engages people in recognizing and developing the social bond inscribed in nature; people who draw upon common sense are automatically united to others who do the same, and the refinement of common sense requires an awareness of social responsibility that naturally strengthens the ties that people have with each other.

For many eighteenth-century theorists, taste exists in a complementary relationship with common sense. Because aesthetic judgment, like common sense, is a fundamental component of human nature, its cultivation enables individuals to appreciate the natural order that exists outside themselves, improve their intellectual capacities, and strengthen their ties with others who possess the same ability. For theorists such as the Earl of Shaftesbury, Hugh Blair, and Henry Home, Lord Kames, the link between taste and common sense provides taste with an ethical as well as aesthetic function.

The implicit connection between taste and common sense creates an additional link between eighteenth-century rhetorical theories and other important Stoic principles: style, propriety, and sympathy. For Blair, as well as other eighteenth-century theorists, the cultivation of taste facilitates a consciousness of style that depends upon an awareness of appropriate responses to specific rhetorical contexts. A refined critical judgment in those rhetorical situations in turn depends upon and strengthens the sympathy that makes meaningful social interaction possible. For eighteenth-century rhetoricians, as for the Stoics, Cicero, and Quintilian, style, propriety, and sympathy further define the inextricable links that bind individuals to their communities.

Propriety, Sympathy, and Style in Ancient Thought

The Stoics were not unique in their emphasis on the concept of propriety. Notions of propriety were important in many classical rhetorical theories, including those of the Sophists and Aristotle, as well as Cicero and Quintilian. Classical treatments of propriety differ significantly, but most of them exemplify the complex intersection between public and private life. As John Poulakos notes, sophistic propriety involves carefully accounting for the converging elements of the rhetorical situation: "A complement to the notion of kairos, *to prepon* points out that situations have formal characteristics, and demands that speaking as a response to a situation be suitable to those very characteristics. Both notions are concerned with the rhetor's response; but while the former is interested in the when, the latter is concerned with the what of speaking. *To prepon* requires that speech must take into account and be guided by the formal structure of the situation it addresses. Like kairos, *to prepon* constitutes not only a guide to what must be said but also a standard of the value of speech."[1] This early concept of propriety establishes the view that rhetorical success requires the rhetor's attention to audience and context.

Aristotle's extensive treatment of the complex interactions among speaker, audience, and context also assumes the rhetor's need to develop a sense of propriety that is responsive to the demands of each rhetorical situation. Stephen McKenna argues that Aristotle assumes that the guidelines for establishing pathos, ethos, and logos shift as rhetors encounter different audiences and contexts, which leads him to conclude that "propriety functions in relation to all three" of Aristotle's proofs.[2] Thus the sophists and Aristotle share the general view that propriety is defined by a complex interplay of each part of the communicative act, which requires people to consider complex factors that affect their presentation of the messages they hope to share with others.

Stoic propriety has features in common with these rhetorical notions of propriety, but its orientation reflects a particular emphasis on the centrality of individual integrity. Individuals develop propriety first through acting in ways that unify their conduct and character. Propriety enters the realm of communication as a reflection of the relationship that develops true understanding between the rhetor and audience. The link between Stoic style and propriety begins with the conviction that style should not draw attention to itself but instead should support the rhetor's message and reflect an awareness of the social connections that foster sensus communis. Such an awareness reflects the Stoic endorsement of language's function in negotiating conduct that can appropriately guide people toward useful participation in social life, which in turn supports their understanding of their position in the divine order. Although this view of language use departs from other classical theories emphasizing rhetoric's role in resolving immediate public questions, the Stoics do not entirely dismiss the significance of expression. Epictetus shares Cicero's view that there is ethical significance in the manner in which ideas are expressed, as he allows both for the value of attractive language in appealing to the audience and acknowledges that attention to rhetorical propriety can potentially develop the rhetor's social awareness and strengthen the relationship between rhetor and audience.[3] Marcia L. Colish explains that for the Stoics, style "must conform to nature and to truth"[4] and must be adapted to meet the needs of the subject.

At the same time, the Stoics' belief that style reflects character leads them to insist that style maintains a certain consistency from one audience to the next, for communication enables the rhetor to address "the *logos* of his hearers, and the *logos* is the same in all men."[5] The Stoic concept that appropriate style simultaneously embodies the connections that unite people universally and reflects the demands of particular situations anticipates belletristic notions of style as responsive to specific rhetorical contexts, even as it seeks to establish common standards of judgment that go beyond the immediate moment. And, like the eighteenth-century rhetoricians who follow them, the Stoics perceive that people develop meaningful social relationships through engaging in conversation about their immediate concerns and reflecting upon the mutual significance of those concerns. Epictetus's expectation that the speaker "makes plain to his hearers that he has need of them"[6] illustrates the Stoic assumption that appropriate discourse inevitably acknowledges and fosters social relationships and builds on the sympathy that exists between speakers and audiences.

For the Stoics, then, style inevitably requires attention to propriety, which in turn depends upon and develops the natural human capacity for sympathy. The sympathy that naturally binds people to each other is a prerequisite to language use; both Epictetus and Marcus Aurelius describe effective communication as encouraging the sympathetic interactions that contribute to society's strength, a point discussed at greater length in chapter 2 of the current volume. Although Epictetus and Marcus Aurelius hold negative views of rhetoric as the empty use of words for show and privilege syllogism as the ideal structure for preserving the necessary emphasis on discursive purpose, it is nevertheless clear that they recognize the importance of argument in constructing notions of appropriate conduct, exploring "how the good man may fitly deal with it and fitly behave towards it."[7] Through such interactions, the rhetor and audience may form a bond that promotes the sympathy that is so crucial to humanity's fulfillment of its true nature. Marcus Aurelius's injunction that people are "caught and held by" their sympathy with each other[8] reveals the power that connects people to each other, and it also suggests that success in social life depends upon acknowledging this organizing principle of human experience.

Cicero's appropriation of Stoic ethics facilitates his development of a concept of propriety that brings together the traditional goals of rhetoric with the moral development emphasized by the Stoics. As argued in chapter 2, Cicero links aesthetic features of style, the rhetor's consciousness of propriety, and the sympathy that binds people together in a manner that reflects assumptions present in Stoic ethics and anticipates developments in eighteenth-century rhetorical theories. Colish notes that Cicero draws upon Panaetius in considering the aesthetic and ethical function of decorum,[9] a relationship that continues to be significant to eighteenth-century rhetorical theorists. His belief that appropriate language use requires the individual to develop both intellectually and as a responsible member of society contributes to Cicero's advocacy for the moral value of language instruction. He argues that language not only reflects the sense of propriety an individual already possesses but serves as a great aid in "the attainment of propriety."[10]

For Cicero, as for the Stoics, an appreciation for propriety derives from human nature itself, although the enactment of propriety always emerges within specific contexts. In other words, people determine what is appropriate according to situations that are ever changing, but the sense that propriety is something to be sought in each situation remains constant. Propriety's visibility "in every deed, in every word, even in every movement and attitude of the body"[11] provides a natural connection between language and moral development and action. Colish notes that for Cicero, "Decorum means truthfulness in action and its antithesis in error. Here Cicero follows the Stoics once again in identifying virtue and vice with correct and incorrect intellectual judgments. In this sense, he says, decorum governs all the virtues."[12] The moral development available through decorum comes about in part because the rhetor's consciousness of propriety applied to communication necessarily involves learning to anticipate and address the needs of others through language.[13]

The connection between moral character and language use leads Cicero explicitly to identify style as that which conveys the orator's character to the audience in a tangible form. Because language defines human nature, individual virtue is necessarily enacted through language, so that "speech seems to represent . . . the character of the speaker,"[14] a statement that strikingly resonates with Seneca's assertions concerning the capacity of style to mirror character. The assumed connection between the individual and the social assures language's capacity both to reveal qualities within the individual and to facilitate cooperation among people, as eloquence creates a notion of ethics that ultimately brings people together in search of "the common good."[15] The intrinsically moral quality of speech extends to every situation in which communication takes place; propriety for Cicero can be seen as both a private internal quality and an external and social one. Cicero's conviction that an individual's moral judgment must manifest itself externally through language that addresses public values provides the link between style and ethos, ethics and rhetoric, individual and social. People are naturally drawn toward the orator whose language touches them, and the virtue of the orator only becomes real through devising language that appropriately meets the needs of the situation and audience. In *De finibus bonorum et malorum,* Cicero explains that the natural ties among people promote sympathy: "From this impulse is developed the sense of mutual attraction which unites human beings as such; this also is bestowed by nature. The mere fact of their common humanity requires that one man should feel another man to be akin to him."[16] Cicero believes that language ultimately creates a relationship that reinforces this "mutual and natural sympathy between humans."[17] Through bringing these perceptions to bear in their ideas of the higher goals of rhetorical interaction, Cicero helps to bring the Stoic perception of the ethical significance of language forward in a way that ultimately supports the development of eighteenth-century rhetorical theories that emphasize the intricate relationships among style, propriety, and sympathy.

The assumed links among the natural order, language, and virtue ultimately led eighteenth-century rhetoricians, in concert with Cicero and Seneca, to the notion that language can be seen as a direct reflection of the individual's internal state. The Stoic assumption that the individual's moral development entails a commitment to humanity, together with the guidance of Cicero and Quintilian concerning the role of language in promoting that link, provided eighteenth-century theorists with a useful framework for responding to the troubling arguments of thinkers such as Thomas Hobbes and Bernard Mandeville, who seemed to set the stage for a chaotic society ruled by self-interest. Writers such as Shaftesbury are drawn to the Stoic notion that individuals are naturally destined to pursue virtue and that this pursuit inevitably entails the cultivation of social responsibility. Through their direct contact with Stoic philosophy and through the rhetorical application of Stoic thought in the theories of Cicero and Quintilian, eighteenth-century theorists developed arguments that emphasize the ethical potential of style to enact propriety, promote sympathy, and strengthen their society.

Shaftesbury's Propriety: Internal Deliberation, Style, and Common Sense

Shaftesbury and rhetorical theorists later in the eighteenth century follow Cicero in identifying a link between refined language skill and the propriety that promotes social harmony. Shaftesbury shares Cicero's interest in considering the way that even private discourse may facilitate the development of a sense of propriety and promote reasoned dialogue. He believes that the social accountability embodied in "polite discourse" provides the ideal setting for reasoned dialogue. Although people innately possess knowledge of the world and of right conduct, their judgment may be endangered by excessive appeals to the emotion that temporarily overwhelm the functioning of reason. In defending the gentle wit that he associates with polite conversation, Shaftesbury insists that people can never be subverted from their own instinctive regard for the truth when opposing views are presented with humor and gentility: "Men indeed may, in a serious way, be so wrought on, and confounded, by different Modes of Opinion, different Systems and Schemes *impos'd by Authority,* that they may wholly lose all Notion or Comprehension of *Truth.* I can easily apprehend what Effect *Awe* has over Mens Understandings. I can very well suppose Men may be frighted out of their Wits: But I have no apprehension they shou'd be laugh'd out of 'em. I can hardly imagine that in a pleasant way they shou'd ever be talk'd out of their Love for Society, or reason'd out of Humanity and *common Sense.*"[18] For Shaftesbury, "the only *Poison* to Reason, is *Passion.*"[19] When reason is given free rein to function through private deliberation, the intuitive human ability to perceive the truth will ultimately prevail. Private deliberation provides individuals with practice in cultivating discourse appropriate to their circumstances and in the process constructs a society governed by standards of propriety that evolve as individuals regularly engage in reasoned conversation.

In emphasizing the rational function of polite conversation, Shaftesbury adapts the Stoic concept of sensus communis to the changing social climate of the eighteenth century in a manner that reflects a consideration of how the link between reasoned discourse and civic responsibility can develop in response to the specific challenges of his age. While the changing public sphere was posing varied challenges to classical notions of consensus, Shaftesbury resists abandoning entirely the goal of social unity. In what may be seen as the beginning of the eighteenth century's effort to counter the move toward the individualism that becomes more fully entrenched in the nineteenth century, Shaftesbury identifies the pleasure of reasoning as a social endeavor developed through conversation with others.

The social quality of reason establishes a vital role for imagination in Shaftesbury's thought, for the imagination is the capacity that enables the individual to establish connections with others through sympathy. For Shaftesbury, as for the Stoics, this process begins with internal dialogue. Nancy S. Struever notes that much of Shaftesbury's ideal of intellectual discipline arises from reasoning carried out in the form of internal inquiry, which "generates an awareness of the values of harmony, order, and proportion, which mark good moral performance as well as aesthetic production."[20] Shaftesbury's "private empiricism"[21] therefore parallels Stoicism in arguing for the development of a moral sense that is refined at least in part through private deliberation. Vivienne Brown describes Shaftesbury's dialogic approach in *Philosophical Regimen* as participating in the Stoic model of "dialogic debate," developed in the writings of both Epictetus and Marcus Aurelius,[22] as it embarks on an intense self-examination for the purpose of acquiring moral judgment.

For Shaftesbury, as for the Stoics, propriety begins as a process of self-discovery that facilitates the development of an ethical sensibility, which is in turn heightened through the individual's participation in sensus communis. Shaftesbury provides detailed guidance about this process in *Soliloquy, or Advice to an Author*. Echoing Epictetus's challenge to "fix your opinions, exercise yourselves in them"[23] and anticipating Adam Smith's "impartial spectator," Shaftesbury advocates a metaphorical surgery that can create a second self capable of engaging in an ongoing critical dialogue concerning the motives that drive an individual's conduct: "By virtue of this SOLILOQUY he becomes two distinct *Persons*. He is Pupil and Preceptor. He teaches, and he learns."[24] Such careful and intensive self-examination naturally leads to greater self-awareness, enabling each individual *"to know my-self, and what belongs to me."*[25]

This type of self-knowledge promotes the development of virtue, as it enables the individual to discover the high values that are held by the true self. Shaftesbury endorses Marcus Aurelius's process of self-interrogation,[26] as he discusses the value of an "inward Rhetorick" that impartially investigates the mind's dispositions.[27] He provides a sample of the interrogatory process that should guide the ethical inquiry he advocates,[28] an "inquisition" that ultimately establishes control over the *"Fancy* and *Opinion"* that could otherwise overwhelm the individual's reason.[29] Tiffany notes that Shaftesbury also follows Marcus Aurelius in advocating severity with oneself accompanied by tolerance to others.[30] Shaftesbury insists that the endeavor of critical self-examination ultimately offers people the true pleasure that he elsewhere describes as derived from "a generous Behaviour, a Regularity of Conduct, and a Consistency of Life and Manners."[31] The outcome of this conduct closely resembles that of Marcus Aurelius's "contemplative way" of viewing the world,[32] which promotes an expansive vision that moves the individual beyond his or her immediate concerns in order to engage constructively with the external world. The final outcome of soliloquy becomes thoughtful rhetorical practice, which Shaftesbury contrasts with those who "discharge frequently and vehemently in publick," behavior that ultimately interferes with the "Controul" made possible through private reflection.[33] Regular engagement in this type of private reflection develops a useful critical perspective, for "unless the Party has been us'd to play the Critick thorowly upon himself, he will hardly be found proof against the Criticisms of others."[34] The regular practice of soliloquy develops critical skills that cannot be acquired in any other way: "'Tis the hardest thing in the world to be *a good Thinker*, without being a strong *Self-Examiner*, and *thorow-pac'd Dialogist*, in this solitary way."[35]

Thus Shaftesbury's notion of self-discovery, like the Stoics, resists the connotation of solipsistic introspection that Romanticism subsequently invested in that term. For both Shaftesbury and the Stoics, as well as for the eighteenth-century rhetoricians who share Shaftesbury's Stoic orientation, private deliberation always has a social dimension. Because sensus communis assumes a natural connection among people, the individual's pursuit of appropriate conduct begins with self-control and self-knowledge but ultimately requires interaction with the judgment of others and the fulfillment of a social duty. Shaftesbury notes that developing control over the passions means that "I must undoubtedly come the better to understand a human Breast, and judg the better both of others and *my-self*."[36] The ultimate aim of propriety resides in "the rational and social Enjoyment" that Shaftesbury pronounces "essential to Happiness."[37] Like the Stoics and later eighteenth-century theorists, Shaftesbury maintains that society with others, which both builds on and furthers sympathy, provides the basis for the individual's fulfillment and happiness.

The individual who has developed the sense of propriety that comes from private virtue and social harmony naturally manifests this propriety externally. For Shaftesbury, as for the Stoics, the connection between individual self-discovery and the social world inevitably affects the manner in which ideas are expressed. He echoes the view of the Stoics, Cicero, and Quintilian that the style of an individual's expression serves as the window into the hidden internal state of the individual's mind and character: "We shou'd find, perhaps, that what we most admir'd, even in the turn of *outward* Features, was only a mysterious Expression, and a kind of shadow of something *inward* in the Temper."[38] Because Shaftesbury is convinced that the individual inevitably has a relationship to others, his notion of style as a manifestation of individual character inevitably has social implications. McKenna argues, "Shaftesbury treated emotion and belief in terms recalling classical propriety: if there are affections appropriate to beliefs, it followed that there are modes of communication appropriate to transmitting those beliefs to various audiences. Key to managing this propriety is a Stoic honesty in self-knowledge, which one develops through the self-conscious interaction of 'natural affection' and social situatedness. Honesty is the key link in a kind of heuristic chain: It abets a form of sociability that is both congenial to others, yet true to self."[39] Shaftesbury's Stoic perspective encourages a vision of propriety as emerging from the intersection of self-discovery, social formation, and communication. Shaftesbury's notion of style therefore reflects the complex interaction between the individual and social that represent one aspect of his appropriation of Stoic thought.

The Centrality of Propriety in Adam Smith's Rhetorical Philosophy

Many eighteenth-century rhetoricians share Shaftesbury's interest in propriety, and they typically describe education as having a crucial role in the individual's development of this social sense. Adam Smith shares Shaftesbury's complex understanding of propriety's personal and social significance. Although he maintains that propriety and virtue are not identical,[40] he insists that propriety has an important part to play in an individual's development of a moral sense: "It is thus that the general rules of morality are formed. They are ultimately founded upon experience of what, in particular instances, our moral faculties, our natural sense of merit and propriety, approve, or disapprove of."[41] He also shares Shaftesbury's adoption of the Stoic appreciation for "superior reason and understanding" and "self-command,"[42] even as he, like his teacher Francis Hutcheson and Shaftesbury, departs from Stoic thought in emphasizing sentiment as a central dimension of moral development that extends beyond the workings of reason alone, a move that at least in part reflects resistance to the conflation of reason and self-interest in the works of Hobbes and Mandeville.

McKenna identifies propriety as central to Smith's rhetorical theory, a unifying principle that carries from his *Lectures on Rhetoric and Belles Lettres* through the ethical system he develops in *Theory of Moral Sentiments*. McKenna argues that for Smith, "propriety mediates virtually all forms of social interaction";[43] this insight leads him to identify rhetoric as the foundation for understanding all of Smith's work, as rhetoric provides the forum through which the sense of propriety is both developed and practiced. McKenna identifies a number of classical strains at work in Smith's thought, including propriety's assumed visual dimension and its heuristic function,[44] with particular emphasis on connections between Smith's notion of propriety and that of Aristotle,[45] particularly in Smith's appreciation for moderation. Although he accurately stresses Smith's refusal to endorse Stoicism wholeheartedly as "an adequate philosophy of morality,"[46] he acknowledges the significance of Smith's debt to Stoic principles, particularly as mediated through Cicero's influence, "which shows *decorum* as useful precisely because it was first of all a norm of speech that cannot be reduced to an absolute but must always be determined with the kind of imprecision endemic to speech situations."[47] As McKenna illustrates, this insight is in keeping with the interest in the rhetorical construction of propriety that Smith demonstrates in both the *Lectures* and *Theory of Moral Sentiments*. It also ties in with Smith's general appreciation for those philosophical systems that make propriety central to virtue, which he summarizes through describing the thought of the emblematic figures of Plato, Aristotle, and Zeno, even as he identifies ways in which each philosophical school falls short of fully accounting for the role of propriety in the development of virtue.

One of Smith's objections to Stoic thought resides in what he perceives to be an ascetic tendency that runs contrary to the dictates of nature. He argues that the Stoic expectation that a concern with the workings of the entire universe should detach people from their immediate interests defines propriety in terms that have no bearing on the reality of human experience: "The man who should feel no more for the death or distress of his own father, or son, than for those of any other man's father or son, would appear neither a good son nor a good father. Such unnatural indifference, far from exciting our applause, would incur our highest disapprobation."[48] He maintains that life within one's immediate sphere naturally holds greatest interest;[49] although the consolation provided by nature comes in part through contemplation, he explicitly counters Stoic ideas in insisting, "Nature has not prescribed to us this sublime contemplation as the great business and occupation of our lives."[50] Although many Stoics would agree that the pursuit of propriety involves an active quest that is fully integrated with the daily business of living, Smith's modern sensibility leads to a greater emphasis on practical affairs. Moreover, his awareness of modern philosophical developments that have detached reason from the pursuit of social virtue also lead him to join with other contemporary theorists in insisting upon the importance of sentiment to the individual's moral development. This emphasis on sentiment ultimately contributes to a modern shift toward personal autonomy, even as Smith sustains in other respects the Stoic vision of individuals whose interests are inextricably bound to each other and to the broader community.

However, in spite of Smith's stated rejection of Stoic extremes in emphasizing reason and contemplation, much of his moral philosophy reflects the influence of Stoic ethics. In her insightful analysis of the classical influences on Smith's thought, Gloria Vivenza notes that strains of ancient influences are difficult to ascertain with absolute precision but describes Stoicism as "the major classical influence operating on Smith."[51] She argues that Smith draws heavily upon a classical foundation in developing a network of original ideas responsive to his own time. Vivenza identifies the natural relationship between individual self-interest and the public good and the virtue of self-control as Stoic principles that hold particular importance for Smith. She ultimately describes the classical influence on Smith as "a composite set of elements, among which we could perhaps identify a Stoic theoretical principle (sometimes called universal harmony, which upholds the principle that the interests of the individual are not opposed to those of the community), with which Aristotelian, Epicurean, or again Stoic elements intertwined to regulate individual behaviour so that harmony could be reached."[52] This convergence of influences on Smith's rhetoric and philosophy in part accounts for the significant presence of Stoic thought in British rhetorical theories through the latter part of the eighteenth century.

Like the Stoics, Smith perceives propriety as manifested in language, a connection that might appear at first glance to establish narrow guidelines for style in keeping with the demands of the subject matter. Certainly Smith perceives propriety as to some extent allied with clarity. His November 19, 1762, lecture on rhetoric begins with practical advice concerning perspicuity, which he summarizes as the careful selection of words "English and agreeable to the custom of the country, but likewise to the custom of some particular part of the nation."[53] He moves immediately from that discussion to explore the way in which context and audience affect the meaning of language, and it is at this point that he introduces the term *propriety* for the first time: "We may indeed naturally expect that the better sort will often exceed the vulgar in the propriety of their language, but where there is no such excellence we are apt to prefer those in use amongst them, by the association we form betwixt their words and the behaviour we admire in them. It is the custom of the people that forms what we call propriety, and the custom of the better sort from whence the rules of purity of style are to be drawn."[54] Smith's willingness to describe a notion of propriety based on class lines appears to support those who charge Smith and his contemporaries with placing rhetoric in the service of bourgeois standards. There is no question that Smith's assumption of the intrinsic value of the language used by "the better sort" here reflects the elitist assumptions he shares with Blair and other educators of his day. Yet, Smith's view of propriety, developed in both his lectures and *Theory of Moral Sentiments,* reveals a tension between the hazardous connections among style, character, and social class that he shares with other eighteenth-century thinkers and the goal of shared social understanding that he appropriates from Stoic ethics.

Style, Propriety, and Sympathy in Smith's Thought

For Smith, as for the Stoics, the complexity that surrounds propriety comes about through its role in simultaneously reflecting an individual's disposition and creating social relationships. The fact that propriety provides the controlling principle of style again demonstrates Smith's participation in the Stoic assumption that the significance of rhetorical style derives from its contribution to the social relationships that the rhetor must establish. Because Smith recognizes the significance of language in human life, he places his theories of language use firmly within the broader context of his moral philosophy. D. D. Raphael argues that "humanity and self-control together constitute for Smith 'the perfection of human nature,' a combination of Christian and Stoic virtue,"[55] and this combination can be seen as the driving force in Smith's description of propriety reflected in style that demonstrates rhetorical discipline and promotes sympathy.

Smith's assumption that propriety determines effective rhetorical interaction is evident in the structure of the lectures, which generally avoid offering specific rules for rhetorical practice. In his lecture dated November 29, 1762, he charges grammarians with mistakenly attributing beauty to the figures found in a passage and goes on to say that although much rhetorical theory has been developed to consider the use of figures, "They are generally a very silly set of books and not at all instructive."[56] Smith replaces such theorizing about the use of figures in the abstract with guidelines that stress the necessity of perceiving rhetoric as acquiring meaning through an immediate relationship between speaker and audience: "When the sentiment of the speaker is expressed in a neat, clear, plain, and clever manner, and the passion or affection he is poss[ess]ed of and intends, *by sympathy,* to communicate to his hearer, is plainly and cleverly hit off, then and then only the expression has all the force and beauty that language can give it."[57] For Smith, language inevitably emerges within contexts that must be examined alongside the words that are uttered or written: "The various styles, instead of being condemned for the want of beauties perhaps incompatible with those they possess, may be considered as good in their kind and suited to the circumstances of the author."[58] The rhetor must be sensitive to audience and context but also strive to maintain a style that suits "his natural character."[59] That Smith devotes so much of his lecture time to critical inquiry into the contexts that surround different rhetorical acts demonstrates his commitment to revealing the complexity of propriety as it forms through a complicated network of interactions, including the rhetor's character, rhetorical moment, and relationship to the audience. For Smith, as for classical theorists, the significance of clear and appropriate speech goes far beyond efficiently getting one's ideas across. There is a strong moral dimension to Smith's emphasis on propriety; when Smith echoes Seneca's view in stating that "the style of an author is generally of the same stamp as their character,"[60] he is not simply describing the way in which the surface features of language reveal the speaker's educational background. He is instead connecting himself to the Stoic insight that communication both forms and reflects the development of propriety and virtue in a manner that is both internally consistent and visible to others. Smith, like the Stoics, sees style as reflecting an individual's character and social consciousness, but he draws upon the rhetorical insights of Cicero and Quintilian in acknowledging that awareness of appropriate style requires flexibility in response to changing rhetorical situations.

Although the Stoics did not endorse the stylistic flexibility that Smith advocates, his perception that appropriate communication both depends upon and strengthens social relationships more generally draws upon Stoic notions of the constant interaction between the personal and social. *Theory of Moral Sentiments* reflects an assumption about the link between individual and social responsibility that draws directly on Stoic thought, as Smith explains that individuals naturally move from their direct apprehension of their own positions and experiences to an appreciation of the perspectives of other people: "Every man, as the Stoics used to say, is first and principally recommended to his own care; and every man is certainly, in every respect, fitter and abler to take care of himself than of any other person. Every man feels his own pleasures and his own pains more sensibly than those of other people. The former are the original sensations, and the latter the reflected or sympathetic images of those sensations. The former may be said to be the substance; the latter the shadow."[61] Although Smith does not fully accept Hutcheson's notion of an inborn moral sense, he shares the conviction of the Stoics, Cicero, Shaftesbury, and Hutcheson that people are granted "original anticipations of nature"[62] that guide their decisions about daily conduct.

This daily conduct begins with the cultivation of specific personal strengths. Smith echoes the Stoics in his appreciation for self-control and the sense of duty: "What noble propriety and grace do we feel in the conduct of those who, in their own case, exert that recollection and self-command which constitute the dignity of every passion, and which bring it down to what others can enter into!"[63] Such self-command connects with Smith's endorsement of the need to acquire a sense of responsibility, as evident in his argument for "general rules of conduct" that "are of great use in correcting the misrepresentations of self-love concerning what is fit and proper to be done in our particular situation."[64] Such discipline perfectly connects with his insistence that "a sense of duty" must be seen as "a principle of the greatest consequence in human life, and the only principle by which the bulk of mankind are capable of directing their actions."[65] Such passages underscore the potential that many critics see in the thought of Smith, as well as the Stoics, to advocate absolute principles of conduct that support a fixed order that is problematically attributed to nature's dictates.

At the same time, Smith, along with the Stoics, leaves substantial room for contingency in insisting that the "original anticipations" that prompt the development of a moral sense assume their tenor through particular human interactions. He insists that "among civilized nations, the virtues which are founded upon humanity are more cultivated than those which are founded upon self-denial and the command of the passions."[66] He therefore seeks to develop a constructive account of the way in which human virtue develops both in individuals and in society as a whole. For Smith, the natural capacity for sympathy plays a crucial role in explaining how people establish connections with each other and maintain social stability. His assumption that sympathy is an integral element in the acquisition of a sense of propriety is evident throughout *Theory of Moral Sentiments,* which begins with a chapter on sympathy, within a section titled, "Of the Sense of Propriety." Smith maintains that sympathy, which he defines as "our fellow-feeling with any passion whatever,"[67] is a natural component of the human psyche.

It is through the quality of sympathy that Smith explains the natural mediation between individual and social that makes Stoic ethics particularly compelling for eighteenth-century thinkers. Although Smith explains that people's sensory natures prevent them from understanding the experiences of others directly, sympathy enables people to understand their situations better "by conceiving what we ourselves should feel in the like situation."[68] This view creates a reciprocal relationship between individuals, as one person learns to identify with others through imaginatively placing him/herself in a similar situation. This type of interaction not only strengthens specific human relationships through facilitating understanding between people but also reinforces for both parties their mutual identity as social beings: "Nothing pleases us more than to observe in other men a fellow-feeling with all the emotions of our own breast."[69] Even affection for one's family members Smith attributes to the practice of "habitual sympathy."[70] Thus sympathy serves as a primary vehicle for society's stability through connecting individuals to each other in a direct way.

This quality also ensures that sympathy reinforces the development of propriety. Smith maintains that people define appropriateness according to the conduct they would adopt if they found themselves in a similar situation: "To approve of the passions of another . . . as suitable to their objects, is the same thing as to observe that we entirely sympathize with them."[71] People develop their sense of propriety as they interact and sympathize with others, define standards of appropriate conduct in particular situations, and together come to a better understanding of their perspectives on the world.

Smith explains that the pleasure that comes from sympathy not only ensures that people are able to arrive at a better understanding of others' situations but also facilitates a stronger understanding of their own positions. This process requires communication and an ongoing assessment of the self from the standpoint of the other. Smith's discussion of the "impartial spectator" describes sympathy as evolving through an ongoing process of social interaction and ethical introspection, a process that builds on Shaftesbury's appropriation of the Stoic internal dialogue. Vivienne Brown argues that Smith's spectator can be seen as a direct descendant of the Stoic internal dialogue, as well as a forerunner of Bakhtinian dialogism.[72] She connects Smith's impartial spectator to what Mikhail Bakhtin identifies as the Stoics' use of dialogue that leads to "the discovery of the *inner man*—'one's own self,' accessible not to passive self-observation but only through an *active dialogic approach to one's own self.*"[73] In supporting this claim, she cites Smith's discussion of Stoicism in book 7 of *Theory of Moral Sentiments,* which she describes as "a model of Smith's own account of the relation between a moral agent and the impartial spectator."[74] In Brown's view, Smith's impartial spectator therefore enacts the Stoic model of an internal reasoning process that develops moral judgment through imaginatively engaging with the perspectives of others.

Although Brown's observation that Smith's emphasis on imagination over reason constitutes a significant departure from Stoicism is accurate,[75] her characterization of this departure as a complete rejection seems overstated, given that the Stoics maintain an important role for the imagination even as they emphasize the primacy of reason.[76] This apparent division becomes particularly complicated when Cicero's adaptation of Stoic thought to rhetoric is taken into account. The imaginative process through which the impartial spectator achieves sympathy with others in many respects sustains the fundamental connection between Smith's theory and Stoicism, as Smith shares Stoic assumptions concerning the necessary relationship between self-knowledge and social responsibility—an assumption that is fully developed as a rhetorical enterprise in the writings of Cicero and Quintilian. The dialogue that defines the impartial spectator's agency is consistently oriented not only toward self-knowledge but also toward an active and meaningful relationship with others. Smith consistently asserts a connection between an individual's self-awareness and his or her ability to understand the behavior of others: "The principle by which we naturally either approve or disapprove of our own conduct, seems to be altogether the same with that by which we exercise the like judgments concerning the conduct of other people."[77] This insight creates a reciprocal arrangement through which people understand others through the lens of their own experience but also strengthen their social consciousness through examining themselves in light of their encounters with other people. Thus people learn to assess their own conduct through learning to hold themselves accountable in the same way they would others. Because people are by nature social creatures, interaction with others is a necessary component of ethical refinement. In a passage that echoes Cicero's description of the "outward, visible propriety" that both shapes and reflects "the good opinion of those with whom and amongst whom we live,"[78] Smith writes, "Bring him into society, and he is immediately provided with the mirror which he wanted before. It is placed in the countenance and behaviour of those he lives with, which always mark when they enter into, and when they disapprove of his sentiments; and it is here that he first views the propriety and impropriety of his own passions, the beauty and deformity of his own mind."[79] In keeping with the example of the Stoics and Cicero, Smith perceives individuals as simultaneously gaining an understanding of themselves and others.

Thus the sympathetic impulse that leads people to identify with others ultimately encourages them to examine themselves through others' eyes: "As nature teaches the spectators to assume the circumstances of the person principally concerned, so she teaches this last in some measure to assume those of the spectators."[80] Developing a stronger moral sense requires people to move beyond their own perceptions in order to judge themselves according to external standards. In discussing the development of a sense of justice, Smith writes, "We must here, as in all other cases, view ourselves not so much according to that light in which we may naturally appear to ourselves, as according to that in which we naturally appear to others."[81] Smith's "impartial spectator" enacts a process of internal examination that trains the individual to mediate between self and society. McKenna compares Smith's notion of propriety with Shaftesbury's inner dialogue, in which "self-knowledge comes about in part through the discovery of requisite fitness in verbal representation,"[82] as propriety in Smith emerges through an "'inward rhetoric,' self-regulating sentiments before an internal 'impartial spectator.'"[83] Like Shaftesbury, Smith perpetuates a long tradition that adheres to the Stoic goal of balancing the pursuit of self-interest with the social impulse natural to humanity.

For Smith, as for Cicero and the Stoics, an individual demonstrates virtue first through developing an internal sense of civic duty and then through demonstrating and developing that ethical consciousness through responsible language use. Smith's emphasis on propriety brings together the rhetor and audience in forming a relationship that promotes sympathy. This practice also leads toward the tranquillity and self-control that ultimately contribute to human happiness. In spite of Smith's resistance to certain aspects of Stoic thought, he agrees that the ability of humans to accept their situations can be seen as evidence that "the Stoics were, at least, thus far very nearly in the right."[84] Such acceptance comes not from a focus on themselves but from methodical attention to their relationships with others. Calling upon the impartial spectator therefore ensures that the individual will benefit from sympathy not only through devising more effective communication that will inspire a sympathetic reaction in others but also through developing disciplined habits and self-awareness that will ultimately lead the individual to merit that understanding. Smith follows Cicero's development of Stoic principles in suggesting that the regular enactment of this rhetorical practice can actually form as well as demonstrate virtue.

This principle generally involves an imaginative process of invention, as it requires shaping the way emotions are expressed so that they achieve sympathetic assent. This anticipation of the need to persuade others affects not only the public appearance of sentiments but also reciprocally shapes the character and conscience of the individual who engages imaginatively with spectators.

Smith explains the interactions between spectator and "the person principally concerned" as a cycle in which both come to a better understanding through their ability to sympathize with each other: "As their sympathy makes them look at it, in some measure, with his eyes, so his sympathy makes him look at it, in some measure, with theirs, especially when in their presence and acting under their observation: and as the reflected passion, which he thus conceives, is much weaker than the original one, it necessarily abates the violence of what he felt before he came into their presence, before he began to recollect in what manner they would be affected by it, and to view his situation in this candid and impartial light."[85] Thus agents who view their interests through the eyes of spectators achieve the moderation that comes from looking at their circumstances through others' eyes. Smith's conception of rhetoric informed by sympathy creates a notion of propriety that McKenna argues "is not simply the self-interested achievement of humans desiring the pleasure of sympathy. By seeking sympathy through propriety, people actively transcend self-interest,"[86] which ultimately makes possible the social relationships that are necessary for a strong community.

The reflective process Smith describes parallels Marcus Aurelius's counsel that regular habits of reflection encourage the moderation of strong feelings that might interfere with the pursuit of social harmony, another respect in which Smith's notion of propriety established by the "impartial spectator" constitutes the rhetorical enactment of internal deliberation found in the Stoics and Cicero. McKenna notes that the critical component of sentiment "implies that stylistic propriety is more than superficial nicety, or, as is often said of style in the period, a managerial device whose role is simply to shape the form of communication once subject matter has been revealed by logic. Instead, propriety must be understood as an integral part of successful communication, one that works in concert with invention and arrangement."[87] For Smith, the tendency to seek the approval of others is a natural strength that should be cultivated: "Nature, when she formed man for society, endowed him with an original desire to please, and an original aversion to offend his brethren. She taught him to feel pleasure in their favourable, and pain in their unfavourable regard. . . . Nature, accordingly, has endowed him, not only with a desire of being approved of, but with a desire of being what ought to be approved of; or of being what he himself approves of in other men."[88] Thus sympathy, enacted in part through acting the part of a spectator observing one's actions from the standpoint of others, encourages the development of true virtue. Rhetoric aimed at gaining an audience's approval does not necessarily involve pandering to the whims of the crowd, as Plato suggests. The individual who carefully cultivates self-knowledge alongside the sympathetic connection with others facilitated by the impartial spectator has the opportunity to acquire the true ethical sense that derives from judging one's own actions in light of an evolving notion of a common good.

Thus Smith develops rhetorical and ethical guidelines that adhere to the Stoic connection between the individual and the social. E. G. West introduces Smith's *Theory of Moral Sentiments* with the observation that "in Smith's comprehensive and panoramic view of society, self-interest lives with perfect propriety side by side with Benevolence."[89] In Smith's view, individuals cannot exist in isolation, because people are naturally programmed to achieve their fulfillment through relationships with others: "Society and conversation . . . are the most powerful remedies for restoring the mind to its tranquillity, if, at any time, it has unfortunately lost it; as well as the best preservatives of that equal and happy temper, which is so necessary to self-satisfaction and enjoyment."[90] He echoes the Stoics and Cicero, as well as other classical rhetoricians, in insisting, "Man, who can subsist only in society, was fitted by nature to that situation for which he was made."[91] Achieving a sense of propriety therefore comes about through social interaction and requires each person to become committed to the well-being of the whole. "Man, it has been said, has a natural love for society, and desires that the union of mankind should be preserved for its own sake, and though he himself was to derive no benefit from it. The orderly and flourishing state of society is agreeable to him, and he takes delight in contemplating it. Its disorder and confusion, on the contrary, is the object of his aversion, and he is chagrined at whatever tends to produce it. He is sensible too that his own interest is connected with the prosperity of society, and that the happiness, perhaps the preservation of his existence, depends upon its preservation."[92] All human activity should therefore be directed toward a consideration of others: "Man was made for action, and to promote by the exertion of his faculties such changes in the external circumstances both of himself and others, as may seem most favourable to the happiness of all."[93]

For Smith, as for the Stoics, the habit of developing a true understanding with others helps to form a strong character. The self-control that people strive to achieve comes about through developing a sense of propriety, which involves sensitivity to others' perspectives. For Smith, the Stoic emphasis on self-control is central to the development of the social sense: "Our sensibility to the feelings of others, so far from being inconsistent with the manhood of self-command, is the very principle upon which that manhood is founded."[94] The conscious practice of sympathy, guided by the impartial spectator, provides the means for self-control, for "the man who feels the most for the joys and sorrows of others, is best fitted for acquiring the most complete control of his own joys and sorrows."[95] Smith therefore suggests that the deliberate development of the character of self-control, which strongly resonates with Stoic values, also reconciles the apparent division between public and private life: "The man of real constancy and firmness, the wise and just man who has been thoroughly bred in the great school of self-command, in the bustle and business of the world, exposed, perhaps, to the violence and injustice of faction, and to the hardships and hazards of war, maintains this control of his passive feelings upon all occasions; and whether in solitude or society, wears nearly the same countenance, and is affected very nearly in the same manner."[96] Developing a sense of propriety inevitably involves bringing the individual's character in line with his or her social responsibilities. In articulating this process, Smith offers a theory that alleviates the divided consciousness of the individual and bridges the apparently growing chasm between public and private life.

Propriety and Social Duty in the Writings of Henry Home, Lord Kames

Kames shares the belief of Shaftesbury, Smith, and Cicero, that propriety is both internally cultivated and socially constructed; like these other theorists, he draws upon a Stoic framework in connecting this notion of propriety to public and private virtue, as he maintains that learning appropriate language use, that is, language that responds effectively to particular audiences and contexts, regulates self-interest through developing an awareness of one's duty to others. In *Essays on the Principles of Morality and Natural Religion,* Kames describes "uniformity of conduct" as a "foundation of the laws of our nature": "Any action, conformable to the common nature of our species, is considered by us as regular and good: it is according to order, and according to nature. . . . These reflections lead us to the foundation of the laws of our nature. They are to be derived from the common nature of man, of which every person partakes who is not a monster."[97] Kames's insistence that a sense of order and fitness is ordained by nature has a decidedly Stoic cast, as does his optimistic assessment of the common judgment people share as a result of their natural appreciation for their appropriate positions in the universe: "We find this to hold in fact; and it is extreme agreeable to observe how accurately the laws of each species, arising from its nature, are adjusted to its external frame, and to the circumstances in which it is placed, so as to procure the conveniencies of life in the best manner, and to produce regularity and consistency of conduct."[98]

Kames's appreciation for the fundamental value of appreciating "regularity and consistency of conduct" is further evident in *Elements of Criticism,* where he devotes an entire chapter to the subjects of congruity and propriety; he defines congruity in broad terms as the human impulse to see that things are fit and proper to the circumstance; his definition of propriety resonates with both Stoic and contemporary thought, as he maintains that propriety pertains specifically to "that congruity or suitableness, which ought to subsist between sensible beings, and their thoughts, words, and actions."[99] Propriety therefore brings the search for congruity into the human realm, and its importance becomes clear as it translates the natural urge for order into a social realm designed to promote the order and justice that provide a foundation for human life. Like the Stoics, Kames assumes both the natural, human desire for order and an automatic link between the individual and the social; even the passions he asserts to be "by nature, modelled and tempered with perfect wisdom, for the good of society as well as for private good."[100] Thus individuals learn propriety through assessing how their awareness of their character prompts them to respond to particular situations.

Kames maintains that such conduct becomes a way of life through education and practice. The beginning of the *Elements of Criticism* chapter on propriety resonates with Stoic thought in drawing explicit connections among sensory experience, the cultivation of the highest human instincts, and an appreciation for regularity that brings individuals into harmony with both the divine order and other people. Citing *De officiis,* Kames suggests that propriety's moral dimension is a consequence of its role in mediating among individuals, the divine, and the social world: "Man is superior to the brute, not more by his rational faculties, than by his senses. With respect to external senses, brutes probably yield not to men; and they may also have some obscure perception of beauty: but the more delicate senses of regularity, order, uniformity, and congruity, being connected with morality and religion, are reserved to dignify the chief of the terrestrial creation. Upon that account, no discipline is more suitable to man, nor more *congruous* to the dignity of his nature, than that which refines his taste, and leads him to distinguish, in every subject, what is regular, what is orderly, what is suitable, and what is fit and proper."[101] He emphasizes the gradual process through which people acquire a "sense" of propriety, as they learn to connect the physical senses that apprehend the external world with their internal moral senses. Like the external sense, the moral sense becomes refined through cultivation, for Kames believes that discipline has the potential to promote the development of virtue. Such virtue inevitably involves the civic sensitivity that accompanies an individual's development of sound moral judgment; Kames notes that social affections are always more refined than selfish ones.[102]

Because individuals acquire a sense of propriety through contact with others, Kames shares the Stoic view that propriety must be acquired through self-examination that maintains a dialogic quality. The appropriateness of each person's actions is therefore measured not only according to an internal compass but also through the lens of a spectator who represents the collective judgment of society: "Let us suppose, for example, a generous action suited to the character of the author, which raises in him and in every spectator the pleasant emotion of propriety: this emotion generates in the author both self-esteem and joy; the former when he considers his relation to the action, and the latter when he considers the good opinion that others will entertain of him: the same emotion of propriety produces in the spectators esteem for the author of the action; and when they think of themselves, it also produces by contrast an emotion of humility."[103] Kames's description outlines a complex web of relationships that contribute to the development of propriety. To think of propriety as simultaneously grounded in self-esteem and external validation automatically creates a bridge between private and public. It also requires a complicated interplay between "author" and "spectators," as authors both apprehend the significance of their actions personally and imagine their reception by spectators.

Meanwhile, spectators both interpret the propriety of an action in terms of their external relationship to the rhetor and put themselves in the place of the rhetor by imagining what it would feel like to accomplish those actions. This endeavor is made possible through the natural human capacity for sympathy, which has a particular role in helping people acquire the understanding that promotes appropriate conduct toward others. He describes sympathy as "the cement of human society";[104] while this natural human capacity is "a principle implanted in the breast of every man,"[105] it can be enhanced through careful cultivation. In the introduction to *Elements of Criticism,* he stresses the role of taste and criticism in promoting sympathy: "Delicacy of taste tends no less to invigorate the social affections, than to moderate those that are selfish. To be convinced of that tendency, we need only reflect, that delicacy of taste necessarily heightens our feeling of pain and pleasure; and of course our sympathy, which is the capital branch of every social passion. Sympathy invites a communication of joys and sorrows, hopes and fears: such exercise, soothing and satisfactory in itself, is necessarily productive of mutual good-will and affection."[106] Their ability to sympathize with each other helps people share their emotions, and this process is both delightful and valuable in strengthening the understanding that exists among people: "Where the countenance, the tones, the gestures, the actions, join with the words in communicating emotions, these united have a force irresistible. Thus all the pleasant emotions of the human heart, with all the social and virtuous affections, are, by means of these external signs, not only perceived, but felt."[107] Although the "painful passion" of sympathy may initially evoke disagreeable sensations in the spectator, it is ultimately beneficial by virtue of the strengthened connections that exist among people.[108] Thus sympathy can be seen as a primary means by which the natural connections among people are reinforced: "The conformity of the nature of man to his external circumstances is in every particular wonderful: his nature makes him prone to society; and society is necessary to his well-being, because in a solitary state he is a helpless being, destitute of support, and in his manifold distresses destitute of relief. But mutual support, the shining attribute of society, is of too great moment to be left dependent upon cool reason: it is ordered more wisely, and with greater conformity to the analogy of nature, that it should be enforced even instinctively by the passion of sympathy."[109] The sense of sympathy, like that of propriety, begins in the internal sensibility of the individual but inevitably draws the individual into a greater awareness of his or her relationships with others.

In Kames's view, the relationship between author and spectator simply entails a conscious awareness of the natural connections that propriety always possesses. In a passage that strikingly resonates with Stoic thought, Kames describes propriety's role as one that supports "the sense of justice, to enforce the performance of social duties. In fact, the sanctions visibly contrived to compel a man to be just to himself, are equally serviceable to compel him to be just to others; which will be evident from a single reflection, that an action, by being unjust, ceases not to be improper: an action never appears more eminently improper, than when it is unjust: it is obviously becoming, and suitable to human nature, that each man do his duty to others; and, accordingly, every transgression of duty to others, is at the same time a transgression of duty to one's self."[110] Thus propriety's mediation between the self and social assigns it a central role in the preservation of society's strength. The pursuit of a sense of propriety ensures attention to the individual's character and to the relationships among people that promote true justice.

Like Cicero and the Stoics, Kames's belief in the natural connection between the internal cultivation of propriety and one's social relations leads to the view that propriety is something that is externally manifested in the conduct and even the appearance of the individual. In *Elements of Criticism,* he echoes Cicero's belief in an "outward, visible propriety," as he notes that "looks and gestures give direct access to the heart, and lead us to select, with tolerable accuracy, the persons who are worthy of our confidence. It is surprising how quickly, and for the most part how correctly, we judge of character from external appearance."[111] Although linking character to personal appearance has obvious hazards, it is at least instructive to understand the Stoic rationale that Kames and his contemporaries use in drawing this connection. The notion that the social sense exists as a visible attribute develops from the conviction that people are naturally created to live in community with others—and that their willing participation in that relationship has tangible—and visible—benefits.

Style and Propriety in Blair's Rhetorical Theory

Blair's interest in the rhetorical capacity of aesthetic judgment reflects the same conviction that the physical world visibly manifests qualities that can help to develop an ethical sensibility. Blair's belief that style, as well as taste, entails the convergence of character and social expectation leads to a rhetorical emphasis that is decidedly different from that found in many classical theories. Although he has little guidance to offer in the canons of invention or arrangement, however, his notion of building character through rhetoric does sustain the view that rhetoric is bound to context. In discussing the origins of language, he sides with the Stoics against Platonists in arguing that the relationship between words and things is not natural but an arbitrary system that develops according to the particular expectations that evolve in different social environments.[112] Blair therefore maintains that "language is generally understood to receive its predominant tincture from the national character of the people who speak it,"[113] building on the foundation provided by preceding generations but acquiring new dimensions from the needs of the present day.

For Blair, as for the Stoics, Shaftesbury, and Kames, the intersection between public and private life that is effected in part through propriety leads to the expectation that individual style visibly exhibits the internal character of the writer or speaker. He acknowledges that "style has always some reference to an author's manner of thinking,"[114] for "Style is nothing else, than that sort of expression which our thoughts most readily assume."[115] Like Seneca and Smith, Blair connects style with character: "There is a certain character imprinted on his Style, which may be denominated his manner."[116] This insight at times contributes to Blair's tendency to dismiss the need for rhetorical training, as it encourages him to emphasize communication as primarily deriving from an individual's relationship with the subject matter. He asserts that figures "must flow from a mind warmed by the object which it seeks to describe,"[117] arguing that "the real and proper ornaments of Style arise from Sentiment."[118] Blair cites Quintilian in insisting that the rule of style is "to think closely of the subject, till we have attained a full and distinct view of the matter which we are to clothe in words, till we become warm and interested in it; then, and not till then, shall we find expression begin to flow."[119]

Blair's notion of style emphasizes perspicuity, which he describes as comprising the elements of purity, propriety, and precision. While both purity and precision primarily involve qualities that are internal to the spoken or written text, propriety must be defined in terms that account for the social conditions that surround the language act: "Propriety, is the selection of such words in the Language, as the best and most established usage has appropriated to those ideas which we intend to express by them. It implies the correct and happy application of them, according to that usage, in opposition to vulgarisms, or low expressions; and to words and phrases, which would be less significant of the ideas that we mean to convey."[120] As with his notion of taste, Blair describes propriety in terms that strengthen the links between individuals and the community that surrounds them. Barbara Warnick aptly describes Blair's conception of propriety as "a general quality that reflected a composer's entire outlook on people and communication in general."[121] Warnick emphasizes that Blair considers propriety to be conceived intuitively, a point supported by statements in which he links style to common sense. However, Blair's Stoic orientation suggests that his notion of propriety includes the assumption that this intuitive sense is strengthened and developed through a social process that helps to shape the rhetor's sense of the "fitness and design"[122] of language. Blair describes the intrinsic connection between an internal sense of propriety and external context in a passage that invokes common sense as the ultimate guide: "Nothing merits the name of eloquent or beautiful, which is not suited to the occasion, and to the persons to whom it is addressed. It is to the last degree awkward and absurd, to attempt a poetical florid Style, on occasions, when it should be our business only to argue and reason; or to speak with elaborate pomp of expression, before persons who comprehend nothing of it, and can only stare at our unseasonable magnificence. These are defects not so much in point of Style, as, what is much worse, in point of common sense."[123]

Thus Blair shares with the Stoics, Cicero, and Quintilian the sense that developing a style suited to the subject matter inevitably involves a complex enterprise that includes awareness of audience and rhetorical context. Communication that does not effectively respond to the expectations of other people inevitably exhibits a lack of social awareness that has significance beyond the immediate concerns of the present. Rhetors who attend to the necessary "decorums of time, place, and character"[124] are not only fostering effective communication at the moment but are also developing the internal sensitivity to appropriate language that strengthens their relationships with others in a more general sense.

Thus for Blair, too, propriety constitutes an effort to capture the complexity that inevitably arises when people attempt to negotiate the potential division between private interests and the collective values that ensure social stability. He maintains the classical view that attention to propriety is a necessary component of ethos: "Let the matter of an author be ever so good and useful, his compositions will always suffer in the public esteem, if his expression be deficient in purity and propriety."[125] Blair's recognition that appropriate language plays a role in audience reception extends beyond the practical concern with the efficacy of a speech. Blair insists that propriety can be seen as a quality that defines the essence of a communicative act. Like the Stoics, Blair describes propriety as a quality that does not operate merely on the surface of communication but inevitably has a tangible effect on the relationship between the audience and speaker.

For this reason, speakers who train themselves to become more attentive to the complex demands of their rhetorical contexts, which includes careful attention to developing discourse that appropriately responds to specific situations, are ultimately drawing upon and strengthening their ethical foundations. Blair cites "ancient rhetoricians," which would include both Quintilian and his Stoic forebears,[126] in maintaining that "in order to be a truly eloquent or persuasive Speaker, nothing is more necessary than to be a virtuous man."[127] For Blair, as for the Stoics, virtuous language appropriately reflects the individual's character and his or her commitment to the welfare of others.

The Complexity of Sensus Communis

The Stoic influence in eighteenth-century British rhetorical theories supports their development of notions of propriety that assume a bridge between individuals and their society. Propriety represents both the individual's firmness of character and the ability to contribute to an orderly and harmonious society. Self-control facilitates the ability to maintain personal integrity and to participate meaningfully in society. This participation is made possible through sympathy, which enables people to have an immediate experience of the social bond that connects them on a deeper level. At the same time, ongoing communication strengthens the capacity people have to sympathize with each other, thereby enhancing the stability of the community. Shaftesbury, Smith, Kames, and Blair draw upon Stoic ethics as well as their systematic appropriation by Cicero and Quintilian to devise notions of propriety that establish rhetoric as the ground for moral development, the resolution of immediate social concerns, and the development of private and public virtue.

In pursuing their notions of virtue, these theorists undoubtedly invoke universal standards that jeopardize the expressions of difference that are vital to a democratic society, a tension always present in the Stoic enterprise of sensus communis. However, nineteenth-century developments suggest that the rejection of sensus communis has other consequences for rhetoric. Nineteenth-century British thinkers acknowledged the oppressive character of the eighteenth-century pursuit of order and harmony. Although many writers of that era continued to use terms consistent with a Stoic vocabulary, they largely abandoned the struggle to negotiate the difficult balance between public and private life that had been a central feature of Stoic thought and that had been a major force in the eighteenth-century appropriation of Stoicism. Although eighteenth-century notions of taste, propriety, and a unity between public and private virtue were imperfect vehicles for promoting democracy, the nineteenth-century pursuit of a private realm distinct from the sordid concerns of daily life also reveals limitations that have had significant consequences for subsequent developments in rhetorical theory and pedagogy. Focusing on the rejection of the Stoic ideal of sensus communis in nineteenth-century British language theories helps to illuminate the nature of the nineteenth-century shift away from earlier versions of rhetoric, both traditional agonistic discourse and the Stoic alternative of rhetoric based in character formation and civic virtue. This shift illuminates rhetoric's gradual transformation during this period—and illustrates persistent challenges that surround rhetoric's role in promoting positive social action.

Chapter 5

VICTORIAN LANGUAGE THEORIES AND THE DECLINE OF SENSUS COMMUNIS

The eighteenth-century appropriation of Stoic thought altered rhetoric's history, as it created a unique synthesis of ancient and modern ideas that emphasized rhetoric's role in developing character and fostering civic virtue. Because rhetoric's nature involves sensitivity to cultural change, it is not surprising that this version of rhetoric did not last because nineteenth-century theorists gradually came to reject the viability of the civic ideal that had sustained earlier generations. This outlook results in language and aesthetic theories that seem to have little to do with earlier conceptions of rhetoric. Perhaps it is for this reason that British rhetoric's transformation in the nineteenth century has not been thoroughly assessed—most accounts of rhetoric's history simply stop with Richard Whately's *Elements of Rhetoric* in 1828. This demarcation is understandable in light of the fact that Whately's theory represents a final example of a traditional treatise aimed at instructing people on persuasive appeals based in "common sense." Whately's theory can therefore be seen as representing a pivotal moment when British language theorists begin to depart in striking ways from a philosophical orientation that pursues communicative goals compatible with traditional rhetorical principles and the pursuit of sensus communis. One value of understanding the function of Stoic principles in eighteenth-century rhetorical theories is that it illuminates the nineteenth-century transition to new conceptions of rhetoric and its public function.

Thomas De Quincey: Unstifling the Rhetorical Impulse

One of the nineteenth century's earliest advocates of the power of imaginative language in the midst of an industrial age was Thomas De Quincey. As a writer whose essays attempt to re-form the relationship between the classical canons of invention and style, De Quincey occupies a pivotal role in shifting British rhetorical theory from its classical roots and from the Stoic orientation found in eighteenth-century theories.

De Quincey's work reflects a suspicion of industrial society that continued to develop throughout the century. His response to the social conditions that surrounded him outlines a disruptive role for rhetoric that directly counters the management of thought that Whately advances in his adaptation of classical principles. For De Quincey, language is inherently unmanageable and functions best when it challenges the monotony that for him characterized the acceptable standards of social discourse. His distrust of industrial society leads De Quincey to create a theory that moves the focus of rhetoric away from creating a successful interaction between the rhetor and audience. He insists that rhetoric's power comes from its ability to spark creativity and reveal the internal strength of the individual—a sharp, inward turn that anticipates the complete transformation of nineteenth-century rhetorical theory.

De Quincey's position in the rhetorical tradition has been vigorously debated by scholars throughout the past century. A striking number of scholarly articles have focused on the question of whether De Quincey's essays on rhetoric offer any coherent and substantive statement about rhetoric's basic function.[1] De Quincey himself would probably be among the first to acknowledge that they do not—and further to assert that any search through his writings for precise and efficient guidelines that explain the function of rhetoric is in itself symptomatic of the utilitarian approach to knowledge that his essays attempt to challenge. Thus for De Quincey the search for order that eighteenth-century theorists had enthusiastically adopted from Stoic thought comes to represent not a value that connects humanity to the natural world but a manifestation of industrial society's artificial imposition of a system that destroys individual creativity.

Although his interest in style resonates with the British rhetorical tradition that preceded him, De Quincey diverges from earlier theorists in demonstrating the intellectual play with words that he advocates rather than methodically describing the central features of rhetoric or providing practical instructions for its proper use. In assuming for his own writing the freedom to explore the subtleties of his topic in an unsystematic fashion, De Quincey directly responds to a modern culture that he diagnoses as too exclusively oriented toward the immediate and practical goals of science and public business. In De Quincey's view, the creative impulse that preserves the vitality of society can only be recaptured through a rhetorical theory that recognizes the essential unity of style and invention.

The unconventional approach to rhetoric that emerges from De Quincey's social consciousness represents a turning point in the evolution of British rhetoric. De Quincey's anxiety over the limitations that industrial society has placed upon the creative use of rhetoric reflects a concern that had also been evident in the work of eighteenth-century theorists. However, his proposed solution—to conceive of rhetorical invention as the dynamic interplay between form and substance that unleashes the individual's creative energy—anticipates a nineteenth-century trend to replace theoretical approaches to rhetorical training with practices that reveal the lasting social value of the individual's imaginative activity. This view alters rhetoric's traditional public function of making judgment possible. Following the tradition of Longinus, De Quincey views rhetoric neither as engaging the rhetor and audience in a common effort to achieve consensus about specific questions nor in fostering an agreement about civic virtue. De Quincey's rhetoric instead provides the means for transforming society indirectly through serving as a site of resistance to the mechanization associated with modern life.

De Quincey serves as an early advocate of the emerging notion of rhetoric's power to overcome the evils of industrialization as he advocates a shift from a theory that emphasizes the specific results of discourse—which had previously been assumed to be the ultimate goal of persuasion—to a process significant primarily because of its ability to engage the intellect in unconventional ways. For De Quincey, rhetoric's power to stimulate the intellect is vital to a society in which creativity has been increasingly sacrificed to scientific materialism. He identifies the early seventeenth century as the last era in which rhetoric flourished in England, for at that time "science was unborn as a popular interest."[2] He argues that from that point forward, the imaginative potential of invention fully developed through style has been limited by a growing emphasis on the mere substance of discourse, dictated by "that same love for the practical and the tangible which has so memorably governed the course of our higher speculations from Bacon to Newton."[3] De Quincey's objective in his writings about rhetoric is to challenge the prevailing view that language must promote the scientific efficiency that governs the rest of the world.

Through this position, De Quincey, like his belletristic predecessors, implicitly counters scientific discourse, which places rhetoric in the service of an accurate and objective accounting of the world of external appearances, with a version of rhetoric that sharpens the intellect through exploring different sides of an issue, without an immediate need for resolution. Central to his challenge to scientific assumptions about the intrinsic value of certainty is his emphasis on rhetoric's importance in mediating between extremes, "amongst that vast field of cases where there is a *pro* and a *con,* with the chance of right and wrong, true and false, distributed in varying proportions between them." Moreover, he adds that "there is also an immense range of truths where there are no chances at all concerned, but the affirmative and negative are both true." The focus of rhetoric therefore should not be upon achieving a definite conclusion, for "where it is possible for the understanding to be convinced, no field is open for rhetorical persuasion." Rhetoric's role involves "giving an impulse to one side, and by withdrawing the mind so steadily from all thoughts or images which support the other as to leave it practically under the possession of a one-sided estimate."[4] Those who seek to free themselves from the constraints of the practical in order to realize the creative potential of rhetoric must be willing to involve themselves in an activity that balances varied perspectives and must recognize the persuasive features of other positions even as they make the advantages of one side more vivid to others.

This view of rhetoric's purpose has an immediate bearing on De Quincey's view of style. He insists that English style has been damaged by the belief that "the right of occupying the attention of the company seems to inhere in *things* rather than in persons."[5] On the other hand, he notes that French style is focused to excess upon feelings without regard for intellectual content, which potentially leads to eloquence that does not necessarily fulfill the objectives of rhetoric: "There is no eddying about their own thoughts . . . but strains of feeling, genuine or not, supported at every step from the excitement of independent external objects."[6] In De Quincey's view, the perfection of style can only come about through the recognition that rhetoric occupies a middle ground distinct from both scientific objectivity and spontaneous personal feelings. Although De Quincey sees the potential of writing for enhancing the development of thought, he recognizes at the same time that writing possesses the danger of focusing too much attention on the mechanical features of discourse, indirectly promoting the perception that style constitutes the extraneous ornamentation of language rather than encompassing the essence of invention. The mark of the "truly splendid rhetorician" is the ability to employ imagery that has "grown up in the loom, and concurrently with the texture of the thoughts."[7] Attention to style provides a source of intellectual pleasure in itself, because style should be seen as inextricably linked to rhetorical invention.

De Quincey repeatedly states his view that the ability to appreciate the vital function of style has been gradually eclipsed by the growing orientation of both print and the public toward science and public business. Greater attention to style can restore society's intellectual vitality through breaking the boundaries of practicality that otherwise "stifle the rhetorical impulses."[8] De Quincey significantly appropriates and transforms the industrial image of the loom, as he notes that although it is a simple matter to construct "a shorthand memorandum of a great truth," the challenge of composing "begins when you have to put your separate threads of thought into a loom; to weave them into a continuous whole."[9] He argues that such careful weaving of thought cannot be found in the print media, which widely distributes written material that lacks the intellectual depth and stylistic quality that encourages critical thought. Blaming newspapers for limiting the intellectual development of society, De Quincey states that texts written hastily with the intention of being merely efficient encourage people to develop habits of "desultory reading," as they rapidly seek out the key words that contain the essential information of a news story. Such habits can have disastrous consequences for the community as a whole, for "it is by the effects reflected upon his judging and reasoning powers, that loose habits of reading tell eventually. And these are durable effects."[10]

While De Quincey sees that the process of composing written texts provides people with an opportunity to develop new insights through reflecting upon their use of language, he expresses his concern that the British orientation toward literary language might eventually limit the imaginative process; although the immediate consequence of the "bookish idiom" that has suffused the nation is pedantic sentences, De Quincey fears that the appropriation of literary language in daily conversation may in time "weave fetters about the free movement of human thought."[11] Although De Quincey's publication of his essays in *Blackwood's Magazine* demonstrates his willingness to capitalize on the power of the press, his unorthodox style reveals his determination to use his authorial presence to challenge the reader's expectations of printed material. De Quincey's prose style represents his attempt to illustrate his theory that written style that self-consciously embarks upon a leisurely course of intellectual exploration, rather than forcefully developing a specific claim to a particular audience, can preserve the power of rhetoric that ultimately can revitalize society.

In spite of his radical notion of rhetoric, De Quincey sustains a long-standing British assumption that there is a direct relationship between rhetorical practices and the strength of the community. The development of British rhetoric is consistently marked by an assumed link between style and moral philosophy, a connection that assumes new force during the eighteenth century as industrialization and the growth of literacy both enhance and challenge traditional approaches to rhetoric. However, although De Quincey's interest in style demonstrates an important link to belletristic rhetorics, his essays at the same time reflect a shift in the way in which nineteenth-century thinkers were beginning to conceive of rhetoric's central function.

Belletristic rhetoric as developed through Adam Smith, Hugh Blair, and Lord Kames generally emphasizes the connection between style and ethos as it relates to moral character. In the view of these theorists, such ethical qualities are to some extent inscribed by the natural order, developed through social consensus, and reflected in the rhetor's ability to assess the needs of the audience. Belletristic rhetoricians share De Quincey's belief that the responsible rhetor's interest in style must arise not simply due to an interest in ornamentation for its own sake; however, they insist that the value of discourse derives not from the internal exploration of the individual's thought but from its merit in fostering connections with others.

De Quincey's disenchantment with nineteenth-century society, together with his awareness of the ways in which the widespread distribution of print complicates the rhetor's ability to define and address the audience, leads to his departure from versions of rhetoric that, influenced by Stoicism, optimistically depict rhetoric as uniting the rhetor and audience in a common search for the most virtuous course of action. He replaces this model with a proposal for intellectual play with language that indirectly enables the individual to challenge others to new ways of thinking. In describing De Quincey's view of rhetoric, Frederick W. Haberman notes that "all of De Quincey's definitions are alive with action: he perceives rhetoric as movement; and the rhetorical product in terms of the rhetorical process."[12] This emphasis on process assumes that rhetoric rests neither with the resolution of particular questions nor with consensus about civic values, a development that significantly alters the rhetorical landscape that had been constructed through centuries of theories and practices. Haberman highlights the introspective quality in De Quincey's theory in comparing De Quincey's view of rhetorical invention as an artistic internal process with John Ruskin's theory that painting landscapes involves a process of personal recollection: "To De Quincey, invention is appropriate recollection flowing through his pen. In the process of rhetoric, it is an 'inner activity' charged with the search for similitudes."[13] While De Quincey's recognition of rhetorical invention provides a link to the past, his notion of rhetoric as "inner activity" provides a bridge to the turn toward an intense and unstructured introspection emphasized by nineteenth-century writers and theorists at the end of the century.

De Quincey's emphasis on rhetoric as an individual process reflects his determination to resist the power of print culture to construct communicative standards that impose upon society an artificial sense of unity, which, as Christopher A. Kent points out, formed "the code of realism that affected the way readers conceived and perceived the world."[14] For De Quincey, the potential of style is achieved not through attending to the demands of the external world but through adopting a subjective perspective, for "the more closely any exercise of mind is connected with what is philosophically termed *subjective* . . . does the style or the embodying of the thoughts cease to be a mere separable ornament."[15] To instruct people in the fine points of rhetorical practice holds the danger of stifling rather than promoting the creative impulse that springs from within. De Quincey insists that even ignorance is preferable to a mechanical style of instruction that teaches everyone to write according to a formula that restricts individuality.[16]

This significant alteration in the conception of rhetorical training has important ramifications for those who follow De Quincey. In arguing for De Quincey's influence on style throughout the nineteenth century, Marie Secor writes, "Almost everything nineteenth-century writers had to say about style, as well as much of what has developed in modern theories, can be seen as filling in details on De Quincey's outline map."[17] In Secor's view, De Quincey's determination to abandon "the hierarchical view of style"[18] constitutes a turning point in which the classical levels of style become blurred due to "the exigencies of mass publication and the ubiquity of jargon."[19] She further points out that De Quincey's broadened perspective leads him to identify style as "more than one science: it can look at words on the page and explore their interrelationships; or it can examine relationships between the elements of the rhetorical triangle, the speaker, the discourse, and the transaction between them."[20] Secor also notes that De Quincey's view that the aesthetic features of style appeal both to the intellect and the emotions in reactivating the power of the subject reinforces the rhetorical principles of early theorists such as George Campbell and Richard Whately, while his final statement that style serves as the incarnation of thought anticipates the thought of Walter Pater late in the century. Thus Secor recognizes De Quincey's theory of style as a turning point between eighteenth-century rhetorical theory and developments in the latter part of the nineteenth century.

De Quincey also anticipates the nineteenth-century trend toward an emphasis on literary criticism as an art form in itself—a new form of argumentation that moves away from the public parameters that had previously defined rhetoric's domain. John E. Jordan states that De Quincey considered "the *subject* of criticism his métier, more than its practice,"[21] a view that foreshadows Matthew Arnold's later notion of the critic as a social prophet. However, the central values De Quincey maintains within his critical approach at the same time hearken to earlier ideas in the rhetorical tradition; Jordan explains that "the common denominator for beauty and a basic aesthetic criteria for all of De Quincey's criticism was appropriateness."[22] Thus De Quincey can be seen as providing a bridge between the Ciceronian view, sustained through the eighteenth century, that beauty must be defined according to an intrinsically social vector that determines "appropriateness" and a nineteenth-century emphasis on the subjective nature of rhetorical practice and criticism. His belief that enhancing the quality of expression has important ramifications for the vitality of the community as a whole also connects his thought with the rhetorical tradition begun by Isocrates, but the particular parameters of his development of that idea have definite relevance for an industrial society whose public identity was increasingly informed by print media. De Quincey's notion of uniting style and invention in a transformative, subjective realm constitutes a social statement that responds to the unique cultural conditions that he faced. These conditions lead De Quincey to a view of rhetoric that maintains some connection with earlier traditions but radically alters the Stoic belief in sensus communis that had provided a foundation for British rhetorics in preceding generations.

Thomas Carlyle's Heroic Intensity and the Transformation of British Rhetoric

The argument for a rhetoric residing in private inspiration is further developed in the influential writings of Thomas Carlyle. Like De Quincey, Carlyle is highly attuned to the tension between the practical concerns of his society and what he conceives of as the transcendent capacity of imaginative language. His determination to confront the tension between the immediate and practical concerns that drive his society and the deeper spiritual reality that lies beneath the surface of everyday life leads Carlyle to emphasize the role of the inspired individual in provoking needed social change. While he shares the Stoic belief in an ultimate truth that transcends human life, he locates that truth in imaginative vision distinct from nature and sensus communis.

Carlyle's role in the development of nineteenth-century thought has been well documented. The force of Carlyle's critical vision derived from his belief in the work he had to perform—whether or not this work would accommodate society's existing expectations. Carlyle's friend and biographer James Anthony Froude describes Carlyle's early financial hardship as a result of his unwillingness to compromise his intellectual mission, for "literature as a profession, followed with a sacred sense of responsibility (and without such a sense he could have nothing to do with it), refused a living to himself and his wife."[23] Nevertheless, Carlyle's determination to make his statement heard did eventually lead to his "unbounded influence on the mind of educated England."[24] Yet, in spite of scholars' widespread recognition of Carlyle's "unbounded influence" in many aspects of British life, his significance as a figure who plays a role in nineteenth-century British rhetoric's transformation has not been acknowledged.

This omission is understandable in light of Carlyle's particularly harsh arguments against the systematic language use traditionally associated with rhetorical training. While Carlyle's rhetorical practices reflect a stronger allegiance to the British rhetorical tradition than he might claim, it is nevertheless the case that his contribution to British cultural history, most strikingly influenced by Johann Wolfgang von Goethe, constitutes a striking departure from eighteenth-century rhetorical instruction grounded in the pursuit of sensus communis. While eighteenth-century theorists such as Thomas Reid, Campbell, Kames, and Blair had assumed that the individual's cultivation of taste and propriety occurred through an ongoing interaction with the external world, Carlyle posits the vision of the inspired and heroic individual against a society that is inherently corrupt. Carlyle can accurately be seen as a nineteenth-century rhetorician whose skill with language exemplifies persuasive discourse at its best. However, his role as "the apostle of aesthetics in England, 1825–27"[25] involves the advocacy of an imaginative aesthetic experience that differs in important ways from earlier efforts to define the symbiotic relationship between the public and private realms. It also signals a transition from treatises specifically addressing rhetoric's civic function to a more general treatment of language and aesthetic experience as the means for intellectual development and social transformation.

Carlyle's educational background can be seen as integral to both his skillful use of rhetoric and his strategic departure from traditional ideas concerning rhetoric's practice and function. His study at the University of Edinburgh, beginning in 1809, certainly made him familiar with the fundamental principles of rhetoric, and his initial study for the ministry and law would have given him reason for a particular emphasis on rhetorical instruction.[26] Carlyle's application for the Regius Chair of Rhetoric at the University of Edinburgh in 1835[27] underscores his interest in rhetoric, and his rejection for that post may have fuelled his determination to denounce what he saw as the uninspired direction that study had taken in nineteenth-century universities. What can be considered his version of a theory of aesthetics has a lasting impact not because he simply substitutes aesthetic experience for the outmoded rules of rhetoric but because he exemplifies the application of rhetorical skill and long-standing rhetorical principles to a vision that he believes to be essential in bringing new vitality to a society in the midst of dramatic change.

Without question, this vision leads to a distinct departure from previous conceptions of rhetoric's function. In an 1834 letter to Ralph Waldo Emerson, Carlyle states that if one has "any earnest meaning which demands to be not only listened to but *believed* and *done*," it is necessary to reach a point where "one leaves the pasteboard coulisses, and three unities, and Blair's Lectures, quite behind; and feels only that there is *nothing sacred*, then, but the *Speech of Man* to believing Men!"[28]—a prescription that signals a change in British rhetoric's focus for the remainder of the century. In replacing theory and training with sincerity and the cultivation of largely subjective aesthetic responses, Carlyle signals rhetoric's transformation from a formal and practical discipline rooted in consensus to a prophetic practice.

Carlyle was outspoken concerning the deep problems that pervaded industrial society and the significant impact those problems could have on the life of the individual. In keeping with the rhetorical tradition's "civilization myth" as depicted by both Isocrates and Cicero, Carlyle insists that people can only achieve their full spiritual potential within society: "It is in Society that man first feels what he is; first becomes what he can be. In Society an altogether new set of spiritual activities are evolved in him, and the old immeasurably quickened and strengthened. Society is the genial element wherein his nature first lives and grows; the solitary man were but a small portion of himself, and must continue forever folded in, stunted and only half alive."[29]

However, he goes on to note that part of the force that breathes life into society involves a cycle of "periods of sickness and vigour, of youth, manhood, decrepitude, dissolution, and new birth,"[30] as "the small Mechanical grows so mysteriously and indissolubly out of the infinite Dynamical, like Body out of Spirit."[31] The rebirth of society therefore has a direct bearing on the well-being of each individual, and Carlyle insists that the key to bringing about his society's rebirth is to recognize that "the grand vital energy, while in its sound state, is an unseen unconscious one."[32] The unconscious therefore becomes the means for seeking the spiritual reality that lies beneath the materialism that has become dominant, for "what is mechanical lies open to us: not what is dynamical and has vitality."[33] Carlyle hopes that the action of the individual's unconscious, sparked by an innate appreciation for beauty, can provide the basis for revitalizing a society whose vision has been damaged by mechanism and materialism. In spite of his pessimism about the society that surrounds him, Carlyle preserves the certainty that there is a divine justice that provides the world with order and meaning[34] and that people who insist upon the discovery of this realm can discover its deeper reality. In a passage that echoes the principles of Stoic philosophy, Carlyle insists, "Institutions are much; but they are not all. The freest and highest spirits of the world have often been found under strange outward circumstances."[35] In spite of the unique challenges of his age, he notes that the potential for restoring what has been lost continues to exist: "Not the invisible world is wanting, for it dwells in man's soul, and this last is still here."[36] It is therefore only through discovering one's inner strength that redemption may eventually occur on a broader scale: "To reform a world, to reform a nation, no wise man will undertake; and all but foolish men know, that the only solid, though a far slower reformation, is what each begins and perfects on *himself*."[37] Carlyle shares De Quincey's belief that the creative individual ultimately holds the key to reinvigorating a society that has been desensitized by materialistic values.

Thus Carlyle defines his task as devising new communicative strategies that can break through the barrier of indifference that industrialism has created. In "Signs of the Times," Carlyle writes that the best single epithet for describing his age would be "not an Heroical, Devotional, Philosophical, or Moral Age, but, above all others, the Mechanical Age."[38] He is forthright in connecting the physical mechanization of society with its intellectual and spiritual decline:

"Not the external and physical alone is now managed by machinery, but the internal and spiritual also. . . . Instruction, that mysterious communing of Wisdom with Ignorance, is no longer an indefinable tentative process . . . but a secure, universal, straightforward business, to be conducted in the gross, by proper mechanism, with such intellect as comes to hand."[39]

Like the Earl of Shaftesbury and Reid, Carlyle blames part of the shift in society's values on modern philosophy, which from Locke's time has emphasized the material world.[40] Although he expresses a certain degree of appreciation for the noble intentions that underlie the work of the Scottish commonsense philosophers, he ultimately concludes that even their attempt to use intuition to counter Hume's skepticism became lost in the technicalities of their theories, which ultimately damaged the vitality of their message.[41] He blames the pervasiveness of machinery in all aspects of life for a basic change in the way people view themselves and the world around them, claiming that people have not only been changed in their behavior but have also "grown mechanical in head and in heart" as well.[42] He goes on to argue that religion itself has been subsumed by the strength of an industrial society: "Our true Deity is Mechanism. It has subdued external Nature for us, and we think it will do all other things."[43] While eighteenth-century theorists had still seen in the Stoic ideal of nature the hope for an alternative to the artificial values found in certain aspects of human society, Carlyle articulates a later generation's pessimistic view that the forces of industry had entirely overwhelmed nature.

Carlyle's conviction that the mechanical forces of industrial society had overtaken the vital inner core of humanity extends to what he perceives as the corruption of language in British society. According to Froude, "England as he saw it was saturated with cant, dosed to surfeit with doctrines half true only or not true at all . . . till the once noble and at heart still noble English character was losing its truth, its simplicity, its energy, its integrity."[44] Although Froude's description of the prose qualities Carlyle values resembles the standards of discourse that had earlier been advocated by classical and belletristic rhetorics, he stresses Carlyle's conviction that these goals were not being upheld in his society. He discusses Carlyle's perception that religious leaders and politicians alike used speech for the purpose of advancing their own self-interest in keeping with the goals of an increasingly materialistic orientation: "They used their faculties only to dress the popular theories in plausible language, and were carried away by their own eloquence, till they actually believed what they were saying. Respect for fact they had none. Fact to them was the view of things conventionally received, or what the world and they together agreed to admit."[45] Challenging convention therefore became a necessary part of Carlyle's mission, as he expresses his certainty that the world is constantly guided by change that is not in itself necessarily a bad thing "but the product simply of *increased resources* which the old *methods* can no longer administer."[46]

The explosion of print production and distribution lay at the heart of the change in language use that Carlyle believed to have moved beyond the limits of "the old methods." He argues even more vehemently than De Quincey that the explosion of print both exemplifies and perpetuates the decline in moral and intellectual vitality that exists throughout society. He notes that the act of writing has become enmeshed in technology, for "books are not only printed, but, in a great measure, written and sold, by machinery."[47] The rise of periodicals associated with print has been particularly significant because of the growing influence of newspapers on the public mind. Carlyle also follows De Quincey's example in publishing his diatribes against the press in the very periodicals he so sweepingly denounces. Like De Quincey, he seems to be convinced that the power of his own rhetoric can transcend the dangers of mechanical production that he perceives as a limitation upon print culture when left to its own devices. He therefore offers his own use of language as an example of the rhetorical transformation that the hero can effect even within a corrupt medium.

In large part, then, Carlyle's dissatisfaction with the traditional rhetorical education exemplified by Blair's lectures relates to his perception that such instruction has been incorporated into a larger mechanical system that precludes the development of the individual's potential. Carlyle's contempt for the "old methods" of rhetoric was undoubtedly fueled not only by what he viewed as the corruption of political speech but also by the fact that rhetorical instruction in the schools of his day did not preserve the vitality of the classical tradition. Winifred Bryan Horner notes that Andrew Brown, the holder of the Regius Chair of Rhetoric at the University of Edinburgh during the time Carlyle attended, would be seen today as "an uninspired and undemanding teacher, who really had no interest in his subject."[48] Meanwhile, the nineteenth-century professors of logic at the University of Edinburgh had come to perceive the study of rhetoric as involving "little more than grammar."[49] Thus, in Carlyle's view, the systematic practice of rhetoric has become symptomatic of a society sickened by intellectual sterility: "Again, in the difference between Oratory and Rhetoric, as indeed everywhere in that superiority of what is called the Natural over the Artificial, we find a similar illustration. The Orator persuades and carries all with him, he knows not how; the Rhetorician can prove that he ought to have persuaded and carried all with him: the one is in a state of healthy unconsciousness, as if he 'had no system'; the other, in virtue of regimen and dietetic punctuality, feels at best that 'his system is in high order.'"[50] In revising

the meaning of *orator* and *rhetor,* Carlyle sustains the eighteenth-century emphasis on nature, reserving the term *orator* for those individuals who communicate
with sincerity and vision, while the rhetorician serves as the spokesperson for
an artificial society with self-interested goals.

Thus Carlyle's version of rhetoric replaces the formal principles that he perceived to be oriented toward fulfilling the practical concerns of industrial society with his own unique style of oratorical language. Although Carlyle willingly
takes on the role of prophet charged with the redemption of society, his rebel-
lion against rhetorical theory reflects his alienation from the social institutions
that traditionally had provided the forum for public judgment. As early as an
1829 letter to Goethe, he laments, "The whole bent of British endeavour, both
intellectual and practical at this time, is towards Utility."[51] He again reflects
this sentiment in "Signs of the Times" when he notes that his age possesses no
philosophers who stress the "infinite worth of moral goodness, the great truth
that our happiness depends on the mind which is within us"[52] but is instead
directed by those such as Jeremy Bentham who define the well-being of individuals in strictly material terms. This spiritual damage is reflected and perpetuated by a change in the way in which people perceive beauty, for they "are no
longer instinctively driven to apprehend, and lay to heart, what is Good and
Lovely, but rather to inquire, as onlookers, how it is produced, whence it comes,
whither it goes."[53] In Carlyle's view, the corruption of values is also reflected
in poetry, which means that "beauty is no longer the god it worships, but some
brute image of Strength; which we may well call an idol, for true Strength is one
and the same with Beauty, and its worship also is a hymn."[54] Carlyle's consistent emphasis on the spiritual regeneration of humanity and of his society is
repeatedly connected to his interest in directing people toward the search for
truth that can be discovered through an unconscious aesthetic engagement with
the world—an engagement that assumes the individual's necessary removal
from the corruption of the external world, which in turn limits the potential
for sensus communis.

In launching his alternative idea of language, Carlyle advances a notion of
sublimity that resides in the rhetor's heartfelt quest for truth that is markedly
distinct from material reality and that may at times require a presentation that
is anything but concise and simple. After assuring Emerson that *Sartor Resartus "was* earnestly meant and written,"[55] he responds to Emerson's comments
concerning his unconventional style: "You say well that I take up that attitude
because I have no known public, am *alone* under the heavens, speaking into
friendly or unfriendly space; add only, that I will not defend such an attitude,
that I call it questionable, tentative, and only the best that I, in these mad
times, could conveniently hit upon. For you are to know, my view is that now
at last we have lived to see all manner of Poetics and Rhetorics and Sermonics,

and one may say generally all manner of *Pulpits* for addressing mankind from, as good as broken and abolished."[56] Although human speech is inevitably sacred and may one day "anew environ itself with fit modes,"[57] Carlyle concludes, "Meanwhile, I know no method of much consequence, except that of *believing*, of being sincere."[58] While Carlyle shares the traditional view that effective rhetoric depends upon the sincerity of the rhetor, nineteenth-century cultural conditions have caused him to question earlier assumptions that meaningful communication is derived from general principles that can be readily adapted to particular situations or that rhetoric can create a sympathetic bond between rhetors and audiences. Although the sincerity of Carlyle's rhetor does carry forward a classical emphasis on ethos, Carlyle's perception that the "Age of Machinery" has corrupted the public's natural judgment leads him to doubt the audience's ability to participate in the construction of a rhetorical ethos. For this reason, the value of rhetoric comes not through its role in fostering sensus communis but through its capacity to transmit the inspired vision of the sincere rhetor to a society in need of moral transformation.

This image becomes the basis for Carlyle's own rhetorical practice. Froude explains that Carlyle's adoption of his prophetic voice derived from a deliberate effort to counter society's malaise: "For the sick body and sick soul of modern Europe there was but one remedy, the old remedy of the Jewish prophets, repentance and moral amendment."[59] He describes Carlyle's unique style as arising from "confidence in his own powers"[60] and notes that Emerson found in Carlyle "a voice speaking real and fiery convictions, and no longer echoes and conventionalisms."[61] Froude explains that in keeping with his conviction that the commercialization of print had encouraged the production of public discourse geared toward achieving no higher goals than entertaining the public, Carlyle accepted financial hardship rather than writing what he knew would be more likely to accommodate the popular taste.[62]

Thus Carlyle places himself as a writer in direct opposition to the practical concerns of his day, a position that reflects a certain social commitment, to be sure, but one that holds little expectation that a natural sense of community has the power to preserve what he sees as the moral malaise of nineteenth-century society. His ethical convictions concerning language use certainly placed him at odds with the practical goals that had in large part come to define formal rhetorical training in the nineteenth century. Carlyle's obscurity and linguistic extravagances are carefully targeted to achieve his broader purpose of reawakening society and asserting the primacy of personality in the midst of a mechanized and impersonal age. Froude insists, "Prophetic utterances seldom fall into harmonious form; they do not need it, and they will not bear it."[63] He accordingly states that his friend's speech, "if he was in earnest, was not smooth and flowing, but turbid like a river in a flood,"[64] and he elsewhere describes

Carlyle's style as the "spurting of volcanic fire."[65] For Carlyle the rhetorical technique of vehemence constitutes a particularly appropriate response to the ills of industrial society.

Carlyle's notion of a heroic detachment from history may also reflect his perception of himself as consistently isolated from his cultural surroundings; in his letter to Emerson of February 3, 1835, he repeats a frequent theme in discussing his "solitary existence"[66] and his belief that few others have a true understanding of his ideas. Carlyle's embodiment of the lonely artistic vision also anticipates Pater's view that the writer's goal should be not to transcribe fact but to convey his superior sense of it "and in selecting assert something of his own good humour, something that comes not of the world without but of a vision within."[67] For Pater as for Carlyle, artistic genius is defined by its capacity for achieving new insight into the nature of human experience. Oscar Wilde also shares Carlyle's view that the hero forms history, as he states categorically that "behind everything that is wonderful stands the individual, and that it is not the moment that makes the man, but the man who creates the age."[68] William Butler Yeats echoes this view in defining truth as the "dramatically appropriate utterance of the highest man,"[69] a man who can be assumed to possess the artistic vision that enables him to break away from bondage to the everyday world. For Carlyle, as well as for many intellectuals who follow him, the imaginative individual's vision necessarily leads to a certain alienation from the social sphere.

The hero's critical ability to see the truth and to make that truth known to others is an important part of Carlyle's legacy to nineteenth-century rhetoric. Belletristic rhetoric had already introduced the notion that there was a relationship between criticism and the practice of rhetoric. Blair defends criticism from its detractors, insisting that, "True criticism is a liberal and humane art,"[70] because "it teaches us, in a word, to admire and to blame with judgment, and not to follow the crowd blindly."[71] Carlyle's belletristic heroism builds upon Blair's belief in the importance of textual criticism, as he further elaborates the way in which a critical vision illuminates the world's falsehood and insists that the insight that critical powers provide must be accompanied by the act of communicating the truth to others.

Carlyle, like De Quincey, avoids the intense introspection of Romanticism in order to position the individual's creative use of language within a rhetorical engagement with the world. Carlyle's pivotal role in the transition to a new conception of rhetoric in the nineteenth century comes about as he reestablishes and transforms earlier links among the imagination, criticism, and the moral well-being of society. In spite of his disparagement of rhetoric, Carlyle's proclamation that "greater than all recorded miracles have been performed by Pens"[72] reflects his ongoing faith in the power of language to inspire change. Carlyle's idealism did not sustain itself in the face of the cynicism of the fin de siècle, but his determination to turn away from rhetorical theory had the miraculous result of creating a powerful new rhetoric that would reverberate through periodicals, pamphlets, and novels throughout the course of the century.

Matthew Arnold: The Evolution of Disinterestedness

The educated individual's role in shaping public judgment is further developed in Matthew Arnold's emphasis on criticism. Shaftesbury had argued for a type of intellectual disinterestedness as a component of sensus communis, as he advocated the use of gentle wit and polite conversation as opposed to philosophical wrangling. Smith's "impartial spectator" provides another dimension of the idea that adopting a disinterested perspective promotes communication that ultimately strengthens community. According to this eighteenth-century view, a cultivated disinterestedness can prevent people from being narrowly focused on their biases, which provides the intellectual freedom necessary to pursue sensus communis. This notion of disinterestedness evolves in the writings of De Quincey and Carlyle into a detachment from an absorption in commercial life that they believed to be detrimental to the search for higher forms of knowledge.

The influential aesthetic theory of John Ruskin, a disciple of Carlyle, ties "disinterested pleasure" to sympathy, as he perceives the beauty and pleasure of art as deriving from the individual's ability to connect his own feelings to the experience of others. At the same time, Ruskin maintains that the natural sympathy between the artist and the audience should not be corrupted by economic concerns that lead people to base their artistic production or judgment upon financial necessity. Consequently Ruskin's conception of "disinterested pleasure" perpetuates Shaftesbury's assumption that the sympathetic detachment of art promotes shared understanding between people and anticipates the emphasis later in the Victorian period on a notion of disinterestedness that requires those who seek artistic appreciation to remove themselves from the economic concerns that might inhibit their critical judgment.

The ideal of disinterestedness becomes particularly compelling as the century wears on, as continuing concern over the effects of industrial capitalism and increasing religious skepticism lead people to pursue art as an alternative both to the sordid world of commerce and to spiritual commitments that now seemed to be called into question by science. The writings of Matthew Arnold reveal a subtle ideological shift from the theories of De Quincey, Carlyle, and Ruskin. While those writers continue to advance the fundamental premise of earlier arguments that artistic expression and reception are components of an ethical enterprise that offers social stability, the relentless changes that had been taking place since the end of the previous century forced constant adjustments of the terms in which aesthetic experience could plausibly be described. According to Robin Gilmour, by 1850, "no one, not even the conservatives, believed that the old attitudes and institutional structures could be sustained without exposure to the spirit of the age: they might be reaffirmed or they might be overthrown, but they had to come to terms with the most significant intellectual development of the previous fifty years, which was the growth of the *expectation* of change."[73] The acknowledged inevitability of change helps to account for new expressions of the role of language and aesthetic experience in society around the middle of the century. The strident and confident assertions of Carlyle and Ruskin concerning the objective basis upon which art may be judged were seen to have less currency in a world beset by the "acid rain of historical relativism,"[74] a society that was coming to see itself driven by the impersonal agency of the process of natural selection "through random variations and towards no predetermined end."[75] Although both Carlyle and Ruskin were major influences on the thought of later Victorians, Arnold's theories also reflect his immersion in a culture that can no longer find solace in the accessibility of a fixed and unchanging Stoic order.

This shift can be seen as the reflection of a broader evolution in Victorian thought. Gerald L. Bruns argues that although Victorians largely continued to believe in the existence of a higher order, their awareness of themselves as participants in a historical progression of events made them less certain that life was under the benevolent control of a divine presence. He explains that many Victorians perceived themselves "as being in possession of not a cosmos but a history, not a transcendent system of laws or power of mind that synchronizes the levels of creation into universal harmony, but simply an irreversible succession of events."[76] Although Bruns identifies Carlyle as an early representative of this historical perspective, the evolution of language theories illustrates the increasing impact of the force of history on Victorian thought over the course of the century. In response to this trend, Arnold provides a bridge to fin de siècle figures such as Pater and Wilde by establishing criticism's inward turn, emphasizing the critical process that leads to perfection apart from the objective reality that Carlyle and Ruskin, as well as Cicero, the Stoics, and eighteenth-century theorists, had believed to lie at the heart of rhetorical communication.

Arnold by no means abandons the belief that an objective standard provides expression with its ethical force, but he shares the view of his contemporaries that a corrupt society threatens the pursuit of that truth. In Arnold's view, only a mental process detached from self-interested opinion provides the basis for the type of engagement with the world that can ultimately create new knowledge; his view that criticism takes form as "the play of the mind" strikingly resonates with De Quincey's notion that style should provide the basis for rhetorical invention. This type of criticism naturally depends upon the proper spirit of disinterestedness, a patient attitude that maintains a distance from "'the practical view of things.'"[77] In Arnold's view, criticism has both an analytical and communicative function, "simply to know the best that is known and thought in the world, and by in its turn making this known, to create a current of true and fresh ideas."[78] He goes on to add that, once criticism detaches itself from that which is "polemical and controversial," it can go on to attain its true purpose, leading humanity toward the perfection that comes from focusing upon "what is excellent in itself, and the absolute beauty and fitness of things."[79] Arnold therefore does share with the Stoics, Cicero, Quintilian, and eighteenth-century theorists the perception that moral improvement inevitably comes about through encounters with beauty and propriety.

However, Arnold's concerns about society heighten his interest in disinter-estedness as a resource in transcending a world in which the print media, too often controlled by self-interest, has come to dominate public discourse. He argues that materialism inhibits true criticism, for "our organs of criticism are organs of men and parties having practical ends to serve, and with them those practical ends are the first thing and the play of the mind the second."[80] In Arnold's view, the practical orientation of newspapers has fostered a cynical attitude in the public at large; in *Culture and Anarchy,* he denounces philoso-phies that claim "that there is no such thing at all as a best self and a right rea-son having claim to paramount authority,"[81] adding, "The great promoters of these philosophical theories are our newspaper, which, no less than our Parlia-mentary representatives, may be said to act the part of guides and governors to us."[82] Thus the pursuit of sensus communis becomes increasingly complicated by a public sphere that not only encourages competing perspectives but also includes the ascendancy of a press that hovers among all parties involved, sub-tly influencing them in ways that seem to lie outside anyone's control. Arnold expresses his despair over these conditions in an 1849 letter to Arthur Hugh Clough: "These are damned times—everything is against one—the height to which knowledge is come, the spread of luxury, our physical enervation, the absence of great *natures,* the unavoidable contact with millions of small ones, newspapers, cities, light profligate friends, moral desperadoes like Carlyle, our own selves, and the sickening consciousness of our difficulties; but for God's sake let us neither be fanatics nor yet chalf [*sic*] blown in the wind."[83] Arnold shares Shaftesbury's view that debate only exacerbates social problems, which involves the corollary view that society will benefit most from judgment reached through the disinterested search for knowledge that lies at the heart of the criti-cal enterprise. He recognizes that people often assess the relative merits of ideas only with respect to their utility in addressing existing political or material goals, which makes them unable to seek knowledge with the open minds necessary for self-improvement and discovery. The ability to engage freely in thinking about all subjects regardless of their immediate utility, to define "curiosity . . . as a high and fine quality of man's nature,"[84] ultimately leads the individual to the internal development that provides the basis for cultural transformation.

Although many of these ideas hearken to the Stoics, particularly as mediated through Shaftesbury and later eighteenth-century theorists, Arnold does not share their optimism concerning the rhetorical potential of sensus communis. Although Arnold's appreciation for the outcome of belletristic education has something in common with eighteenth-century theorists, his ultimate hope resides in cultural revitalization through the truth that resides in literary texts rather than through an interactive process that involves rhetorical encounters that negotiate the interpretation of those texts in keeping with standards embedded in nature and community life. Arnold's "disinterestedness" represents a deliberate departure from "an interested, rhetorical" way of dealing with ideas;[85] his lament that English literature has not yet produced a "supposed centre of correct information, correct judgment, correct taste"[86] stands in sharp contrast with earlier views that taste evolves over time and is inevitably shaped by social context. Arnold's famous definition of criticism as that which enables the disinterested individual to "see the object itself as it truly is" strikingly resonates with Thomas Sprat's goal of devising a discipline dedicated to the pursuit of "uninterested Truth." Hans-George Gadamer attributes the shifting ideas of taste to the influence of Immanuel Kant's *Critique of Judgment,* which transformed belletristic conceptions of taste as an element of sensus communis to a view of taste as an independent process that replaces the negotiated political interests of the community with an autonomous aesthetic judgment.[87] Arnold's perspective on criticism participates in this nineteenth-century trend, which shifts taste from its grounding as an interested ethical enterprise to the realm of pure beauty, which ideally removes cultured individuals from the worldly confusion that might destroy their objectivity. Arnold does not acknowledge it, but his version of criticism must be seen as a scientific enterprise that removes aesthetic experience from the rhetorical pursuit of sensus communis.

Although Arnold strongly believes that culture possesses a moral component, he replaces the critic's role of engaging with society with the notion that moral strength develops through a more subtle process of cultural indoctrination. Arnold's thought signals the transition to the fin de siècle by representing the ideal of the critic who acquires cultural authority through a perspective that transcends the self-interest of the industrial world and facilitates the gradual discovery of truth through a cultural search for perfection. In the process, he shifts the focus of criticism from message to attitude, as he transcends the Carlylean claim that the hero is obligated above all to proclaim the truth by arguing that society's redemption can best be effected by those who demonstrate an intellectual outlook that will promote a superior understanding of culture.

Fin de Siècle Aestheticism and the Death of Sensus Communis

A number of language theories at the end of the nineteenth century build upon this insight in their adherence to the notion of perfection through culture rather than community. The ethical commitments of these theories generally depart in dramatic ways from the rhetorical enactment of sensus communis. Theorists such as Walter Pater continue to emphasize the cultural conditions that give rise to criticism. However, Pater insists that critical insights develop most fully under "the comparatively inexplicable force of a personality, resistant to, while it is moulded by, them."[88] Although he acknowledges that changing circumstances inevitably affect the formation of personality, Pater at the same time maintains that personality derives its own strength and ultimately becomes a force that cannot be contained, due to its flexibility in responding to the fluid conditions that surround the individual. Ethos that is self-consciously based upon this "inexplicable force" therefore establishes for later theorists a foundation that is necessarily unstable and incoherent; when Wilde points out that "what people call insincerity is simply a method by which we can multiply our personalities,"[89] he is also articulating the final rejection of the Stoic pursuit of natural harmony and social unity that characterizes British aesthetic theories at the end of the nineteenth century. Because personality can be multiplied, even the perspectives of theorists shift as they channel the force of their own personalities to respond to different exigencies—a development that grants them a degree of liberty that had not been enjoyed by those writers whose philosophical positions placed them under an obligation to an ethos grounded in external truth.

Thus the freedom that theorists late in the century assume through the flexibility of personality generates not only theoretical perspectives but also identities that can be adapted to particular moments in time. This flexibility further complicates the ambivalent relationships between the prophets of culture and the public that they simultaneously renounce and rely upon for their validation. Many eighteenth-century and early nineteenth-century writers assumed responsibility for educating their society about the insights they had achieved through their awareness of ethical principles found in the natural order. By the latter decades of the nineteenth century, the entrenched social changes brought on by industrialism led theorists to identify society's central weakness not as a changeable character that had led to a detachment from nature but as a rigid and monolithic defiance of nature and personal agency. Fin de siècle theorists rejected earlier notions of an externally ordained moral code, choosing instead to confront society's misguided values on their own terms; they offered aesthetic experience not as the vehicle for achieving sensus communis but as a liberatory and supple alternative to the uncompromising austerity of industrial society. Within their secular framework, redemption comes not from the certainty of a divine order but from the fluidity of personality catalyzed through cultivated aesthetic experiences.

The unresolved conflicts constantly present in aestheticism are therefore consciously invoked as the century ends—a move that lies at the heart of the notion of Decadence associated with that period. Ruth Robbins defines Decadent aesthetics as "an attitude exhibited towards contradiction,"[90] a willingness to accept the logical flaw in using language, "an inconsistent and time-bound tool,"[91] for the purpose of achieving an idealized realm that lies outside the bounds of time. Robbins identifies "the site of Decadence"[92] as the acknowledged tension between the terms established within a number of binary relationships—real and ideal, instability and truth, worldly and eternal. The aestheticism of the 1880s and 1890s therefore converges around an ideological position that values instability, a point Jonathan Freedman underscores in arguing that "the defining quality of British aestheticism—the only way these various and distinctive writers and artists may be seen to share any characteristic at all—is the desire to embrace contradictions, indeed the desire to seek them out the better to play with the possibilities they afford."[93] Fin de siècle theorists are not totally devoid of the idealism of those writers who precede them, but their vision is complicated by their open recognition of the problematic nature of any effort to define and enact moral judgments. Their recognition of and appreciation for contradiction contrast sharply with the Stoic search for order, harmony, and unity that had maintained a hold on language theorists throughout the preceding century.

In Robbins's view, the deliberate appropriation of the contradictions implicit in aestheticism constitutes for the Decadent aesthetes a challenge to "that attitude which belongs to the male heterosexual middle classes, the individuals who make up the speakers and ideologues of dominant discourse."[94] Cultural conditions at the end of the century placed in strong relief the social fissures that had always existed; intellectuals such as Pater, Wilde, and Vernon Lee insisted upon reconceiving the boundaries of appropriate conduct and discursive practices within their society, seeking to devise notions of language that could subvert the oppressive social structures that they experienced in different ways.

The writings of Pater, Lee, and Wilde in some respects reveal the continuation of the long-standing search for sensus communis. Freedman notes that aestheticism explores cultural contradictions "without abandoning the option of contradicting contradiction itself, without the loss of the nostalgia for a lost unity and the desire to project such a unity into the vision of a future consummation."[95] However, these writers faced the difficult task of locating that source of shared understanding apart both from the divine realm they had rejected and from the community that restricted their participation in public life. They responded to this dilemma by validating an internal aesthetic sense that facilitates the development of a consciousness that transcends the limitations surrounding ordinary human experience. This principle of late Victorian aestheticism in some respects parallels the eighteenth-century notion that the development of the intuitive capacity of taste involves the individual in a natural relationship with other people who share the same innate gift. However, the subjectivity that lies at the heart of this version of aestheticism maintains a radically subversive tenor, involving neither the straightforward idealism associated with earlier visions of civic virtue nor the total retreat from society into an idealized world that is stereotypically identified as the end of "art for art's sake" aestheticism. Pater, Lee, and Wilde advocate aesthetic experience that simultaneously withdraws from and confronts society, willingly offering themselves as examples of the unreconciled opposition between aesthetic experience as a vehicle for cultural criticism and the commodification of art and criticism. Under their guidance, the common ethical bond of humanity becomes expressed in terms of the particularity that individuals discover within themselves through their experience with beauty. Although aesthetic experience is shared with others, the intense individualism of their doctrine leaves people free from confusing sensus communis with conformity to their society's established moral system.

Pater's thought is clearly connected with Arnold's, then, through his advocacy of a disinterested critical temperament, his emphasis upon the life of aesthetic contemplation above political action, and his hope for a refined culture that assumes the place that at one time had been occupied by religion. Graham Hough acknowledges the philosophical link between Arnold and Pater, illustrated by the view of T. S. Eliot and others that both writers attempt "to usurp the throne of religion and put culture in its place."[96] However, Hough goes on to note the contrast between the two: "Pater has none of Arnold's nostalgia for the age of faith; on the contrary, he quite complacently identifies himself with modernity; he has none of Arnold's longing for certitude; instead, he shows considerable willingness to involve himself in the flux."[97] Although Pater's questions about religion parallel Arnold's effort to redefine redemption in terms of a secular culture, the exigencies of his own temperament and experience, as well as the circumstances of life in the latter half of the century, prompt him to remove himself further from what both men perceived to be an outdated spiritual ideal.

Certainly Pater's contemporaries perceived this attitude as a marked departure from the accepted religious standards of their society. His radicalism is most evident in one of his earliest and most controversial works, *The Renaissance: Studies in Art and Poetry* (1873), which Gerald Monsman and Samuel

Wright characterize as "the manifesto of the Aesthetic Movement,"[98] and Wilde repeatedly cites as a major influence on his subsequent thought. In an 1873 letter following the publication of that book, John Wordsworth expresses his personal regret at the necessity of criticizing Pater's work but adds, "After a perusal of the book I cannot disguise from myself that the concluding pages adequately sum up the philosophy of the whole; and that that philosophy is an assertion, that no fixed principles either of religion or of morality can be regarded as certain, that the only thing worth living for is momentary enjoyment and that probably or certainly the soul dissolves at death into elements which are destined never to reunite."[99] Pater's work can therefore be seen as a departure from Arnold's cultural ideal due to Pater's more absolute break from the fundamental principles that had previously defined British culture, a schism that leads him more completely to immerse himself in what he perceived to be the redemptive intensity of momentary experience.

This momentary and exclusively personal notion of aesthetic experience represents a marked departure from the social orientation embedded in the eighteenth century's rhetorical appropriation of Cicero and Stoic ethics. Pater's notion that beauty must be experienced rather than merely discussed eliminates the role of language in negotiating standards of beauty, a crucial premise of eighteenth-century theories of taste; he posits a recipient of aesthetic experience who makes judgments that are completely independent of others. Pater begins his preface to *The Renaissance* with his agreement with Arnold's belief that the goal of criticism is "to see the object as in itself it really is," but he adds that it is only possible to achieve such a certain sense of that object through determining the impression it makes on oneself. The facts that lie within the critic's province are therefore derived from questions about his or her impressions of the art object: "What is this song or picture, this engaging personality presented in life or in a book, *to me?* What effects does it really produce on me? Does it give me pleasure? And if so, what sort of degree of pleasure? How is my nature modified by its presence, and under its influence?"[100]

A number of critics have noted the crucial alteration of Arnold's doctrine of criticism that Pater effects in this passage, from one that emphasizes the obligation to come to terms with art as an objective external reality to one that instead defines the encounter with art in purely subjective terms. Jay B. Losey notes that Pater breaks new theoretical ground in that he "shifts the critic's mode of perception and argues that the impression produced by the object is more significant than the object itself."[101] In Losey's view, this move "makes him a significant contributor to Victorian thought"[102] through making the principles of the French "art for art's sake" movement present in English aesthetic theory.[103] Jesse Matz echoes this view, explaining that Pater's shift from criticism focused on an objective assessment of artistic expression to criticism represented as the discovery of one's own impression "is otherwise and better known as the first misstep down the slippery slope of Decadence."[104] Pater's doctrine clearly encourages this interpretation, as he insists that criticism must be viewed as a solitary endeavor, placing individuals in "intellectual isolation" from each other.[105] Pater's intensely personal exploration of feeling stands in sharp contrast to Smith's idea of communicable sentiments and illustrates the dramatic late nineteenth-century shift away from the ideal of a common aesthetic and ethical sense.

It is this same quality of intense individual experience that Pater advocates in the conclusion to *The Renaissance,* the document Steven Marcus refers to as the "specimen text of modernism."[106] Pater stresses the value of experience for its own sake, insisting upon the need to replace the pursuit of theories and conventional knowledge with "the splendour of our experience and of its awful brevity, gathering all we are into one desperate effort to see and touch."[107] As David Bromwich points out, this emphasis on the immediacy of experiences again modifies Pater's appropriation of Arnoldian disinterestedness, for it requires "an attitude not of patient humility before a given object, but passionate apprehension of a chosen one."[108] Pater's famous line "To burn always with this hard, gemlike flame, to maintain this ecstasy, is success in life"[109] has rightly come to be viewed as a summation of his own subjective approach to aestheticism and as the starting point for Wilde's even more radical view that an individual's experience with art transcends life and therefore cannot be prescribed by standards grounded in nature.

Thus Pater builds on a long-standing line of thought that connects aesthetic apprehension to an individual's development, but his radical subjectivity effectively eliminates the Ciceronian and Stoic strains that had connected this development to language and the development of sensus communis. A number of scholars have aptly pointed out that Pater's theory does maintain a certain interest in the social. Linda Dowling observes that Pater envisions "the social transformation of Victorian life through an enlarged and emboldened sensuousness —his own version of the liberal ideal of aesthetic democracy,"[110] and Jennifer Uglow qualifies her assessment that Pater emphasizes the value of culture for the individual soul with an insistence that he cannot be considered a proponent of "art for art's sake."[111] Yet, while Pater's view that the individual's cultivation holds some social benefit does have certain tenets in common with eighteenth-century rhetorical theories, he departs from those precedents in his determination to place the imaginative intuition in direct opposition to what Uglow describes as "the rational philosophy and codified standards of taste of the eighteenth century."[112] Dowling identifies Pater's process description of the individual's intuitive development as an insular, private as a sharp departure from belletristic rhetorical theories that participate in a long tradition of assuming that society can be transformed through the development of a common aesthetic sense.

Pater does modify his position over the course of his life. Billie Andrew Inman argues that Pater's responsiveness to the reader causes a shift in Pater's style from the radicalism of the conclusion to *The Renaissance* to the more traditional view espoused in *Marius the Epicurean.*[113] Twenty years after publication of *The Renaissance,* Pater certainly appears to reclaim a belief in some degree of shared understanding in *Plato and Platonism,* an unconventional interpretation of Plato, as shown in a passage that appears to invoke the vocabulary of Stoic and eighteenth-century thought.

> There is a general consciousness, a permanent common sense, independent indeed of each one of us, but with which we are, each one of us, in communication. It is in that, those common or general ideas really reside. And we might add just here . . . that those abstract or common notions come to the individual mind through language, through common or general names, *Animal, Justice, Equality,* into which one's individual experience, little by little, drop by drop, conveys their full meaning or content. . . . Between our individual experience and the common experience of our kind, we come to understand each other, and to assist each other's thoughts, as in a common mental atmosphere, an "intellectual world," as Plato calls it.[114]

However, it is significant that Pater's invocation to "common sense" is placed within a framework of what he describes as a Platonic "intellectual world," which differs from the Ciceronian vision of a community established in nature and strengthened through skillful, sympathetic, and ethical language use. Pater's direct engagement with Stoic thought in *Marius the Epicurean* similarly focuses on the individual's capacity to achieve a transcendent vision, which is in keeping with key Stoic principles but emphasizes the intensely inward nature of that experience without attention to the social commitment that is central to Roman Stoicism, advanced and developed through Cicero and Quintilian, and adapted as a consistent strain of eighteenth-century rhetorical theories.

For Pater, then, inner vision removes enlightened individuals from the corruption of society, rather than obligating them to engage with it as committed citizens. Although he invokes something of the idea of sensus communis in *Plato and Platonism,* he cites Plato in defining his ultimate goal as the establishment of "a very exclusive community, which shall be a refuge for elect souls from an ill-made world."[115] Such a refuge seems to be compelling for both Lee, whose emphasis on artistic appreciation as a contemplative process divorced from the world of action also reveals an intellectual debt to Pater, and Wilde, whose alienation from society encourages a view of art that stands in more complete opposition to ordinary life: "Art finds her own perfection within, and not outside of, herself. She is not to be judged by any external standard of resemblance."[116]

Vernon Lee provides a rare example of a woman engaged in nineteenth-century conversations about aesthetic theory. That position provides her with a unique perspective on the objectives and inherent conflicts that constitute late Victorian aesthetic and language theories—a perspective that was not always appreciated by her contemporaries. Lee's activism exposed her to conflict on a regular basis, and she draws upon that experience in articulating the potential role of aesthetic experience in transforming society. Like Pater, Lee defines aesthetic appreciation as an internal process that must in some respects be unique to the individual. This point of view reflects the relativism she also holds in common with Pater; she maintains that "we have learned that we human creatures shall never know the absolute or the essence, that notions, which Plato took for realities, are mere relative conceptions."[117] In contrast with the Stoic emphasis on the need to cultivate an awareness of an external order, Lee argues that the benefit to be received from beauty comes about not through its embodiment of a particular external reality but through the internal process that the individual experiences in the presence of beauty.

This process possesses the advantage of resisting the incursion of external authority that might restrict the individual's freedom of judgment. Lee identifies style, which she defines as "the organic correspondence between the various parts of a work of art, the functional interchange and interdependence thereof,"[118] as the central basis for artistic appreciation. Offering the personal assessment of art's organic functionality as an alternative to external judgments about its quality, Lee argues that style intrinsically depends upon individual judgment, for "there is no *style* when people set to building pseudo-Gothic in obedience to the Romantic movement and to Ruskin."[119] Rather than acquiring things that are conventionally considered beautiful, Lee insists that people should strive to cultivate "the habit of beauty . . . engrained in our nature by the unnoticed experiences of centuries, of *life* in our surroundings and in ourselves."[120] In keeping with Pater's philosophy, Lee insists upon an awareness of beauty that evolves through the individual's commitment to a heightened consciousness that is largely independent of external constraints.

In certain respects, Lee maintains the connection between aesthetics and ethics that had provided one link between eighteenth-century rhetorical theorists and Stoic thought, as she contends that true aesthetic experience inevitably leads to "preference of the spiritual, the unconditional, the durable, to the temporal, the uncertain, and the fleeting"[121] and cultivates the desire to invest "our life into the life universal."[122] She also sustains the view that this "life universal" is possible through qualities endemic to human nature, including "the instinct of congruity, of subordination of part to whole, the desire for harmony which is fostered above all things by art."[123] In Lee's view, the human capacity to appreciate art enables people to accommodate their natural need for harmony through art as well as life, a process she refers to as "empathy" and that encompasses the imagination, sympathy, and the way in which people interpret the world through their own experience.[124]

However, Lee has particular reasons for departing from other fundamental eighteenth-century perspectives. Eighteenth-century theorists had argued for definitions of beauty grounded in fitness, propriety, and usefulness, which perpetuated classical and Stoic links among language, aesthetics, and ethics—a network that provides a foundation for the argument for sensus communis. In concert with other nineteenth-century language theorists, Lee's suspicion of the industrial world prompts her to challenge the value of fitness, which has come to be associated with modern efficiency and utilitarianism, by asserting the worth of that which cannot immediately be put to practical use. She objects to any claim that beauty should be aligned with goodness, because she perceives the term *good* to connote "satisfactory in the way of use and advantage."[125] She notes, "Life hurries us into recognizing *Things*" rather than allowing us to enjoy the beautiful "aspects" of those things;[126] the "practical man" and "man of science" are so concerned with results and action, with "what might be done and of how it had all come about" that they are unable to enjoy beauty in itself.[127] Thus Lee's "psychological aesthetics"[128] emphasizes the process by which individual perceptions are enhanced through contemplating beautiful objects.

Lee's endorsement of a universal appreciation for harmony hearkens back to earlier iterations of Stoic principles, but her optimistic assessment of universal standards exists in striking tension with her insistence upon subjective standards of aesthetic judgment, an opposition that reflects the contradictions of fin de siècle aestheticism. Robbins argues, "Vernon Lee's writings constantly exhibit contradictory attitudes" central to Decadent aestheticism.[129] Lee's construction of her own identity provides one example of her commitment to Decadent instability. René Wellek notes that Lee's rejection of "the Ruskinian morality of art" includes the radical view that "artistic and private personality need not be the same,"[130] a view that is also evident in Wilde's work. John McGowan's characterization of Wilde as an "emblematic figure of the attempt to wriggle out from under Victorian earnestness"[131] seems particularly apt in examining Wilde's statements about the relationship between art and nature. Wilde reverses the argument made by the Stoics, Cicero, Shaftesbury, and commonsense rhetoricians who argue that beauty reflects and makes accessible the harmony found in the natural world, insisting instead that art should be seen as "our spirited protest, our gallant attempt to teach Nature her proper place."[132] He further claims that the concept of "the infinite variety of Nature" does not exist but actually "resides in the imagination, or fancy, or cultivated blindness of the man who looks at her."[133] Art has no obligation to represent the truth of life; in Wilde's view, "Life imitates art far more than Art imitates life."[134]

Wilde builds on the foundation of Pater's skepticism about the integrity of "the object" posited by Arnold's ideal for criticism; he agrees with Pater that any knowledge of an object must be subjective, additionally noting that Arnold's error in seeking more objective knowledge reflects a failure to recognize the nature of "criticism's most perfect form, which is in its essence purely subjective, and seeks to reveal its own secret and not the secret of another."[135] Thus Pater's more tentative assertion that subjective impression might serve as a limitation on Arnoldian criticism crystallizes as a major critique under Wilde's creed of artistic autonomy.

Like both Pater and Arnold, Wilde insists upon drawing a distinction between art and practical activity. Although society demands "productive labour,"[136] art exists apart from the demands of practical life and exists for the sake of emotion. However, the quality of that emotion assumes a new dimension for Wilde, who argues that art "is superbly sterile, and the note of its pleasure is sterility. If the contemplation of a work of art is followed by activity of any kind, the work is either of a very second-rate order, or the spectator has failed to realize the complete artistic impression."[137] Although he essentially agrees with Pater concerning the need for artistic contemplation, his language does not convey the element of passion that Pater advocates in speaking of the "hard, gemlike flame" of momentary experience but instead reflects a serene withdrawal into a world of beauty that reflects Wilde's expansion of Pater's thought. As Wendell Harris notes, after accepting Pater's relativism and subjectivism, Wilde inverts Pater's views in order to suggest that "the critical spirit, through its very creativity, can get outside the individual consciousness that Pater so eloquently describes."[138] Although Wilde shares Pater's view that creativity begins with individual experience, his own version of the subjectivity of art ultimately transcends even the intensity of individual identity. Wilde's awareness of the complexity of the human personality leads him to move beyond Pater's exploration of the individual's deep and sincere response to art. Like other nineteenth-century critics, he believes that materialism has corrupted industrial society, arguing that economic concerns have come to dominate human life and have limited "the full expression of a personality"[139] through encouraging people to focus on the accumulation of property. He insists that humanity must no longer be "the slave of machinery"[140] but must instead enlist machinery in the service of humanity so that people can be free to do their rightful work of creating beauty.[141]

Wilde also advances strident criticisms of the press that reflect the nineteenth century's ongoing difficulty with defining the parameters of public discourse. He perceives society to operate in a vicious cycle in which journalists promote the worst impulses of the public. In "The Soul of Man under Social-ism," he writes, "The fact is, that the public have an insatiable curiosity to know everything, except what is worth knowing. Journalism, conscious of this, and having tradesmanlike habits, supplies their demands."[142] He maintains that journalism inevitably has a negative impact on the true artist not only because it lowers the level of civic discourse through satisfying the public's worst instincts but also because it serves as a mouthpiece for those who would restrict artistic freedom. After insisting in "The Critic as Artist" that art and ethics should not be viewed as dependent on each other, Wilde adds that "though our modern Puritans cannot destroy a beautiful thing, yet, by means of their extraordinary prurience, they can almost taint beauty for a moment. It is chiefly, I regret to say, through journalism that such people find expression."[143] In "The Soul of Man," he returns to this theme, as he laments, "In France . . . they limit the journalist, and allow the artist almost perfect freedom. *Here we allow absolute freedom to the journalist, and entirely limit the artist.*"[144]

Wilde's frustration with the press in part reflects an economic concern aris-ing from his awareness of its power to control public opinion of his own artis-tic production. His expression of this problem highlights the surfacing late in the century of some of the tensions inherent in aesthetic theories—tensions that eighteenth-century theorists had failed to acknowledge or perhaps delib-erately suppressed. Much of the traditional English vision of the redemptive capacity of art had relied upon glossing over its properties as commodity. In describing the way in which artistic images of rural scenes functioned both as commodities and cultural artifacts during the early nineteenth century, Eliza-beth K. Helsinger notes that "the nation imagined as market and the nation imagined as audience are understood as different kinds of collectivity—the latter, especially, often recognizes and resists the former."[145] Wilde delights in challenging this well-entrenched pattern, as he openly confronts the commod-ification of art and acknowledges his own complicity in it. He forces people to recognize his own artistic endeavors as partly related to his desire for pros-perity; after admitting to a friend that he is sometimes attracted by the "earnest-ness and purity" of religion, he concludes that he cannot convert to Catholicism since that would obligate him to abandon the "two great gods 'Money and Ambition.'"[146] Wilde's deliberate commodification of himself forces society's reassessment of its established mode of viewing art, part of his argument that the artist and critic must assert control over art in a society that values all the wrong things.

One of Wilde's vehicles for asserting this control lies in his emphasis on personality, which Robbins identifies as a term that refers "not to the essential being but to a role which can be assumed and cast off at will."[147] For Wilde, the ultimate goal of aesthetic experience is not to enable people to discover a unified essence within themselves but to move outside themselves in order to explore new identities. In Wilde's view, the adoption of masks provides people with the only means of self-realization, because masks enable them to conceal aspects of their identities that have been externally imposed upon them, replacing a false reality with a truer one comprising fictions of their own creation. Wilde's letters from his tour of America reveal that, at least initially, he reveled in shaping his identity in response to the public taste. In an 1882 letter, he requests that his American agent go to a costumier to purchase the requisite wardrobe items: "Two coats . . . they should be beautiful; tight velvet doublet, with large flowered sleeves and little ruffs of cambric coming under the collar. . . . The sleeves are to be flowered—if not velvet then plush—stamped with large pattern. They will excite a great sensation. . . . They were dreadfully disappointed at Cincinnati at my not wearing knee-breeches."[148]

Wilde's appropriation of a persona largely responsive to the audience's expectations marks his willingness to adapt his rhetoric to the constraints of the moment without regard for consistency, a strategy that he deliberately adopts in protesting "Victorian utility, rationality, scientific factuality, and technological progress."[149] Ian Small argues that Wilde's radicalism lies not in the content of his writings but in his method, as his texts undermine the "search for consistency, originality, and authority"[150] that he recognized as forming the basis for Victorian reading practices. Wilde himself is the first to acknowledge his effort to confound society with his posturing, as he reveals in an 1894 letter to Philip Houghton: "To the world I seem, by intention on my part, a dilettante and dandy merely—it is not wise to show one's heart to the world—and as seriousness of manner is the disguise of the fool, folly in its exquisite modes of triviality and indifference and lack of care is the robe of the wise man. In so vulgar an age as this we all need masks."[151] For Wilde, the mask becomes the vehicle for a desperate attempt to maintain control over his own identity in the face of a society that could not bear to see him as he really was.

Ironically the control over personality that Wilde seeks to achieve is only possible through his accommodation to the very public that he ostensibly despises. The problem Wilde faces is that his attempt to control his artistic identity through complying with the public's expectations sometimes stifles his art; in an 1883 letter to R. H. Sherard, he laments that the social life he has been leading as a London sensation has prevented him from writing and concludes, "I wish I was back in Paris, where I did such good work. However, society must be amazed, and my Neronian coiffure has amazed it."[152] Meanwhile, Wilde's manifesto for artistic autonomy completes the gradual transformation of ethos from the sincerity of the Stoic and belletristic traditions to the ironic detachment of Matthew Arnold and finally to a masked representation of an artistic identity that potentially overwhelms the artist himself. The Stoic goal of propriety grounded in individual integrity and directed outward toward sympathetic relationships with others is radically transformed in Wilde's masks.

Wilde's theory reflects the late nineteenth century's rejection of the stability that eighteenth-century theorists had sought in the Stoic ethical system. Wilde replaces sensus communis with a more radical version of Pater's ideal of an intellectual community removed from the mundane affairs of daily life, identifying in the artist's role a defensive rejection of the rhetorical world of production. Wilde's theory exhibits the loss of all vestiges of hope for a sensus communis that can facilitate society's reformation through the community's ongoing interactions.

As the nineteenth century draws to a close, so does the trace of the eighteenth-century view that rhetoric can help to preserve Stoic intersections among the natural order, disciplined individuals, and sensus communis. Nineteenth-century writers have varied reasons for questioning the motives that govern the type of discipline that eighteenth-century writers invoked. Their characterization of rhetorical instruction as prescriptive and their resistance to technology and industry led them to view rhetoric as contributing to society's problems rather than constructively addressing them. While the pursuit of sensus communis had always included the recognition that particular societies inevitably fall short of its promise, many nineteenth-century intellectuals recognized that eighteenth-century assumptions about universal values were no longer tenable. Theorists such as Pater, Lee, and Wilde rejected the notion of collectively negotiating values, advocating instead a withdrawal into a subjective realm of judgment, "a refuge for elect souls."

Earlier versions of nineteenth-century British rhetoric can be seen as reflecting the changing conception of ethos that S. Michael Halloran identifies as a feature of rhetoric's transition to the modern era. According to Halloran, ethos in classical rhetoric "consisted in the degree to which the speaker embodied the virtues most revered by the culture,"[153] but as modern fragmentation increasingly calls shared cultural values into question, ethos instead "is generated by the seriousness and passion with which the speaker articulates his own world."[154] In some respects, eighteenth-century rhetorical theorists both supported and resisted this shift, drawing upon Stoic ideas in order to maintain the notion of an ethos grounded in sensus communis, in contrast with the individualistic ethos that had gained significant ground during the seventeenth century. However, De Quincey and Carlyle more fully exemplify the transformation that Halloran describes, as they define rhetoric as socially transformative through the agency of gifted individuals. De Quincey's argument for rhetoric defined by intellectual play is distinct from Carlyle's sermonic appeals, but both perceive rhetoric as performing the serious task of reforming a hostile world through the individual's rhetorical agency.

By the end of the century, major theorists call into question the value of "seriousness and passion" in a society so fragmented that sincerity can no longer provide the basis for a stable ethos. Wilde's insistence on fiction's superiority to fact and his reliance upon masks that convey a truth deeper than reality demonstrate a further shift beyond the ethos of authentic personal vision Halloran describes. The conflicts present in this shift highlight the internal tensions that pervade nineteenth-century attempts to replace the elusive image of sensus communis with visions grounded in individual subjectivities. This transformation reflects the nineteenth-century rejection of the Stoic foundations of community and nature. Walter J. Ong argues that opposition to nature is an intrinsic function of a technological age even among those who attempt to challenge technology. In *Rhetoric, Romance, and Technology*, Ong maintains that technology plays a fundamental role in Romantic notions of the individual whose vision surpasses the commonplaces that had grounded knowledge in oratorical cultures, arguing that Romanticism and technology can be seen as "mirror images of each other, both being products of man's dominance over nature and of the noetic abundance which had been created by chirographic and typographic techniques of storing and retrieving knowledge and which had made this dominance over nature possible."[155] This view complicates the Romantic affiliation with nature, just as the practical need to commodify knowledge through the press exists in tension with arguments for the purity of the individual's vision.

Theorists early in the nineteenth century attempt to circumvent these complications. Carlyle's strident claims and De Quincey's elaborate exploration of opposing perspectives represent rhetorical strategies that question the optimism of sensus communis but still hold out hope for language's power to generate vibrant ideas that can revitalize a stagnant society. At the end of the century, language theorists acknowledge and even embrace the deep conflicts that emerge in the midst of efforts to resolve social problems, as their identities and intellectual interests lead them to recognize the oppressive potential inherent in the universal values that sensus communis assumes. Their use of paradox underscores their deliberate rejection of the apparent coherence of modern society— a rejection that includes a detachment from the rhetorical engagement that had maintained a tenuous presence in the writings of theorists earlier in the century. The final decline of nineteenth-century British rhetoric comes about in intellectual discourse that creates a "refuge for elect souls" strategically detached from civic life.

CONCLUSION

Eighteenth-century rhetoricians drew upon Stoic ethical philosophies, including their adaptations by Cicero and Quintilian, in order to respond to a complicated array of contemporary questions concerning the individual's relationship with society. These theorists found in Stoic thought a potential remedy for self-interest and individual isolation. The Stoic vision of a higher reality found in the natural order, available to people individually but necessarily bringing them together in fulfillment of a divinely ordained human community, was variously conceived as an alternative to the cynicism of Thomas Hobbes, the esoteric philosophies of John Locke and David Hume, scientific materialism and rationalism, and a bourgeois value system emphasizing individual accomplishment. The classical training of eighteenth-century theorists not only facilitated their turn to Stoic thought but also supported their view that language held the key to the vibrant community life they held as their ideal. Consequently their appropriation of Stoic ethics, alongside the rhetorical theories of Cicero and Quintilian, led them to generate theories of rhetoric and language based in character development and aimed at fostering sensus communis. That this represents a departure from a classical tradition focused on rhetoric's function in resolving immediate public questions in the law courts and legislative assemblies helps to illuminate the diverse ways in which rhetoric's civic work has been conceived across centuries of its development.

Such variations are inevitable in light of rhetoric's flexibility in responding to social change. Given the nature of the changes taking place in the eighteenth century, it is neither surprising that rhetoric would respond to that change nor that it would do so in a way that would remain firmly situated in the classical thought in which eighteenth-century intellectuals were steeped. Much textual evidence indicates that eighteenth-century rhetorical theorists were attentive to the implications of the social change that surrounded them, including uncertain boundaries between oral and written discourse, public and private life, scientific insight and religious belief, and technology and personal agency. Their use of a Stoic framework reflected the way they had been trained to view the world. Through fusing ancient and modern ideas, the theorists examined in this book sought security in the midst of social change even as they assured themselves that they were participating in modern progress. Their appropriation of Stoic thought helped them emphasize the importance of community in spite of a growing trend toward individualism, an outgrowth of a conservative impulse to strengthen earlier British claims concerning the relationship between civic virtue and the rhetorical proficiency of individuals. Classical rhetorical theories offered some guidance in their effort to strengthen this link, but British theorists found in Stoic ethics an important philosophical foundation for articulating the relationship between private deliberation and public discourse, a foundation that gained particular rhetorical force through appropriations of Stoic ideas found in the writings of Cicero and Quintilian. Understanding the presence of Stoic thought in eighteenth-century theories that seek to account for the public significance of private perception helps to elucidate the civic commitment that pervades rhetoric's apparent inward turn during this period, along with revealing more fully the ancient roots of ideas that contemporary scholars have often interpreted as reflecting a more fully modern perspective.

In arguing that eighteenth-century British rhetorical theories are significantly shaped by Stoic ethics, this book seeks to complicate existing narratives of British rhetorical history. Exploring the rhetorical significance of this apparently antirhetorical philosophical strain within British rhetorical theories of this period highlights the complexity that surrounds rhetoric's evolution and offers a more complete understanding of the philosophical principles that undergird this transitional moment in the history of British rhetoric. The complex evolution of thought about rhetoric's civic role resists a straightforward assessment of the nature of rhetoric's transformation during the late eighteenth and early nineteenth centuries. Thomas Miller acknowledges the connection between eighteenth-century rhetorical theories and Stoic thought but suggests that this connection provides evidence of the eighteenth century's turn away from traditional rhetoric. Miller's statement that "the Stoics helped to create a context in which the individual could be conceived apart from his, or even her, public duties"[1] assumes a direct opposition between the model of individual and civic refinement emphasized in eighteenth-century rhetorical theories and the civic debate taught in much of the classical rhetorical canon. However, this assessment assumes distinct boundaries between public and private life that neither the Stoics nor eighteenth-century theorists would have accepted. It also defines rhetoric in terms grounded in a particular classical model of civic action achieved through the use of agonistic discourse. The civic orientation of Stoic ethics and its presence in the rhetorical theories of Cicero and Quintilian reveals that eighteenth-century developments in British rhetoric by no means remove individuals from a commitment to public life but maintain this commitment through emphasizing rhetoric's transformative role in cultivating public and private virtue. Eighteenth-century theorists' use of Stoic thought for the demands of a new era involved pointing toward the potential for deeper significance embedded in contemporary terms such as common sense, taste, sympathy, and propriety and revealing how the notion of a culture of politeness could be incorporated into the goals of social awareness and cultural agreement. Although this vision of rhetoric departs from important classical models that involve direct negotiation about matters of civic importance, it offers an alternative model that emphasizes relationship and a strengthened community as a necessary foundation for social stability.

In addition to offering an alternative interpretation of British rhetoric's history, the study of the Stoic presence in rhetoric's history leads to a more complete understanding of the intellectual strains that inform developments in the history of rhetoric. This inquiry is particularly useful in exploring the histories of both rhetoric and philosophy, as it illustrates the complex interplay between those disciplines from the classical period forward. Additionally this insight into this significant era in the history of rhetorical studies ultimately creates a more nuanced view of the factors that have helped to shape developments in literary and rhetorical theories and pedagogy in the United States. This study of this period challenges contemporary tendencies to assume that the elevation of individualistic expression can be defined as a discrete turning point that occurred at one moment in rhetoric's history. In fact, the tenacity with which eighteenth-century British intellectuals clung to Stoic expressions of the intrinsic connections between the individual and society, even as they participated in a cultural shift that was increasingly oriented toward personal knowledge and agency, illustrates rhetoric's very gradual transformation in response to the practical demands of modern industrial society.

The link between Stoic thought and eighteenth-century rhetorical theories also illustrates the pervasive presence of the past in the evolution of rhetorical history. Enlightenment thinkers were certainly committed to full participation in intellectual advances made possible through modern scientific and philosophical discoveries, but they nevertheless integrated these modern developments with ancient principles that they found compelling. At the same time, their uses of Stoicism involved interpretations and the development of a vocabulary that were unique to their particular era. The examination of the dynamic interplay between past and present in the work of these theorists points toward ways in which later appropriations of the past simultaneously celebrate history and alter its terms for the purposes of the present.

There is no question that the lofty philosophical principles of many eighteenth-century theorists stand in stark contrast with the reality of what their theories represent in practice. The goal of a harmonious society embodied in the Stoic notion of sensus communis might sound compelling, until one asks what voices that apparent harmony obliterates and how many perspectives are dismissed as idiosyncratic because they seem to have no place in common sense. Exclusionary discourses are by no means justified simply because they have complex philosophical roots; however, developing an awareness of those roots can at least help to bring into focus the objectives that guide those discourses and can provide the basis for a more sensitive understanding of the complicated network of ideas that helped to obscure the problematic nature of those discourses.

Such an understanding can also encourage reflective examination of current perspectives on the relationship between rhetoric and society. There is a long and complex history surrounding rhetoric's perceived capacity to promote individual and social objectives. The values of individual autonomy and the emphasis on rights that pervade contemporary discourse have not always been seen as central priorities, and this insight is in itself useful in efforts to consider alternatives to current ways of thinking about the individual's relationship to the collective. As Janet Atwill notes in "Rhetoric and Civic Virtue," there is reason to critique the established alternatives of civic republicanism, in which "the 'common good' more accurately reflects the specific values of the propertied, educated classes,"[2] and liberalism, which "has been criticized for providing no positive ethical base for political community and encouraging a brash rhetoric of 'rights' over discourses of responsibility."[3] Although the eighteenth century certainly does not provide a formula for avoiding the hazards found in these positions, its historical location at least offers insight into the complexity that has surrounded these discourses for centuries. Certainly the problematic elements of common sense illustrate the difficulty of successfully negotiating the gaps between public and private experience in a way that adequately protects individuals from the oppressive character of consensus. However, considering the intellectual aftermath of this period illustrates the rhetorical losses that come about when the individual's subjective experience entirely replaces the quest for sensus communis. This study offers no clear solutions to the questions that pervade rhetorical education today, but it at least suggests that history offers multiple alternatives to current conceptions of individual autonomy and social responsibility. While Stoic thought is not necessarily a desirable alternative, it can be seen as a point of resistance against the detachment from community that the elect souls of the nineteenth century saw as an alternative to sensus communis—an approach that seriously diminished rhetoric's potential.

The goal of realizing rhetoric's democratic potential has proven to be an elusive enterprise across many centuries. This new reading of history does not offer a model for achieving that goal, but I hope that it serves a useful purpose in demonstrating the complex challenges that always surround efforts to support individual expression and sympathetic interactions among people in a community. An awareness of the intersection between Stoic thought and eighteenth-century theories about language does not lead to insight about the precise course of action that rhetoric might take in constructing a democratic community. However, this awareness nevertheless holds the benefit of calling into question the apparent clarity between the boundaries of personal and social that we sometimes believe to be inscribed in history. The awareness that these categories have never been firmly fixed may help us become more aware of alternatives to current configurations of those terms. Awareness of these alternatives can help to fulfill Richard Graff and Michael Leff's call for consistent attention to the link among theory, philosophy, and rhetorical pedagogy, a process that can invigorate efforts to practice and teach rhetoric in ways that challenge the oppressive capacity of common sense without resorting to the alternative of offering students a "refuge for elect souls in an ill-made world."

NOTES

Preface

1. Haakonssen, introduction, 35.

Introduction

1. Vivenza, *Adam Smith and the Classics,* 6–7.

2. Haakonssen, introduction, 35.

3. George T. Buckley quoted in Herrick, *Radical Rhetoric of the English Deists,* 13.

4. Sher states, "Hutcheson's brand of Christian Stoicism exerted a powerful influence on Scottish moral philosophy and religion throughout the eighteenth century" (*Church and University in the Scottish Enlightenment,* 117). He traces the ongoing presence of this influence in the work of the Scottish moderate literati, a group that included Adam Ferguson and Hugh Blair, both of whom Sher identifies as particularly drawn to Hutcheson's fusion of Christianity with Stoicism.

5. Warner, *Publics and Counterpublics,* 28.

6. Habermas, *Structural Transformation,* 27.

7. Ibid., 34.

8. Ibid., 37.

9. Smollett, *Adventures of Roderick Random,* 260.

10. Ibid., 261.

11. Warner, *Publics and Counterpublics,* 39.

12. Warner, *Letters of the Republic,* xiii.

13. Sheridan, *Course of Lectures on Elocution,* xi–xiii, 1.

14. Blair, *Lectures on Rhetoric and Belles Lettres,* 3.

15. Ibid., 74.

16. Ibid., 74.

17. Campbell, *Philosophy of Rhetoric,* 97.

18. Whately, *Elements of Rhetoric,* 254n*.

19. Wood, "Science in the Scottish Enlightenment," 103.

20. Reid, *Inquiry into the Human Mind,* 21.

21. Smith, *Theory of Moral Sentiments,* 6.

22. Clark and Halloran, introduction, 2.

23. Herrick, *Radical Rhetoric of the English Deists,* 15.

24. Stoicism was the dominant school of the Hellenistic age (Inwood, *Cambridge Companion,* 11) and played a significant role in the development of Roman ethics (Gill, "School in the Roman Imperial Period," 33).

25. Colish, *Stoic Tradition from Antiquity,* 36.

26. George Kennedy's reference to the presence of *vir bonus* in Stoic thought is fully developed and effectively argued as a foundation for Quintilian's "good man speaking well" in Arthur E. Walzer, "Quintilian's 'Vir Bonus' and the Stoic Wise Man."

27. In his introduction to *De officiis,* Walter Miller states, "The more he [Cicero] studied and lived, the more of a Stoic in ethics he became" (xv).

28. Hugh Blair quoted in Sher, *Church and University in the Scottish Enlightenment,* 201.

29. Sher, *Church and University in the Scottish Enlightenment,* 200.

30. Howell, *Eighteenth-Century British Logic,* 511.

31. Ibid., 529.

32. Conley, *Rhetoric in the European Tradition,* 203.

33. Ibid., 192–93.

34. Ibid., 221.

35. Warnick, *Sixth Canon,* 11.

36. Ibid., 136.

37. Ulman, *Things, Thoughts, Words, and Actions,* 5.

38. Bitzer, introduction, xxx.

39. Ehninger, "Campbell, Blair, and Whately Revisited," 169, 173–82.

40. T. Miller, *Formation of College English,* 8.

41. See, for example, Carol S. Lipson and Roberta A. Binkley, *Rhetoric before and beyond the Greeks;* Richard Leo Enos, "Recovering the Lost Art of Researching the History of Rhetoric"; Ekaterina V. Haskins, *Logos and Power in Isocrates and Aristotle;* Susan Jarratt, *Rereading the Sophists;* John Poulakos, *Sophistical Rhetoric in Classical Greece;* and Jeffrey Walker, *Rhetoric and Poetics in Antiquity.*

42. Jarratt, *Rereading the Sophists,* 9.

43. Enos, "Recovering," 14.

44. Graff and Leff, "Revisionist Historiography and Rhetorical Tradition(s)," 14.

45. Berlin, *Writing Instruction,* 33.

46. Crowley, *Composition in the University,* 34.

47. Clark and Halloran, introduction, 13.

48. Potkay, *Fate of Eloquence,* 1.

49. Walzer, "Blair's Ideal Orator," 275.

50. Pocock, "Political Thought," 273.

51. Sher, *Church and University in the Scottish Enlightenment,* 175.

52. Warner, *Publics and Counterpublics,* 40.

53. Gilmour, *Victorian Period,* 2.

54. Ibid., 19.

55. Ibid., 93.

56. Ibid., 19.
57. Adams, *Dandies and Desert Saints,* 13.
58. Crowley, *Composition in the University,* 36.
59. Ibid., 43–45.
60. Bourdieu, *Distinction,* 41.
61. Ibid., 44.
62. Ibid., 42.
63. Ibid., 43.
64. Ibid., 56.
65. Ibid., 54.
66. Ibid., 31.
67. De Quincey, "Rhetoric," 100.
68. Carlyle, "Signs of the Times," 62.
69. Ibid., 63.
70. Engstrom and Whiting, introduction, 3.

Chapter 1. Stoic Ethics and Rhetoric

1. Long, "Stoicism in the Philosophical Tradition," 365.
2. Chew, *Stoicism in Renaissance English Literature,* 1.
3. Annas, *Voices of Ancient Philosophy,* 16.
4. Long, "Stoicism in the Philosophical Tradition," 367.
5. Ibid., 366.
6. Schofield, "Stoic Ethics," 253.
7. Long, "Stoicism in the Philosophical Tradition," 367.
8. Ibid.
9. Diogenes Laertius, "Zeno," 87–88.
10. Gill, "School in the Roman Imperial Period," 47–48.
11. Schofield, "Stoic Ethics," 254.
12. Gill, "School in the Roman Imperial Period," 37.
13. Inwood, "Introduction: Stoicism, an Intellectual Odyssey," 1.
14. Ibid.
15. Ibid.
16. Epictetus, *Arrian's Discourses of Epictetus,* 239.
17. Christensen, *Essay,* 56.
18. Oates, introduction, xxi.
19. Diogenes Laertius, "Zeno," 46–47.
20. Epictetus, *Arrian's Discourses of Epictetus,* 224.
21. Ibid., 261–62.
22. E. Vernon Arnold, *Roman Stoicism,* 136.
23. Ibid., 136–37.
24. Ibid., 137.
25. Ibid., 138.
26. Flory, "Stoic Psychology, Classical Rhetoric," 147.

27. Ibid., 149–53.
28. Ibid., 150.
29. Ibid., 158.
30. Epictetus, *Arrian's Discourses of Epictetus,* 281.
31. Ibid., 233–34.
32. Ibid., 234.
33. Copleston, *History of Philosophy,* 139.
34. Rist, *Stoic Philosophy,* 68.
35. Seneca, "Moderation," *Stoic Philosophy of Seneca,* 170.
36. Epictetus, *Arrian's Discourses of Epictetus,* 234.
37. Ibid., 354.
38. Ibid., 272.
39. Ibid., 271.
40. Algra, "Stoic Theology," 161–62.
41. Epictetus, *Arrian's Discourses of Epictetus,* 300.
42. Ibid., 317.
43. Rist. *Stoic Philosophy,* 107.
44. Gill, "School in the Roman Imperial Period," 43.
45. Rist, *Stoic Philosophy,* 190.
46. Cooper, "Eudaimonism," 268.
47. Ibid., 269.
48. Epictetus, *Arrian's Discourses of Epictetus,* 227.
49. Marcus Aurelius, *Meditations,* 547.
50. Ibid., 560.
51. Seneca, "On Anger," *Moral Essays,* 5.
52. Marcus Aurelius, *Meditations,* 565.
53. Ibid.
54. Frede, "Stoic Determinism," 205.
55. Epictetus, *Arrian's Discourses of Epictetus,* 229.
56. Ibid., 233.
57. Frede, "Stoic Determinism," 205.
58. Sandbach, *Stoics,* 16.
59. Diogenes Laertius, "Zeno," 121.
60. Epictetus, *Arrian's Discourses of Epictetus,* 240.
61. Ibid., 259.
62. Seneca, "On the Happy Life," *Moral Essays,* 3.
63. Epictetus, *Arrian's Discourses of Epictetus,* 325.
64. Ibid., 356–57.
65. Ibid., 347–48.
66. Marcus Aurelius, *Meditations,* 508.
67. Ibid., 509.
68. Ibid., 517.
69. Ibid., 547.

70. Ibid.

71. Gill, "School in the Roman Imperial Period," 34.

72. Annas, *Voices of Ancient Philosophy*, 335.

73. Christensen, *Essay*, 73.

74. Epictetus, *Arrian's Discourses of Epictetus*, 250.

75. Seneca, "On Master and Slave," *Ad Lucilium Epistulae Morales*, 2.

76. Epictetus, *Arrian's Discourses of Epictetus*, 251.

77. Annas, *Voices of Ancient Philosophy*, 60; Gill, "School in the Roman Imperial Period," 46.

78. Rist, *Stoic Philosophy*, 176.

79. Annas, *Voices of Ancient Philosophy*, 335.

80. Rist, *Stoic Philosophy*, 187.

81. Ibid., 208.

82. Annas, *Voices of Ancient Philosophy*, 207.

83. Blank and Atherton, "Stoic Contribution to Traditional Grammar," 316.

84. E. Vernon Arnold, *Roman Stoicism*, 143.

85. Epictetus, *Arrian's Discourses of Epictetus*, 262.

86. E. Vernon Arnold, *Roman Stoicism*, 143.

87. Cooper, "Eudaimonism," 278.

88. Kennedy, *Art of Rhetoric*, 4.

89. Diogenes Laertius, "Zeno," 42.

90. Epictetus, *Arrian's Discourses of Epictetus*, 234.

91. Ibid., 236.

92. Seneca, "On the Proper Style for a Philosopher's Discourse," *Ad Lucilium Epistulae Morales*, 4.

93. Diogenes Laertius, "Zeno," 18.

94. Ibid., 20.

95. Epictetus, *Arrian's Discourses of Epictetus*, 239.

96. Ibid.

97. Ibid., 397.

98. Marcus Aurelius, *Meditations*, 491–92.

99. Ibid., 548.

100. Epictetus, *Arrian's Discourses of Epictetus*, 334.

101. Ibid.

102. Ibid., 336.

103. Ibid., 338.

104. Seneca, "On the Proper Style for a Philosopher's Discourse," *Ad Lucilium Epistulae Morales*, 8.

105. Epictetus, *Arrian's Discourses of Epictetus*, 237.

106. Marcus Aurelius, *Meditations*, 510.

107. Ibid., 512.

108. Ibid., 543.

109. Epictetus, *Arrian's Discourses of Epictetus*, 317.

110. Ibid., 316.

111. Ibid., 387.

112. Ibid., 388.

113. Ibid., 389.

114. Ibid., 390.

115. Marcus Aurelius, *Meditations,* 534.

116. Ibid., 555.

117. Epictetus, *Arrian's Discourses of Epictetus,* 236.

118. Seneca, "On Style as a Mirror of Character," *Ad Lucilium Epistulae Morales,* 2.

119. Seneca, "On the Proper Style for a Philosopher's Discourse," *Ad Lucilium Epistulae Morales,* 6.

120. Seneca, "On Style as a Mirror of Character," *Ad Lucilium Epistulae Morales,* 3.

121. Seneca, "On the Happy Life," *Moral Essays,* 3–4.

122. Seneca, "On Style as a Mirror of Character," *Ad Lucilium Epistulae Morales,* 20.

123. Ibid., 21.

124. Ibid., 21–22.

125. Seneca, "On Tranquillity of Mind," *Moral Essays,* 6.

126. Seneca, "On Style as a Mirror of Character," *Ad Lucilium Epistulae Morales,* 13.

127. Ibid., 11–12.

128. Seneca, "On the Proper Style for a Philosopher's Discourse," *Ad Lucilium Epistulae Morales,* 11.

129. Seneca, "On Anger," vol. 1, *Moral Essays,* 1.

130. Chrysippus, quoted in Diogenes Laertius, "Zeno," 100.

131. Oates, introduction, xxiv.

132. Oates, introduction, xxiv–xxv.

133. Kennedy, *Art of Rhetoric,* 503.

134. Cicero, *De finibus bonorum et malorum,* 79.

135. Ibid., 7.

136. Ibid., 19.

137. Ibid., 20.

138. Cicero, *De natura deorum,* 15.

139. Cicero, *De legibus,* 46–47.

140. Cicero, *De finibus,* 31.

141. Cicero, *De oratore,* 244.

142. Cicero, *De legibus,* 45.

143. Cicero, *De finibus,* 20–21.

144. Ibid., 45.

145. Cicero, *De officiis,* 148.

146. Ibid., 69.

147. Cicero, *De finibus,* 63.

148. Ibid., 64.
149. Cicero, *De inventione*, 2.
150. Ibid., 3.
151. Cicero, *De finibus*, 65–66.
152. Cicero, *De oratore*, 207.
153. Cicero, *De officiis*, 136.
154. Ibid., 93–94.
155. Ibid., 132.
156. Cicero, *De oratore*, 254–55.
157. Ibid., 20.
158. Cicero, *De officiis*, 126.
159. Cicero, *De finibus*, 63.
160. Cicero, *De officiis*, 32.
161. Ibid., 146.
162. Ibid., book 1, ch. 40.
163. Cicero, *De oratore*, 133.
164. Ibid., 259.
165. Ibid.
166. Cicero, *De officiis*, 132.
167. Kennedy, *Art of Rhetoric*, 135.
168. Flory, "Stoic Psychology, Classical Rhetoric," 152.
169. Walzer, "Quintilian's 'Vir Bonus,'" 25.
170. Ibid., 35.
171. Quintilian, *Institutio Oratoria*, 9.
172. Ibid., 20–21.
173. Ibid., 1.
174. Ibid., 8.
175. Ibid., 38–44.
176. Walzer, "Moral Philosophy and Rhetoric," 275.
177. Ibid.
178. Ibid., 278.
179. Quintilian, *Institutio Oratoria*, 8–10.
180. Ibid., 20, 35.
181. Ibid., 10.
182. Ibid., 9.
183. Ibid., 25.
184. Ibid., 15.
185. Walzer, "Quintilian's 'Vir Bonus'" and "Moral Philosophy and Rhetoric"; Kennedy, *Art of Rhetoric*, 498.
186. Wenley, *Stoicism and Its Influence*, 160.
187. Hanley, *Stoicism in Major English Poets*, 40.
188. Wenley, *Stoicism and Its Influence*, 110.
189. Skinner, *Reason and Rhetoric*, 1.

Chapter 2. Eighteenth-Century Common Sense and Sensus Communis

1. See *De Anima* and *Physics.* For a discussion of Aristotle's common sense as a counter to idealism, see Frederick S. J. Copleston's *History of Philosophy* and David Knowles's *Evolution of Medieval Thought.*

2. Schaeffer, *Sensus Communis,* 3.

3. Ibid., 2.

4. Shaftesbury, *Sensus Communis,* 57.

5. Ibid., 82–83.

6. Ibid., 45.

7. Ibid., 83.

8. Reid to Henry Home, Lord Kames, King's College, February 14, 1763, in Reid, *Correspondence,* 27.

9. Reid, *Inquiry into the Human Mind,* 18.

10. Campbell, *Dissertation on Miracles,* 21.

11. Shaftesbury, treatise 3, "The Picture of Cebes, Disciple of Socrates," *Second Characters or the Language of Forms,* 87.

12. Reid to Kames, Glasgow College, February 27, 1778, in Reid, *Correspondence,* 97.

13. Gadamer, *Truth and Method,* 22.

14. Ibid.

15. Ibid., 24.

16. Ibid., 25.

17. T. Miller, *Formation of College English,* 209–15.

18. Ibid. 215.

19. Ibid., 216.

20. Clark and Halloran, introduction, 5.

21. Horner, *Nineteenth-Century Scottish Rhetoric,* 16–17.

22. Reid to Skene, Glasgow, November 14, 1764, in Reid, *Correspondence,* 37.

23. Reid to Skene, Glasgow, December 30, 1765, in ibid., 45.

24. Bacon, *Of the Advancement of Learning,* 2.

25. Sprat, *History of the Royal Society,* 18.

26. Ibid., 102.

27. Ibid., 117.

28. Ibid., 18.

29. Shaftesbury, Sensus Communis: *An Essay,* 61.

30. Hutcheson, *Inquiry Concerning Beauty,* 8–11, 1–3.

31. Reid, *Inquiry into the Human Mind,* 17.

32. James McCosh, the author of *Scottish Philosophy* (1875), studied philosophy at the University of Edinburgh from 1829 to 1833 and received an M.A. after writing what his *New York Times* obituary described as a "remarkable essay on the Stoic philosophy." He served as president of Princeton University from 1868 to 1887.

33. McCosh, *Scottish Philosophy,* 75–76.

34. Rand, prefatory introduction, ix.

35. Ibid., xi.

36. Ibid., xi.

37. Tiffany, "Shaftesbury as Stoic," 645.

38. Ibid., 644–45.

39. Rand, prefatory introduction, xii.

40. McCosh, *Scottish Philosophy,* 33.

41. Shaftesbury, *Philosophical Regimen,* 4.

42. Epictetus quoted in Shaftesbury, *Philosophical Regimen,* 7–8.

43. Epictetus quoted in ibid., 41.

44. Epictetus quoted in ibid.

45. Epictetus quoted in ibid., 6.

46. Ibid., 13.

47. Ibid., 17.

48. Shaftesbury to a university student, quoted in McCosh, *Scottish Philosophy,* 31.

49. Shaftesbury, *Philosophical Regimen,* 17.

50. Ibid., 18.

51. Ibid., 169.

52. Ibid., 172.

53. Shaftesbury, *Sensus Communis,* 67–68.

54. Ibid., 72.

55. Ibid., 71.

56. Shaftesbury, *Soliloquy,* 116.

57. Shaftesbury, treatise 4, "Plastics or the Original Progress and Power of Designatory Art," *Second Characters or the Language of Forms,* 174.

58. Shaftesbury, *Sensus Communis,* 66.

59. Ibid., 173.

60. Shaftesbury, *Philosophical Regimen,* 181.

61. Ibid., 49.

62. Ibid., 73.

63. Ibid.

64. Nienkamp, *Internal Rhetorics,* 58.

65. Knud Haakonssen argues that many eighteenth-century thinkers, including Reid, blend Socrates, Stoicism, and Christianity in developing their philosophical ideas. In this respect, Shaftesbury could be characterized as combining Platonic and Stoic thought in certain respects; however, to describe him strictly as a Platonist because of his belief in some type of universal truth overly simplifies the complexity of his use of ancient sources.

66. Haakonssen, introduction, 35.

67. Thomas Reid quoted in ibid., 16–17.

68. Ibid., 17.

69. Ibid., 33.

70. Broadie, introduction, xxix.

71. Reid to Kames, [Glasgow], December 16, 1780, in Reid, *Correspondence,* 141.

72. Reid, *Inquiry into the Human Mind,* 32.

73. Reid to Kames, Glasgow College, December 1, 1778, in Reid, *Correspondence,* 107.

74. Reid, *Inquiry into the Human Mind,* 33.

75. Ibid., 44.

76. Haakonssen, introduction, 41.

77. Reid, March 7, 1766, *Practical Ethics,* 121.

78. Ibid., March 19, 1766, 193.

79. Ibid., April 15, 1765, 181.

80. Reid, *Inquiry into the Human Mind,* 171.

81. Ibid., 193, 194.

82. Ibid., 71.

83. Ibid., 67, 68.

84. Ibid., 68, 69.

85. Kames, *Elements of Criticism,* 164.

86. Ibid., 163.

87. Reid, *Inquiry into the Human Mind,* 192.

88. Reid to James Gregory, [Glasgow], August 26, 1787, in Reid, *Correspondence,* 192–93, 38–41.

89. Walzer, *George Campbell,* 2.

90. Campbell, *Philosophy of Rhetoric,* 40.

91. Ibid., lxvii.

92. Whately, *Elements of Rhetoric,* introduction, 38.

93. Ibid., 32.

94. Whately, *Elements of Rhetoric,* 140.

95. Ibid., 218.

96. Ibid., 221.

97. Ibid., 222.

98. Reid, *On Logic, Rhetoric, and the Fine Arts,* 35.

99. Ibid., 75.

100. Weinsheimer, "Philosophy of Rhetoric," 232.

101. Thomas Miller, *The Formation of College English,* 216.

102. Campbell, "Duty of Allegiance," 264.

103. Reid, "On the Active Powers," 638.

104. Epictetus, *Arrian's Discourses of Epictetus,* 354.

105. Campbell, *Philosophy of Rhetoric,* 40.

106. Ibid., "Influence of Religion on Civil Society," 233.

107. Ibid., 237.

108. Ibid., 234.

109. Herrick, *Radical Rhetoric of the English Deists,* 16.

110. Campbell, *Dissertation on Miracles,* 11.

111. Ibid., 29.

112. Ibid., *Philosophy of Rhetoric*, 56.
113. Ibid.
114. Ibid.
115. Ibid., *Dissertation on Miracles*, 18.
116. Ibid., 12.
117. Ibid., *Philosophy of Rhetoric*, 96.
118. Weinsheimer,"Philosophy of Rhetoric," 240.
119. S. C. Brown and Willard, "George Campbell's Audience," 60.
120. Ibid.
121. Campbell, *Philosophy of Rhetoric*, 71.
122. Epictetus, *Arrian's Discourses of Epictetus*, 390.
123. Campbell, *Philosophy of Rhetoric*, 71.
124. Ibid., 72.
125. Ibid.
126. Ibid., 95.
127. Ibid.
128. Ibid.
129. Ibid., 100.
130. Bitzer, "Re-Evaluation of Campbell's Doctrine of Evidence," 139.
131. Campbell, *Philosophy of Rhetoric*, 43.
132. Ibid., 40.

Chapter 3. Taste and Sensus Communis

1. Diogenes Laertius, "Zeno," 100.
2. Ibid.
3. Cicero, *De officiis*, 126.
4. Ibid., 32.
5. Ferreira-Buckley, "Influence of Hugh Blair's *Lectures*," 61.
6. Ibid.
7. For examples of those who have charged Blair with diminishing the focus on rhetoric through emphasizing the application of taste to literary texts, see Warren Guthrie ("The Development of Rhetorical Theory in America, 1635–1850: Domination of the English Rhetorics"), Clarence Edney ("Hugh Blair's Theory of *Dispositio*"), William A. Covino ("Blair, Byron, and the Psychology of Reading"), and James A. Berlin ("John Genung and Contemporary Composition Theory").
8. T. Miller, *Formation of College English*, 166.
9. Ibid., 235.
10. Ibid.
11. Johnson, *Nineteenth-Century Rhetoric*, 35.
12. H. Lewis Ulman states that Blair "tends to reify written and even spoken language as fixed systems that embody equally stable truths and virtues, thus constituting the historical culmination of a mythos of progress" (*Things, Thoughts, Words, and Actions*, 145); see also Thomas N. Conley, *Rhetoric in the European Tradition*, and

Dottie Broadus, "Authoring Elitism: Francis Hutcheson and Hugh Blair in Scotland and America."

13. Sher, *Church and University in the Scottish Enlightenment*, 36.

14. Ibid., 18.

15. Ibid., 182.

16. T. Miller, *Formation of College English*, 235.

17. Seneca, "Philosopher's Mean," *Ad Lucilium Epistulae Morales*, 4–5.

18. Ferreira-Buckley and Halloran, editors' introduction, xlvi.

19. Gadamer, *Truth and Method*, 33.

20. Ibid., 31.

21. Ulman, *Things, Thoughts, Words, and Actions*, 145.

22. Seneca, "On the Proper Style for a Philosopher's Discourse," *Ad Lucilium Epistulae Morales*, 11.

23. Cohen, "Hugh Blair's Theory of Taste," 266.

24. "Taste: An Essay," 242.

25. Ibid.

26. Ibid.

27. [Miller], "Of Politeness," 222.

28. Tiffany, "Shaftesbury as Stoic," 663.

29. Rand, prefatory introduction to *Second Characters or the Language of Forms*, xxiv.

30. Ibid., xxvii.

31. Shaftesbury, *Second Characters or the Language of Forms*, xiii.

32. Shaftesbury, *Sensus Communis*, 195.

33. Tiffany, "Shaftesbury as Stoic," 660.

34. Ibid., 659.

35. Reid, *On Logic, Rhetoric, and the Fine Arts*, 50.

36. Ibid., 51.

37. Gerard, 38.

38. "Taste: An Essay," 244.

39. Ibid., 246.

40. Tiffany, "Shaftesbury as Stoic," 665.

41. Shaftesbury, *Soliloquy, or Advice to an Author*, 208.

42. Shaftesbury, treatise 2, "A Notion of the Historical Draught or Tablature of the Judgment of Hercules," *Second Characters or the Language of Forms*, 61.

43. Ibid., treatise 4, "Plastics, or the Original Progress and Power of Designatory Art," 167.

44. Ibid., 114.

45. Tiffany, "Shaftesbury as Stoic," 649.

46. Shaftesbury, treatise 4, "Plastics, or the Original Progress and Power of Designatory Art," *Second Characters or the Language of Forms*, 174.

47. Shaftesbury, *Sensus Communis*, 89.

48. Tiffany, "Shaftesbury as Stoic," 645.

49. Kames, *Elements of Criticism,* 22.

50. Ibid.. 14–15.

51. Ibid., 21.

52. Ibid., 15.

53. Ibid., 28.

54. "The Happy Life," 157.

55. "Taste: An Essay," 254.

56. [Miller], "Of Politeness," 224.

57. "Taste: An Essay," 252–53.

58. Shaftesbury, *Soliloquy,* 307.

59. Gadamer, *Truth and Method,* 41.

60. Ibid.

61. Reid, *On Logic, Rhetoric, and the Fine Arts,* 73.

62. Gerard, *Essay on Taste,* 71.

63. Kames, *Elements of Criticism,* 60.

64. Ibid., 94.

65. Smith, *Theory of Moral Sentiments,* 11.

66. Kames, *Elements of Criticism,* 471.

67. Ibid.

68. Ibid., 470.

69. Ibid., 176.

70. Blair, *Lectures on Rhetoric and Belles Lettres,* 10.

71. Ibid., 19.

72. Ibid., 21.

73. Ibid., 22.

74. Ibid., 49.

75. Ibid., 5.

76. Ibid.

77. Ibid., 11.

78. Ibid.

79. Ibid., 344–45.

80. Halloran, "Hugh Blair's Use of Quintilian," 184.

81. Ferreira-Buckley and Halloran, editors' introduction, xxxviii.

82. Blair, *Lectures on Rhetoric and Belles Lettres,* 9.

83. Ibid., 13.

84. Ibid.

85. Ibid., 3.

86. Ibid., 55.

87. Ibid., 9.

88. Ibid., 33.

89. Ibid., 48.

90. Ianetta, "To Elevate I First Must Soften," 407–8.

91. Blair, *Lectures on Rhetoric and Belles Lettres,* 18.

92. Ferreira-Buckley and Halloran, editors' introduction, xl.

93. Ibid., xlii.

94. Blair, *Lectures on Rhetoric and Belles Lettres,* 17.

95. Ibid., 22.

96. Ibid.

97. Ibid.

98. Ibid., 18.

99. Ibid., 19.

100. Ibid., 18.

101. Ibid., 170.

102. Ibid., 7.

103. Bitzer, "Rhetoric and Public Knowledge," 74.

104. Sher, *Church and University in the Scottish Enlightenment,* 179.

105. "Taste: An Essay," 270–71.

Chapter 4. Propriety, Sympathy, and Style—Fusing the Individual and Social

1. Poulakos, "Toward a Sophistic Definition of Rhetoric," 29.

2. McKenna, *Adam Smith,* 37.

3. Epictetus, *Arrian's Discourses of Epictetus,* 23.

4. Colish, *Stoic Tradition from Antiquity,* 59.

5. Ibid.

6. Epictetus, *Arrian's Discourses of Epictetus,* 390.

7. Ibid., 236.

8. Marcus Aurelius, *Meditations,* 555.

9. Colish, *Stoic Tradition from Antiquity,* 147.

10. Cicero, *De officiis,* 132.

11. Ibid., 126.

12. Colish, *Stoic Tradition from Antiquity,* 147.

13. Cicero, *De oratore,* 55.

14. Ibid., 43.

15. Cicero, *De inventione,* 3.

16. Cicero, *De finibus bonorum et malorum,* 63.

17. Ibid.

18. Shaftesbury, *Sensus Communis,* 96.

19. Ibid., 58.

20. Struever, "Conversable World," 85.

21. Ibid.

22. V. Brown, "Dialogic Experience of Conscience," 239.

23. Epictetus, *Arrian's Discourses of Epictetus,* 370.

24. Shaftesbury, *Soliloquy, or Advice to an Author,* 100.

25. Ibid., 184.

26. Marcus Aurelius, *Meditations,* 560.

27. Shaftesbury, *Soliloquy, or Advice to an Author,* 117.

28. Ibid., 108.
29. Ibid., 115.
30. Tiffany, "Shaftesbury as Stoic," 654.
31. Shaftesbury, *Sensus Communis*, 88.
32. Marcus Aurelius, *Meditations*, 565.
33. Shaftesbury, *Soliloquy, or Advice to an Author*, 105.
34. Ibid.
35. Ibid., 106.
36. Ibid., 182.
37. Ibid., 192.
38. Shaftesbury, *Sensus Communis*, 86.
39. McKenna, *Adam Smith*, 58–59.
40. Smith, *Theory of Moral Sentiments*, 1.
41. Ibid., 8.
42. Ibid., 6.
43. McKenna, *Adam Smith*, 1.
44. Ibid., 26.
45. Ibid., 44.
46. Ibid., 50.
47. Ibid.
48. Smith, *Theory of Moral Sentiments*, 13.
49. Ibid., 1.
50. Ibid., 46.
51. Vivenza, *Adam Smith and the Classics*, 81.
52. Ibid., 185.
53. Smith, *Lectures on Rhetoric and Belles Lettres*, 2.
54. Ibid., 2–3.
55. Raphael, *Impartial Spectator*, 34.
56. Smith, *Lectures on Rhetoric and Belles Lettres*, 23.
57. Ibid., 22–23.
58. Ibid., 30–31.
59. Ibid., December 3, 1762, 36.
60. Ibid., December 1, 1762, 31.
61. Smith, *Theory of Moral Sentiments*, 1.
62. Ibid., 5.
63. Ibid., 3.
64. Ibid., 12.
65. Ibid., 1.
66. Ibid., 8.
67. Ibid., 5.
68. Ibid., 2.
69. Ibid., 1.
70. Ibid., 7.

71. Ibid., 1.

72. V. Brown, "Dialogic Experience of Conscience," 234–35.

73. Mikhail Bakhtin quoted in ibid., 237.

74. Ibid., 242.

75. Ibid., 244.

76. See Dan Flory, "Stoic Psychology, Classical Rhetoric, and Theories of Imagination in Western Philosophy," for a discussion of the significant role of imagination in Stoic thought.

77. Smith, *Theory of Moral Sentiments,* 2.

78. Cicero, *De officiis,* 126.

79. Smith, *Theory of Moral Sentiments,* 3.

80. Ibid., 8.

81. Ibid., 1.

82. McKenna, *Adam Smith,* 59.

83. Ibid.

84. Smith, *Theory of Moral Sentiments,* 30.

85. Ibid., 8.

86. McKenna, *Adam Smith,* 119.

87. Ibid., 90.

88. Smith, *Theory of Moral Sentiments,* 6–7.

89. West, introduction, 30.

90. Smith, *Theory of Moral Sentiments,* 10.

91. Ibid., 1.

92. Ibid., 6.

93. Ibid., 3.

94. Ibid., 34.

95. Ibid., 36.

96. Ibid., 25.

97. Kames, *Essays on the Principles of Morality,* 37–38.

98. Ibid., 38–39.

99. Kames, *Elements of Criticism,* 166.

100. Ibid., 96.

101. Ibid., 164.

102. Ibid., 62.

103. Ibid., 168.

104. Kames, *Essays on the Principles of Morality,* 24.

105. Ibid., 68.

106. Kames, *Elements of Criticism,* 15.

107. Ibid., 212.

108. Ibid., 213.

109. Ibid.

110. Ibid., 171–72.

111. Ibid., 212.

112. Blair, *Lectures on Rhetoric,* 57–62.

113. Ibid., 94.

114. Ibid., 99.

115. Ibid.

116. Blair, *Lectures on Rhetoric and Belles Lettres,* 197.

117. Ibid., 195.

118. Ibid., 196.

119. Ibid., 215.

120. Ibid., 100–101.

121. Warnick, *Sixth Canon,* 71.

122. Blair, *Lectures on Rhetoric and Belles Lettres,* 49.

123. Ibid., 217.

124. Ibid., 293.

125. Ibid., 97–98.

126. See Kennedy, *Art of Rhetoric;* Walzer, "Moral Philosophy" and "Quintilian's 'Vir Bonus.'"

127 Blair, *Lectures on Rhetoric and Belles Lettres,* 381.

Chapter 5. Victorian Language Theories and the Decline of Sensus Communis

1. For commentaries on De Quincey's contribution to rhetoric, see Paul M. Talley, "De Quincey on Persuasion, Invention, and Style," Hoyt Hudson, "De Quincey on Rhetoric and Public Speaking," William A. Covino, "Thomas De Quincey in a Revisionist History of Rhetoric," Frederick Burwick, introduction, *Essays on Rhetoric* by Thomas De Quincey, and Weldon B. Durham, "The Elements of Thomas De Quincey's Rhetoric." René Wellek offers a more negative assessment of De Quincey's rhetorical theory in "De Quincey's Status in the History of Ideas," a perspective shared by Wilbur Samuel Howell.

2. De Quincey, "Rhetoric," 100.

3. De Quincey, "Style," 141.

4. De Quincey, "Rhetoric," 91.

5. De Quincey, "Style," 156.

6. De Quincey, "Rhetoric," 121.

7. Ibid., 110.

8. Ibid., 121.

9. De Quincey, "Style," 181.

10. Ibid., 162.

11. Ibid., 152.

12. Haberman, "De Quincey's Theory of Rhetoric," 196.

13. Ibid., 196–97.

14. Kent, "Victorian Periodicals and the Constructing of Victorian Reality," 4.

15. De Quincey, "Style," 229.

16. Ibid., 193.

17. Secor, "Legacy of Nineteenth Century Style Theory," 79.

18. Ibid.

19. Ibid., 80.

20. Ibid.

21. Jordan, introduction, 34.

22. Ibid., 36.

23. Froude, *Froude's Life of Carlyle,* 351.

24. Ibid., 323.

25. apRoberts, "Carlyle," 60.

26. Froude, *Froude's Life of Carlyle,* 104, 116–17.

27. Horner, *Nineteenth-Century Scottish Rhetoric,* 62, 271.

28. Carlyle to Emerson, August 12, 1834, Carlyle, *Correspondence of Thomas Carlyle and Ralph Waldo Emerson,* 1.22–23.

29. Carlyle, "Characteristics," 339–40.

30. Ibid., 342.

31. Ibid.

32. Ibid., 339.

33. Ibid., 333.

34. Cate, introduction, 55.

35. Carlyle, "Signs of the Times," 72.

36. Ibid., 81.

37. Ibid., 82.

38. Ibid., 59.

39. Ibid., 60–61.

40. Ibid., 64.

41. Ibid., 64–65.

42. Ibid., 63.

43. Ibid., 74.

44. Froude, *Froude's Life of Carlyle,* 400.

45. Ibid., 492.

46. Carlyle, "Characteristics," 371.

47. Carlyle, "Signs of the Times," 62.

48. Horner, *Nineteenth-Century Scottish Rhetoric,* 62.

49. Ibid., 68.

50. Carlyle, "Characteristics," 335.

51. Carlyle to Goethe, December 22, 1829, Carlyle, *Correspondence between Goethe and Carlyle,* 164.

52. Carlyle, "Signs of the Times," 67.

53. Ibid., 74.

54. Ibid., 78.

55. Carlyle to Emerson, August 12, 1834, Carlyle, *Correspondence of Thomas Carlyle and Ralph Waldo Emerson,* 1.22.

56. Ibid.

57. Ibid., 1.23.

58. Ibid.

59. Froude, *Froude's Life of Carlyle,* 331.

60. Ibid., 210.

61. Ibid., 285.

62. Ibid., 292.

63. Ibid., 415.

64. Ibid., 362.

65. Ibid., 357.

66. Carlyle to Emerson, February 3, 1835, Carlyle, *Correspondence of Thomas Carlyle and Ralph Waldo Emerson,* 1.43.

67. Pater, "Style," 9.

68. Wilde, "Critic as Artist," 356.

69. Yeats, *Autobiography of William Butler Yeats,* 80.

70. Blair, *Lectures on Rhetoric and Belles Lettres,* 6.

71. Ibid., 7.

72. Carlyle, *Sartor Resartus,* 158.

73. Gilmour, *Victorian Period,* 19.

74. Ibid., 93.

75. Ibid., 129.

76. Bruns, "Formal Nature," 905.

77. M. Arnold, "Function of Criticism at the Present Time," 270.

78. Ibid.

79. Ibid., 271.

80. Ibid., 270.

81. Ibid., "Barbarians, Philistines, and the Populace," 153.

82. Ibid.

83. Arnold to Clough, 23 September 23, [1849], in Lang, *Letters of Matthew Arnold,* 1.156.

84. M. Arnold, "Function of Criticism at the Present Time," 268.

85. Arnold to Alexander Macmillan, April 18, 1865, in Lang, *Letters of Matthew Arnold,* 2.408.

86. M. Arnold, "Literary Influence of Academies," 245.

87. Gadamer, *Truth and Method,* 30–39.

88. Pater, *Plato and Platonism,* 111.

89. Wilde, "Critic as Artist," 393.

90. Robbins, "Vernon Lee: Decadent Woman?" 141.

91. Ibid.

92. Ibid.

93. Freedman, *Professions of Taste,* 6.

94. Robbins, "Vernon Lee: Decadent Woman?" 145.

95. Freedman, *Professions of Taste,* 9.

96. Hough, *Last Romantics,* 134.

97. Ibid., 137.

98. Monsman and Wright, "Walter Pater," 113.

99. Wordsworth to Pater, March 17, 1873, Wordsworth, *Letters of Walter Pater,* 12.

100. Pater, *Renaissance,* viii.

101. Losey, "Pater's Epiphanies and the Open Form," 30.

102. Ibid., 31.

103. Ibid., 40.

104. Matz, "Walter Pater's Literary Impression," 434.

105. Pater, *Renaissance,* x.

106. S. Marcus, "Conceptions of the Self in an Age of Progress," 445.

107. Pater, *Renaissance,* 237.

108. Bromwich, "Genealogy of Disinterestedness," 77.

109. Pater, *Renaissance,* 236.

110. Dowling, *Vulgarization of Art,* 76.

111. Uglow, introduction, xi.

112. Ibid.

113. Inman, "Pater's Appeal," 643–65.

114. Pater, *Plato and Platonism,* 135–36.

115. Ibid., 17.

116. Wilde, "Decay of Lying," 306.

117. V. Lee, "Art and Life III," 695.

118. Ibid., 698.

119. Ibid., 699.

120. Ibid., 707.

121. Ibid., "Art and Life I," 694.

122. Ibid., "Art and Life III," 706.

123. Ibid., 702.

124. Ibid., *Beautiful,* 68.

125. Ibid., 3.

126. Ibid., 84.

127. Ibid., 11.

128. Ibid., 57.

129. Robbins, "Vernon Lee: Decadent Woman?" 148.

130. Wellek, "Vernon Lee, Bernard Berenson, and Aesthetics," 235.

131. McGowan, "From Pater to Wilde to Joyce," 426.

132. Wilde, "Decay of Lying," 291.

133. Ibid.

134. Ibid., "Critic as Artist," 307.

135. Ibid., 366.

136. Ibid., 380.

137. Wilde to R. Clegg, [April? 1891], Wilde, *Letters of Oscar Wilde,* 292.

138. Harris, "Arnold, Pater, and Wilde and the Object," 745.

139. Wilde, "Soul of Man under Socialism," 262.

140. Ibid., 268.

141. Ibid.

142. Ibid., 276–77.

143. Wilde, "Critic as Artist," 393.

144. Wilde, "Soul of Man," 277.

145. Helsinger, introduction, 13.

146. Wilde to William Ward, [week ending March 3, 1877], Wilde, *Letters of Oscar Wilde,* 31.

147. Robbins, "'Judas Always Writes the Biography,'" 112.

148. Wilde to Colonel W. F. Morse, [?February 26, 1882], Wilde, *Letters of Oscar Wilde,* 97.

149. Gagnier, *Idylls of the Marketplace,* 3.

150. Small, "Literary Radicalism in the British *Fin de Siecle,*" 213.

151. Wilde to Houghton, [late February? 1894], Wilde, *Letters of Oscar Wilde,* 353.

152. Wilde to Sherard, [week ending March 3, 1883], Wilde, *Letters of Oscar Wilde,* 147–48.

153. Halloran, "On the End of Rhetoric," 86.

154. Ibid.

155. Ong, *Rhetoric, Romance, and Technology,* 264.

Conclusion

1. T. Miller, *Formation of College English,* 185.

2. Atwill, "Rhetoric and Civic Virtue," 84.

3. Ibid., 85.

WORKS CITED

Adams, James Eli. *Dandies and Desert Saints.* Ithaca, N.Y.: Cornell University Press, 1995.

Algra, Keimpe. "Stoic Theology." In Inwood, *Cambridge Companion,* 153–78.

Annas, Julia. *Voices of Ancient Philosophy.* New York: Oxford University Press, 2001.

apRoberts, Ruth. "Carlyle and the Aesthetic Movement." *Carlyle Annual* 12 (1991): 57–64.

Aristotle. *De Anima.* Translated by R. D. Hicks. Cambridge: Cambridge University Press, 1907.

———. *On Rhetoric: A Theory of Civic Discourse.* Translated by George A. Kennedy. New York: Oxford University Press, 1991.

———. *Physics.* Translated by Philip H. Wicksteed and Francis M. Cornford. Cambridge, Mass.: Harvard University Press, 1957.

Arnold, E. Vernon. *Roman Stoicism.* London: Routledge and Kegan Paul, 1911.

Arnold, Matthew. "Barbarians, Philistines, and the Populace." *Culture and Anarchy.* 1869. Vol. 5. In Super, *Complete Prose,* 137–62.

———. "The Function of Criticism at the Present Time." 1864. Vol. 3. In Super, *Complete Prose,* 258–85.

———. "The Literary Influence of Academies." 1864. Vol. 3. In Super, *Complete Prose,* 232–57.

Atwill, Janet. "Rhetoric and Civic Virtue." In *The Viability of the Rhetorical Tradition.* Edited by Richard Graff, Arthur E. Walzer, and Janet M. Atwill, 75–92. Albany: State University of New York Press, 2005.

Bacon, Francis. *Of the Advancement of Learning.* Edited and with an introduction by G. W. Kitchin. London: J. M. Dent and Sons, n.d.

Berlin, James A. "John Genung and Contemporary Composition Theory: The Triumph of the Eighteenth Century." *Rhetoric Society Quarterly* 11, no. 2 (1981): 74–84.

———. *Writing Instruction in Nineteenth-Century American Colleges.* Carbondale: Southern Illinois University Press, 1984.

Bitzer, Lloyd F. Editor's introduction. In Campbell, *Philosophy of Rhetoric,* vii–li.

———. "A Re-Evaluation of Campbell's Doctrine of Evidence." *Quarterly Journal of Speech* 46 (1960): 135–40.

———. "Rhetoric and Public Knowledge." In *Rhetoric, Philosophy and Literature: An Exploration.* Edited by Don M. Burks, 67–93. West Lafayette, Ind.: Purdue University Press, 1978.

Blair, Hugh. *Lectures on Rhetoric and Belles Lettres.* Edited by and with an introduction by Linda Ferreira-Buckley and S. Michael Halloran. Carbondale: Southern Illinois University Press, 2005.

Blank, David, and Catherine Atherton. "The Stoic Contribution to Traditional Grammar." In Inwood, *Cambridge Companion,* 310–27.

Bourdieu, Pierre. *Distinction: A Social Critique of the Judgment of Taste.* Translated by Richard Nice. Cambridge: Harvard University Press, 1984.

Broadie, Alexander. Introduction. In Reid, *On Logic, Rhetoric, and the Fine Arts,* xiii–l.

Broadus, Dottie. "Authoring Elitism: Francis Hutcheson and Hugh Blair in Scotland and America." *Rhetoric Society Quarterly* 24, no. 3–4 (1994): 39–52.

Bromwich, David. "The Genealogy of Disinterestedness." *Raritan* 1, no. 4 (1982): 62–92.

Brown, Stuart C., and Thomas Willard. "George Campbell's Audience: Historical and Theoretical Considerations." In *A Sense of Audience in Written Communication.* Edited by Gesa Kirsch and Duane H. Roen, 58–118. Written Communication Annual. Vol. 5. Newbury: Sage, 1990.

Brown, Vivienne. "The Dialogic Experience of Conscience: Adam Smith and the Voices of Stoicism." *Eighteenth-Century Studies* 26 (Winter 1992–1993): 233–60.

Bruns, Gerald L. "The Formal Nature of Victorian Thinking." *PMLA* 90 (1975): 904–18.

Burwick, Frederick, ed. Introduction. In De Quincey, *Essays on Rhetoric,* xi–xlviii.

Campbell, George. *A Dissertation on Miracles, Containing an Examination of the Principles Advanced by David Hume, Esq., in an Essay on Miracles, with a Correspondence on the Subject by Mr. Hume, Dr. Campbell, and Dr. Blair, to Which Are Added Sermons and Tracts.* London: Thomas Tegg, 1839.

———. "The Duty of Allegiance." In Campbell, *Dissertation on Miracles,* 261–98.

———. "The Influence of Religion on Civil Society." In Campbell, *Dissertation on Miracles,* 233–48.

———. *Philosophy of Rhetoric.* Edited by Lloyd Bitzer. Carbondale: Southern Illinois University Press, 1963.

Carlyle, Thomas. "Characteristics." In *Critical and Miscellaneous Essays.* Vol. 8. *The Works of Thomas Carlyle,* 329–76. Edited by H. D. Traill. 30 vols. London: Chapman & Hall, 1869.

———. *Correspondence between Goethe and Carlyle.* Edited by Charles Eliot Norton. London: Macmillan, 1887.

———. *The Correspondence of Thomas Carlyle and Ralph Waldo Emerson, 1834–1872.* 2 vols. Edited by Charles Eliot Norton. Boston: Ticknor, 1886.

———. *Sartor Resartus: The Life and Opinions of Herr Teufelsdröckh.* Vol. 1. *The Works of Thomas Carlyle.* Edited by H. D. Traill. 30 vols. New York: Scribner, n.d.

———. "Signs of the Times." *Critical and Miscellaneous Essays.* Vol. 27, *The Works of Thomas Carlyle,* 56–82. Edited by H. D. Traill. 30 vols. New York: Scribner, n.d.

Cate, George Allen. Introduction. In *The Correspondence of Thomas Carlyle and John Ruskin.* Edited by George Allen Cate, 1–58. Stanford: Stanford University Press, 1982.

Chew, Audrey. *Stoicism in Renaissance English Literature.* Vol. 82. American University Studies. New York: Peter Lang, 1988.

Christensen, Johnny. *An Essay on the Unity of Stoic Philosophy.* Munksgaard, Copenhagen: Scandinavian University Books, 1962.

Cicero, Marcus Tullius. *De finibus bonorum et malorum.* Trans. H. Rackham. Loeb Classical Library Series. London: William Heinemann, 1914.

———. *De inventione.* Translated by H. M. Hubbell. Loeb Classical Library Series. Cambridge, Mass.: Harvard University Press, 1968.

———. *De legibus.* Translated by Clinton Walker Keyes. Loeb Classical Library Series. Cambridge, Mass.: Harvard University Press, 1928.

———. *De natura deorum.* Translated by H. Rackham. Loeb Classical Library Series. Cambridge, Mass.: Harvard University Press, 1933.

———. *De officiis.* Translated by Walter Miller. Loeb Classical Library Series. London: William Heinemann, 1913.

———. *De oratore.* Translated by J. S. Watson. Carbondale: Southern Illinois University Press, 1970.

Clark, Gregory, and S. Michael Halloran. "Introduction: Transformations of Public Discourse in Nineteenth-Century America." In *Oratorical Culture in Nineteenth-Century America: Transformations in the Theory and Practice of Rhetoric.* Edited by Clark and Halloran, 1–26. Carbondale: Southern Illinois University Press, 1993.

Cohen, Herman. "Hugh Blair's Theory of Taste." *Quarterly Journal of Speech* 44 (October 1958): 265–74.

Colish, Marcia L. *The Stoic Tradition from Antiquity to the Early Middle Ages.* Vol. 1: *Stoicism in Classical Latin Literature.* Leiden: E. J. Brill, 1990.

[Concanen, Matthew, and Leonard Welsted.] "A Miscellany on Taste. By Mr. Pope, etc. I. Of Taste in Architecture. With Notes Variorum, and a Compleat Key." In Gilmore, *Early Eighteenth Century Essays,* 3–30.

Conley, Thomas M. *Rhetoric in the European Tradition.* New York: Longman, 1990.

Cooper, John M. "Eudaimonism, the Appeal to Nature, and 'Moral Duty' in Stoicism." In Engstrom and Whiting, *Aristotle, Kant, and the Stoics,* 261–84.

Copleston, Frederick. *A History of Philosophy.* Vol. I: *Greece and Rome.* New York: Image, 1962.

Covino, William A. "Blair, Byron, and the Psychology of Reading." *Rhetoric Society Quarterly* 11, no. 4 (1981): 236–42.

———. "Thomas De Quincey in a Revisionist History of Rhetoric." *Pre/Text* 4, no. 2 (1983): 121–36.

Crowley, Sharon. *Composition in the University: Historical and Polemical Essays.* Pittsburgh, Penn.: University of Pittsburgh Press, 1998.

De Quincey, Thomas. *Essays on Rhetoric.* Edited by Frederick Burwick. Landmarks in Rhetoric and Public Address Series. General editor, David Potter. Carbondale: Southern Illinois University Press, 1967.

———. "Rhetoric." In De Quincey, *Essays on Rhetoric,* 81–133.

———. "Style." In De Quincey, *Essays on Rhetoric,* 134–245.

Diogenes Laertius. "Zeno." In *Lives of Eminent Philosophers,* vol. 2, 110–263. Translated by R. D. Hicks. Cambridge: Harvard University Press, 1925.

Dowling, Linda. *The Vulgarization of Art: The Victorians and Aesthetic Democracy.* Charlottesville: University Press of Virginia, 1996.

Durham, Weldon B. "The Elements of Thomas De Quincey's Rhetoric." *Speech Monographs* 37 (November 1970): 240–48.

Edney, Clarence. "Hugh Blair's Theory of *Dispositio.*" *Speech Monographs* 23 (March 1956): 38–45.

Ehninger, Douglas. "Campbell, Blair, and Whately Revisited." *Southern Speech Journal* 28 (Spring 1963): 169–82.

Engstrom, Stephen, and Jennifer Whiting, eds. *Aristotle, Kant, and the Stoics: Rethinking Happiness and Duty.* Cambridge: Cambridge University Press, 1996.

———. Introduction. In Engstrom and Whiting, *Aristotle, Kant, and the Stoics,* 1–15.

Enos, Richard Leo. "Recovering the Lost Art of Researching the History of Rhetoric." *Rhetoric Society Quarterly* 29, no. 4 (1999): 7–20.

Epictetus. *Arrian's Discourses of Epictetus.* Translated by P. E. Matheson. In *The Stoic and Epicurean Philosophers.* Edited by Whitney J. Oates, 223–487. New York: Modern Library, 1940.

Ferreira-Buckley, Linda. "The Influence of Hugh Blair's *Lectures on Rhetoric and Belles Lettres* on Victorian Education: Ruskin and Arnold on Cultural Literacy." Ph.D. diss., Pennsylvania State University, 1990.

Ferreira-Buckley, Linda, and S. Michael Halloran. Editors' introduction. In Blair, *Lectures on Rhetoric and Belles Lettres,* xv–liv.

Flory, Dan. "Stoic Psychology, Classical Rhetoric, and Theories of Imagination in Western Philosophy." *Philosophy and Rhetoric* 29, no. 2 (1996): 147–67.

Frede, Dorothea. "Stoic Determinism." In Inwood, *Cambridge Companion,* 179–205.

Freedman, Jonathan. *Professions of Taste: Henry James, British Aestheticism, and Commodity Culture.* Stanford, Calif.: Stanford University Press, 1990.

Froude, James Anthony. *Froude's Life of Carlyle.* Abridged and edited by John Clubbe. Columbus: Ohio State University Press, 1979.

Gadamer, Hans-Georg. *Truth and Method.* New York: Seabury, 1975.

Gagnier, Regenia. *Idylls of the Marketplace: Oscar Wilde and the Victorian Public.* Stanford, Calif.: Stanford University Press, 1986.

Gerard, Alexander. *An Essay on Taste.* 1759. A facsimile of the third edition (1780) with an introduction by Walter J. Hipple Jr. Gainesville, Fla.: Scholars' Facsimiles and Reprints, 1963.

Gill, Christopher. "The School in the Roman Imperial Period." In Inwood, *Cambridge Companion,* 33–58.

Gilmore, Thomas B., ed. *Early Eighteenth Century Essays on Taste.* Delmar, N.Y.: Scholars Facsimiles and Reprints, 1972.

Gilmour, Robin. *The Victorian Period: The Intellectual and Cultural Context of English Literature, 1830–1890.* London: Longman, 1993.

Graff, Richard, and Michael Leff. "Revisionist Historiography and Rhetorical Tradition(s)." In *The Viability of the Rhetorical Tradition.* Edited by Richard Graff, Arthur E. Walzer, and Janet M. Atwill, 11–30. Albany: State University of New York Press, 2005.

Guthrie, Warren. "The Development of Rhetorical Theory in America, 1635–1850: Domination of the English Rhetorics." *Speech Monographs* 15 (1948): 61–71.

Haakonssen, Knud. Introduction. In Reid, *Practical Ethics,* 3–94.

Haberman, Frederick W. "De Quincey's Theory of Rhetoric." In *Eastern Public Speaking Conference, 1940: Papers and Addresses Delivered at the Thirty-first Annual Meeting: March 28, 29, 30, 1940, Washington, D.C..* Edited by Harold F. Harding, 191–203. New York: H. W. Wilson, 1940.

Habermas, Jürgen. *The Structural Transformation of the Public Sphere: An Inquiry into a Category of Bourgeois Society.* Translated by Thomas Burger with the assistance of Frederick Lawrence. Cambridge, Mass.: MIT Press, 1991.

Halloran, S. Michael. "Hugh Blair's Use of Quintilian and the Transformation of Rhetoric in the 18th Century." In *Rhetoric and Pedagogy: Its History, Philosophy, and Practice.* Edited by Winifred Bryan Horner and Michael Leff, 183–95. Mahwah, N.J.: Lawrence Erlbaum, 1995.

———. "On the End of Rhetoric: Classical and Modern." In *Landmark Essays on Rhetorical Invention in Writing.* Edited by Richard E. Young and Yameng Liu, 79–90. Davis, Calif.: Hermagoras, 1994. First published in *College English* 36 (February 1975): 621–31.

Hanley, Evelyn A. *Stoicism in Major English Poets of the Nineteenth Century.* New York: Haskell, 1964.

"The Happy Life. An Epistle to the Honourable Lieutenant General Wade." 1733. In Gilmore, *Early Eighteenth Century Essays,* 150–59.

Harris, Wendell. "Arnold, Pater, and Wilde and the Object as in Themselves They See It." *Studies in English Literature 1500–1900: Nineteenth Century* 11, no. 4 (1971): 733–47.

Haskins, Ekaterina V. *Logos and Power in Isocrates and Aristotle.* Columbia: University of South Carolina Press, 2004.

Helsinger, Elizabeth K. *Rural Scenes and National Representation: Britain, 1815–1850.* Princeton, N.J.: Princeton University Press, 1997.

Herrick, James. *The Radical Rhetoric of the English Deists: The Discourse of Skepticism, 1680–1750.* Columbia: University of South Carolina Press, 1997.

Horner, Winifred Bryan. *Nineteenth-Century Scottish Rhetoric.* Carbondale: Southern Illinois University Press, 1993.

Hough, Graham. *The Last Romantics.* 1947. London: Methuen, 1961.

Howell, Wilbur Samuel. "De Quincey on Science, Rhetoric, and Poetry." *Speech Monographs* 13 (1946): 1–13.

———. *Eighteenth-Century British Logic and Rhetoric.* Princeton, N.J.: Princeton University Press, 1971.

Hudson, Hoyt. "De Quincey on Rhetoric and Public Speaking." In *Historical Studies of Rhetoric and Rhetoricians.* Edited by Raymond F. Howes, 198–214. Ithaca, N.Y.: Cornell University Press, 1961.

Hutcheson, Francis. *An Inquiry Concerning Beauty, Order, Harmony, Design.* Edited by Peter Kivy. The Hague: Martinus Nijhoff, 1973.

Ianetta, Melissa. "'To Elevate I Must First Soften': Rhetoric, Aesthetic, and the Sublime Traditions." *College English* 67 (March 2005): 400–420.

Inman, Billie Andrew. "Pater's Appeal to His Readers: A Study of Two of Pater's Prose Styles." *Texas Studies in Literature and Language* 14, no. 4 (1973): 643–65.

Inwood, Brad, ed. *The Cambridge Companion to the Stoics.* Cambridge: Cambridge University Press, 2003.

———. "Introduction: Stoicism, an Intellectual Odyssey." In Inwood, *Cambridge Companion,* 1–6.

Jarratt, Susan. *Rereading the Sophists.* Carbondale: Southern Illinois University Press, 1998.

Johnson, Nan. *Nineteenth-Century Rhetoric in North America.* Carbondale: Southern Illinois University Press, 1991.

Jordan, John E. Introduction. In *De Quincey as Critic,* 1–48. London: Routledge and Kegan Paul, 1973.

Kames, Henry Home, Lord. *Elements of Criticism.* Edited by Abraham Mills. New York: Sheldon, 1871.

———. *Essays on the Principles of Morality and Natural Religion.* Hildesheim, N.Y.: Georg Olms Verlag, 1976.

Kennedy, George A. *The Art of Rhetoric in the Roman World: 300 B.C.–A.D. 300.* Princeton, N.J.: Princeton University Press, 1972.

Kent, Christopher A. "Victorian Periodicals and the Constructing of Victorian Reality." In *Victorian Periodicals: A Guide to Research.* Edited by J. Don Vann and Rosemary T. VanArsdel, 1–12. New York: Modern Language Association, 1989.

Knowles, David. *The Evolution of Medieval Thought.* New York: Vintage, 1962.

Lang, Cecil Y., ed. *Letters of Matthew Arnold.* 2 vols. Charlottesville: University Press of Virginia, 1996.

Lee, Vernon. "Art and Life I." 1896. In *Prose by Victorian Women.* Edited by Andrea Broomfield and Sally Mitchell, 681–94. New York: Garland, 1996.

———. "Art and Life III." 1896. In *Prose by Victorian Women.* Edited by Andrea Broomfield and Sally Mitchell, 695–710. New York: Garland, 1996.

———. *The Beautiful: An Introduction to Psychological Aesthetics.* Cambridge: Cambridge University Press, 1913.

Lipson, Carol S., and Roberta A. Binkley, eds. *Rhetoric before and beyond the Greeks.* Albany: State University of New York Press, 2004.

Locke, John. *An Essay Concerning Human Understanding.* Edited by and with an introduction by Peter H. Nidditch. Oxford: Clarendon, 1975.

Long, A. A. "Stoicism in the Philosophical Tradition: Spinoza, Lipsius, Butler." In Inwood, *Cambridge Companion,* 365–92.

Losey, Jay B. "Pater's Epiphanies and the Open Form." *South Central Review* 6, no. 4 (1989): 30–50.

Marcus Aurelius. *The Meditations of Marcus Aurelius Antoninus.* Translated by G. Long. *The Stoic and Epicurean Philosophers.* Edited by Whitney J. Oates, 491–587. New York: Modern Library, 1940.

Marcus, Steven. "Conceptions of the Self in an Age of Progress." In *Progress and Its Discontents.* Edited by Gabriel A. Almond, Marvin Chodorow, and Roy Harvey Pearce, 431–48. Berkeley: University of California Press, 1982.

Matz, Jesse. "Walter Pater's Literary Impression." *Modern Language Quarterly* 56 (1995): 433–56.

McCosh, James. *The Scottish Philosophy, Biographical, Expository, Critical, from Hutcheson to Hamilton.* New York: Robert Carter, 1875.

McGowan, John. "From Pater to Wilde to Joyce: Modernist Epiphany and the Soulful Self." *Texas Studies in Literature and Language* 32, no. 3 (1990): 417–45.

McKenna, Stephen. *Adam Smith: The Rhetoric of Propriety.* Albany: State University of New York Press, 2006.

[Miller, James.] "Of Politeness. An Epistle to the Honourable William Stanhope, Lord Harrington. The Author of Harlequin Horace." In Gilmore, *Early Eighteenth Century Essays,* 206–24.

Miller, Thomas. *The Formation of College English: Rhetoric and Belles Lettres in the British Cultural Provinces.* Pittsburgh, Penn.: University of Pittsburgh Press, 1997.

Miller, Walter. Introduction. In Cicero, *De officiis,* xiii–xvi.

Monsman, Gerald, and Samuel Wright. "Walter Pater: Style and Text." *South Atlantic Quarterly* 71, no. 1 (1972): 106–23.

Nienkamp, Jean. *Internal Rhetorics: Toward a History and Theory of Self-Persuasion.* Carbondale: Southern Illinois University Press, 2001.

Oates, Whitney J. Introduction. In *The Stoic and Epicurean Philosophies.* Edited by Oates, xiii–xxv. New York: Modern Library, 1940.

Ong, Walter J. *Rhetoric, Romance, and Technology.* Ithaca, N.Y.: Cornell University Press, 1971.

Pater, Walter. *Marius the Epicurean: His Sensations and Ideas.* New York: Garland, 1975.

———. *Plato and Platonism: A Series of Lectures.* London: Macmillan, 1928.

———. *The Renaissance: Studies in Art and Poetry.* 1873. London: Macmillan, 1910.

———. "Style." In *Appreciations, with an Essay on Style,* 5–38. London: Macmillan, 1910.

Pocock, J. G. A. "Political Thought in the English-Speaking Atlantic, 1760–1790: The Imperial Crisis." In *The Varieties of British Political Thought, 1500–1800.* Edited by J. G. A. Pocock, with the assistance of Gordon J. Schochet and Lois Schwoerer, 246–82. Cambridge: Cambridge University Press, 1993.

Potkay, Adam. *The Fate of Eloquence in the Age of Hume.* Ithaca, N.Y.: Cornell University Press, 1994.

Poulakos, John. *Sophistical Rhetoric in Classical Greece.* Columbia: University of South Carolina Press, 1995.

———. "Toward a Sophistic Definition of Rhetoric." In *Contemporary Rhetorical Theory: A Reader.* Edited by John Louis Lucaites, Celeste Michelle Condit, and Sally Caudill, 25–34. New York: Guilford, 1999.

Quintilian. *Institutio Oratoria.* Translated by Donald A. Russell. 5 vols. Loeb Classical Library Series. Cambridge, Mass.: Harvard University Press, 2001.

Rand, Benjamin. Prefatory introduction. In *The Life, Unpublished Letters, and Philosophical Regimen of Antony, Earl of Shaftesbury.* Edited by Rand, i–xii. New York: Macmillan, 1900.

———. Preface. In Shaftesbury, *Second Characters or the Language of Forms.* Edited by Rand, xi–xxvii. New York: Greenwood, 1914.

Raphael, D. D. *The Impartial Spectator: Adam Smith's Moral Philosophy.* Oxford, U.K.: Clarendon, 2007.

Reid, Thomas. *The Correspondence of Thomas Reid.* Edited by Paul Wood. University Park: Pennsylvania State University Press, 2002.

———. *An Inquiry into the Human Mind, on the Principles of Common Sense.* 1764. Edited by Derek R. Brookes. University Park: Pennsylvania State University Press, 1997.

———. *On Logic, Rhetoric, and the Fine Arts: Papers on the Culture of the Mind.* Edited by Alexander Broadie. University Park: Pennsylvania State University Press, 2004.

———. "On the Active Powers of the First Principles of Morals." In *The Works of Thomas Reid, D.D.,* vol. 2., 637–79. 8th ed. Edinburgh: James Thin, 1895.

———. *Practical Ethics: Being Lectures on Natural Religion, Self-Government, Natural Jurisprudence, and the Law of Nations.* 1764–96. Princeton, N.J.: Princeton University Press, 1990.

Rist, J. M. *Stoic Philosophy.* Cambridge: Cambridge University Press, 1969.

Robbins, Ruth. "'Judas Always Writes the Biography': The Many Lives of Oscar Wilde." In *Victorian Identities: Social and Cultural Formations in Nineteenth-Century Literature.* Edited by Ruth Robbins and Julian Wolfreys, 97–115. London: Macmillan, 1996.

———. "Vernon Lee: Decadent Woman?" In Stokes, *Fin de Siecle,* 139–61.

Sandbach, F. H. *The Stoics.* New York: W. W. Norton, 1975.

Schaeffer, John D. *Sensus Communis: Vico, Rhetoric, and the Limits of Relativism.* Durham, N.C.: Duke University Press, 1990.

Schofield, Malcolm. "Stoic Ethics." In Inwood, *Cambridge Companion,* 233–56.

Secor, Marie. "The Legacy of Nineteenth Century Style Theory." *Rhetoric Society Quarterly* 12 (Spring 1982): 76–94.

Seneca. *Ad Lucilium Epistulae Morales.* Translated by Richard M. Gummere. 3 vols. Loeb Classical Library Series. London: William Heinemann, 1934.

———. *Moral Essays.* Translated by J. W. Basore. 3 vols. Loeb Classical Library Series. London: William Heinemann, 1965.

———. *Stoic Philosophy of Seneca.* Translated and with an introduction by Moses Hadas. Garden City, N.Y.: Doubleday, 1958.

Shaftesbury, Anthony Ashley Cooper, Earl of. *Characteristicks of Men, Manners, Opinions, and Times.* 1711. Vol. 1 of 3 vols. Indianapolis: Liberty Fund, 2001.

———. *Philosophical Regimen.* In *The Life, Unpublished Letters, and Philosophical Regimen of Antony, Earl of Shaftesbury.* Edited by Benjamin Rand, 1–272. New York: Macmillan, 1900.

———. *Second Characters or the Language of Forms.* Edited by Benjamin Rand. New York: Greenwood, 1914.

———. *Sensus Communis: An Essay on the Freedom of Wit and Humour.* In Shaftesbury, *Characteristicks of Men,* treatise 2, 30–93.

———. *Soliloquy, or Advice to an Author.* In Shaftesbury, *Characteristicks of Men,* treatise 3, 95–224.

Sher, Richard B. *Church and University in the Scottish Enlightenment: The Moderate Literati of Edinburgh.* Princeton, N.J.: Princeton University Press, 1985.

Sheridan, Thomas. *A Course of Lectures on Elocution.* 1762. New York: Benjamin Blom, 1968.

Skinner, Quentin. *Reason and Rhetoric in the Philosophy of Hobbes.* Cambridge: Cambridge University Press, 1996.

Small, Ian. "Literary Radicalism in the British *Fin de Siecle.*" In Stokes, *Fin de Siecle,* 210–29.

Smith, Adam. *Lectures on Rhetoric and Belles Lettres Delivered in the University of Glasgow by Adam Smith Reported by a Student in 1762–63.* Edited by John M. Lothian. Carbondale: Southern Illinois University Press, 1971.

———. *The Theory of Moral Sentiments.* 1759. Edited by Knud Haakonssen. Cambridge Texts in the History of Philosophy. Series editors, Karl Ameriks and Desmond M. Clarke. Cambridge: Cambridge University Press, 2002.

Smollett, Tobias. *The Adventures of Roderick Random.* New York: Oxford, 1999.

Sprat, Thomas. *History of the Royal Society.* 1667. St. Louis, Mo.: Washington University Studies, 1959.

Stokes, John, ed. *Fin de Siecle / Fin du Globe: Fears and Fantasies of the Late Nineteenth Century.* New York: St. Martin's, 1992.

Struever, Nancy S. "The Conversable World: Eighteenth-Century Transformation of the Relation of Rhetoric and Truth." In *Rhetoric and the Pursuit of Truth: Language Change in the Seventeenth and Eighteenth Centuries,* 77–119. Los Angeles: William Andrews Clark Memorial Library, UCLA, 1985.

Super, R. H., ed. *The Complete Prose Works of Matthew Arnold.* 11 vols. Ann Arbor: University of Michigan Press, 1965.

Talley, Paul M. "De Quincey on Persuasion, Invention, and Style." *Central States Speech Journal* 16 (1965): 243–54.

"Taste. An Essay. By J. S. D. S. P. The Second Edition." In Gilmore, *Early Eighteenth Century Essays,* 240–89.

Tiffany, Esther A. "Shaftesbury as Stoic." *Publications of the Modern Language Association of America* 38, no. 3 (1923): 642–84.

Uglow, Jennifer. Introduction. In Walter Pater, *Essays on Literature and Art.* Edited by Jennifer Uglow, vii–xxiii. London: J. M. Dent, 1973.

Ulman, H. Lewis. *Things, Thoughts, Words, and Actions: The Problem of Language in Late Eighteenth-Century British Rhetorical Theory.* Carbondale: Southern Illinois University Press, 1994.

Vivenza, Gloria. *Adam Smith and the Classics: The Classical Heritage in Adam Smith's Thought.* New York: Oxford University Press, 2001.

Walker, Jeffrey. *Rhetoric and Poetics in Antiquity.* Oxford: Oxford University Press, 2000.

Walzer, Arthur E. "Blair's Ideal Orator: Civic Rhetoric and Christian Politeness in Lectures 25–34." *Rhetorica* 25 (Summer 2007): 269–95.

————. *George Campbell: Rhetoric in the Age of Enlightenment.* Albany: State University of New York Press, 2003.

————. "Moral Philosophy and Rhetoric in the *Institutes:* Quintilian on Honor and Expediency." *Rhetoric Society Quarterly* 36, no. 3 (2006): 263–80.

————. "Quintilian's 'Vir Bonus' and the Stoic Wise Man." *Rhetoric Society Quarterly* 33, no. 4 (2003): 25–41.

Warner, Michael. *The Letters of the Republic: Publication and the Public Sphere in Eighteenth-Century America.* Cambridge, Mass.: Harvard University Press, 1990.

————. *Publics and Counterpublics.* New York: Zone, 2002.

Warnick, Barbara. *The Sixth Canon: Belletristic Rhetorical Theory and Its French Antecedents.* Columbia: South Carolina University Press, 1993.

Weinsheimer, Joel. "The Philosophy of Rhetoric in Campbell's *Philosophy of Rhetoric.*" *1650–1850: Ideas, Aesthetics, and Inquiries in the Early Modern Era* 1 (1994): 227–46.

Wellek, René. "De Quincey's Status in the History of Ideas." *Philological Quarterly* 23 (July 1944): 248–72.

————. "Vernon Lee, Bernard Berenson, and Aesthetics." In *Friendship's Garland: Essays Presented to Mario Praz on His Seventieth Birthday.* Edited by Vittorio Gabrieli, 2:233–51. 2 vols. Roma: Edizioni di Storia e Letteratura, 1966.

Wenley, R. M. *Stoicism and Its Influence.* Boston: Marshall Jones, 1924.

West, E. G. Introduction. In *The Theory of Moral Sentiments,* by Adam Smith, 17–43. Indianapolis, Ind.: Liberty Fund, 1976.

Whately, Richard. *Elements of Rhetoric.* 1828. New York: Sheldon, 1871.

Wilde, Oscar. *The Artist as Critic: Critical Writings of Oscar Wilde.* Edited by Richard Ellman. New York: Random House, 1968.

——. "The Critic as Artist." *Intentions.* In Wilde, *Artist as Critic,* 340–408.

——. "The Decay of Lying." *Intentions.* In Wilde, *Artist as Critic,* 290–320.

——. *The Letters of Oscar Wilde.* Edited by Rupert Hart-Davis. New York: Harcourt, Brace, 1962.

——. "The Soul of Man under Socialism." In Wilde, *Artist as Critic,* 255–89.

Wood, Paul. "Science in the Scottish Enlightenment." In *The Scottish Enlightenment.* Edited by Alexander Broadie, 94–116. Cambridge: Cambridge University Press, 2003.

Wordsworth, John. John Wordsworth to Walter Pater, March 17, 1873. In *Letters of Walter Pater.* Edited by Lawrence Evans, 12. Oxford: Clarendon Press, 1970.

Yeats, William Butler. *The Autobiography of William Butler Yeats: Consisting of Reveries over Childhood and Youth, the Trembling of the Veil, and* Dramatis Personae. New York: Macmillan, 1938.

INDEX

ABOUT THE AUTHOR

Lois Peters Agnew is an assistant professor of writing and rhetoric at Syracuse University, where she teaches courses in writing and rhetorical history and theory. She is coeditor with Richard Leo Enos of *Landmark Essays on Aristotelian Rhetoric*.